PAPER BELT ON FIRE

How Renegade Investors
Sparked a Revolt Against the University

MICHAEL GIBSON

New York • London

First American edition published in 2022 by Encounter Books,
an activity of Encounter for Culture and Education, Inc.,
a nonprofit, tax-exempt corporation.
Encounter Books website address: www.encounterbooks.com

Manufactured in the United States and printed on
acid-free paper. The paper used in this publication meets
the minimum requirements of ANSI/NISO Z39.48-1992
(R 1997) (*Permanence of Paper*).

FIRST AMERICAN EDITION

LIBRARY OF CONGRESS CATALOGING-IN-PUBLICATION DATA

Names: Gibson, Michael, 1977– author.
Title: Paper belt on fire: how renegade investors
sparked a revolt against the university / Michael Gibson.
Identifiers: LCCN 2022004801 (print) | LCCN 2022004802 (ebook)
ISBN 9781641772457 (hardcover) | ISBN 9781641772464 (ebook)
Subjects: LCSH: School bonds—United States. | Education—United
States—Finance | Short selling (Securities)—United States.
Classification: LCC HG4952 .G53 2022 (print) | LCC HG4952 (ebook)
DDC 332.63/2330973—dc23/eng/20220203
LC record available at https://lccn.loc.gov/2022004801
LC ebook record available at https://lccn.loc.gov/2022004802

2 3 4 5 6 7 8 9 20 22

For my Serapion Brothers:
Satoshi, Cowperthwaite, Wolfe, Nozick, Zamyatin, and Mom

CONTENTS

"At first sight it would seem that the deep interior of the sun and stars is less accessible to scientific investigation than any other region of the universe. Our telescopes may probe farther and farther into the depths of space; but how can we ever obtain certain knowledge of that which is hidden behind substantial barriers? What appliance can pierce through the outer layers of a star and test the conditions within?"

—*The Internal Constitution of the Stars*
Arthur S. Eddington (1926)

"But I reckon I got to light out for the Territory ahead of the rest, because Aunt Sally she's going to adopt me and civilize me, and I can't stand it. I been there before."

—*The Adventures of Huckleberry Finn*
Mark Twain (1884)

PROLOGUE

"Oh you guys are *full* of shit," Bill Gates exploded at me. "*Total* shit."

Gates was pissed. His brow had furrowed above his trademark glasses. We were arguing, and every time he scored a point, he did this little hip-sway hop, as though he were raining fact and reason down upon me in a series of overhead tennis smashes. This was not the genial billionaire-scholar that I'd seen on TV, carrying a canvas bag full of books. Nor was he the gentleman philanthropist, patiently explaining his efforts to improve the lives of the world's poor. Gates kept that man in reserve for the magazines and Sunday newspapers. Here was the fire, the indignation I had only read about in memoirs and business histories. This was the CEO who had ruthlessly crushed Apple and IBM over and over for decades, and who, during Microsoft's epic antitrust showdown with the Justice Department, had offered the prosecution nothing but contempt, evasion, and ridicule during three days of direct examination. All it had taken was a single question from me to bring the ferocious entrepreneur in him back to life; and it was abundantly clear that the then-richest man on earth thought I was an idiot for even asking it. My heart leapt. A ripple of exhilarating mischief shot through me. The game was on.

It was June 2014, and we were standing in the perfectly white art gallery of the Villa Simonyi, Charles Simonyi's oddly-jointed mansion on the shores of Lake Washington, just outside Seattle. Simonyi, the chief architect of Microsoft Office, and inventor of Word and Excel, had come a long way since he'd fled Soviet-dominated Hungary in 1966 and arrived in America, aged sixteen, with nothing. In 2007, he'd paid $25 million to enjoy ten days orbiting the earth. He'd arrived in a Soyuz spacecraft at the International Space Station bearing gifts. Martha Stewart, his then-girlfriend, had packed him a gourmet picnic of roasted quail and duck breast to share with the cosmonauts on board.

On this terrestrial night, however, Simonyi was hosting a fundraising dinner for the Institute for Advanced Study at Princeton, the highest temple of theoretical physics. The Institute's first academic hire when it opened in 1933 was Albert Einstein; its second, the polymath John von Neumann. Its scholars have since invented the modern computer, won thirty-three Nobel Prizes, and earned forty-two Fields Medals. Tremendous brains, all of them. But like any other non-profit organization, they had to raise money from donors, which was why Simonyi had gathered thirty of Seattle's brainiest well-to-do—including his old friend Bill Gates—to eat and chat about physics below his collection of Roy Lichtenstein's comic strip paintings. The historian of technology George Dyson had invited me with the hope that I might spark a conversation on the future of education with some of the attendees. I suspect I did not disappoint him.

I'd been seated at dinner next to Simonyi at the head table, three people away from Gates, so I didn't get to talk to him directly as we ate. But once the tables had been cleared and coffee was served, people were milling about. I decided I had to approach Microsoft's founder.

"Hi Mr. Gates. I'm Michael Gibson. I work for Peter Thiel."

"Yes, I know Peter," he said, sounding like your kindest uncle.

Then I asked the question. It was something Thiel had talked about in public since around 2006. Now, more than fifteen years later, many tenured academics have written treatises on the topic and a respectable body of scholarship has formed debating the issue. But for most of the world in 2014, hypnotized by smartphones and tangled up in the Web, it was no more than an eccentric grumble. Very few in the mainstream took the question seriously, though the early murmurs had been amplified by the economist Tyler Cowen in *The Great Stagnation* and later by Robert Gordon in *The Rise and Fall of American Growth.*[1]

So I asked Gates: "What do you think of the idea that we're not seeing as much innovation and scientific progress as we should? That the rate of progress has stalled?"

The change in his demeanor was instantaneous. A fast-moving wave of irritation swept across his face. It was the most alive Gates had looked all night. His sudden intensity caught me by surprise.

"Oh you guys are *full* of shit. *Total* shit…"

You guys! It lit me up how animated he'd become. All at once he became a statistical geyser, spouting positive facts about the improved well-being of billions around the world. He pointed me to decreasing child mortality; lengthening life spans; whole generations in developing countries lifted out of poverty in the blink of a historical eye.

About that much, of course, he was right. Life has been getting better for hundreds of millions of people in the last forty years. That, truly, is progress. But Gates was describing the spread of existing knowledge to the places it had yet to touch, giving the poorest people in the world access to proven best practices in medicine, sanitation, and nutrition.

But what I meant by "progress" was the discovery of things entirely new. I argued, echoing Thiel, that we'd ceased to be a nation of explorers and inventors; that American creativity was drying up, dying of thirst; and that, contrary to all the propaganda about exponential growth, the ever faster clip of progress, this roaring, wild current of change—indeed, contrary to the lecture on physics Gates and I had just heard minutes before—the plain fact was we were no longer advancing into the future as quickly as we'd thought we were.

Forget about the fear of robots taking our jobs. That's misdirection. It's not real. Not any time soon. Quite to the contrary: our present social anxieties stem not from too much change in too little time, but from *not enough*. Nothing works the way it's supposed to; much of everything seems past its peak, gone to seed. Too old, too rigid, grotesquely obese, too complacent... rather than failing to adapt to an accelerating future, we're failing to escape from a moribund past. And worst of all, we haven't even noticed it. Few see that we've stalled, going nowhere fast, and expensively too, like a plump middle-aged man pedaling furiously on a stationary bike in the moments before a heart attack.

Gates and I took a quick tour of various sectors of the economy, volleying point-counterpoint. The topic of education came up.

"We're not very good at educating anyone," I said. "From K-through-12 to college, we spend more and more to get the same or worse results than we used to."

"Well, you know," Gates said. Then there was a pause. "I'm *trying* to do something about that."

Indeed. The Gates Foundation has pledged billions to help students and reform schools. Buildings at Stanford, Cornell, Carnegie Mellon, the University of Cambridge, and MIT all bear his name.

Whereas my effort to reform schools constituted...what?

Who was I to argue about education and technological progress with the man who had arguably done the most to push them forward during my lifetime?

Long ago, back in 2006, when I was a grad student at Oxford, I was on my way to becoming a professor. My focus was on ancient and moral philosophy, but I dropped out before earning my doctorate. By and by, I met Peter Thiel and took a job with him, an unlikely event I describe in the chapters to come. On my first day, we started a fellowship that each year awarded twenty young people $100,000 to work on independent projects, startups, and research. It was a no-strings grant, but the program had two newsworthy conditions: you couldn't be enrolled in a university, and you had to be aged nineteen or under when you applied. When we selected our first group of twenty in 2011, the establishment acted as though we had raised the pirate's black flag. Overnight, I became the anti-professor.

Like the Oxford don I'd almost become, I had incredibly brilliant young people under my tutelage. But as the anti-professor, my students were not writing essays or taking tests. Any intelligent person with a strong work ethic (or a Hollywood Mom paying a scammer) can do that.[2] We were going to leave that dog race to the "well-rounded" pack competing for conventional prestige, credentials, and other mechanical lures on the dog track. Instead, our fellows were going to do something rare and difficult: they would build things.

And, my Lord, how they built! In 2013, I met a gaunt Russian teenager from Waterloo, Canada, named Vitalik Buterin. He had some ideas about how the technology underlying Bitcoin could be adapted to create smart contracts and digital assets. We awarded him a Thiel Fellowship and he launched Ethereum, which today has a market capitalization of $255 billion. As India succumbed to a more virulent form of Covid-19 in the spring of

2021, Buterin donated $1 billion in cryptocurrency to the India Covid Relief Fund. A *Time* magazine cover story in March 2022 dubbed Vitalik "the most influential person in crypto."[3]

In 2011, we met Laura Deming when she was sixteen and already enrolled as a sophomore at MIT. Even we, the heretics, thought she was bonkers. She wanted to leave MIT's labs in order to start a venture capital fund to invest in cutting-edge therapies that would extend youth and health, even while our birthdays piled up. It is possible to get older without getting old, if only we pursued the right discoveries, she pleaded to us. In the end, her genius was so astonishing that we gave her a grant despite our concerns about her young age. Seven years on after its founding, her Longevity Fund is doing spectacularly: three of the six companies she invested in have gone public through IPOs. Two of the other companies have drugs undergoing clinical trials.

After one recent workshop I led on philosophy and technology for a small group of our eccentrics, Laura Deming wrote to me: "Perhaps you have become a better professor of philosophy by eschewing academia?"

No doubt I've mulled it over. In the absolute best-case scenario—which was improbable to be sure—I might have become a professor at a top school like Harvard. Over a forty-year career, I might have advised three undergraduates per year on their senior theses. Perhaps two doctoral dissertations a year as well. All told that might be 200 or so works I would have shepherded through. Perhaps my hypothetical students would have added a decimal place to the work of Aristotle or Nietzsche. Whatever the value of that work might be—I can imagine it collecting dust in Emerson Hall on Harvard's campus—it pales in comparison to what this motley crew will produce, even if they don't have a single college degree between them. But more than that, they represent not some group of extraordinary outliers, who cannot be taken as a model for the average student, but the beginning of a new era in education.

Just over five hundred years ago, tradition has it that Martin Luther nailed his ninety-five theses to a church door in Wittenberg, Germany, to protest the sale of indulgences. These indulgences were pieces of paper the Catholic Church sold at great cost, telling people it would save their souls. The church made a fortune selling them, mere Mad Libs filled out by your holy grace. Likewise, universities today sell pieces of paper at great cost and tell young people that buying them is the only way they can save their souls. Universities call this piece of paper a diploma, and they're rolling in money selling them, building extravagant monuments to their glory and power.

The year 1517 was a moment in history when a great social transformation was accelerated by technology. Though Gutenberg's revolution had been underway for more than fifty years, the mass adoption and diffusion of the printing press meant Luther's message could influence all of Europe, and not only the people of a small town in Germany. Kings and priests no longer had a monopoly of authority on the great questions. Equal authority could be found in books and, even more dangerously for establishment institutions, from an individual's own judgment.

There's a famous quote from the science fiction writer William Gibson: "The future is already here—it's just not very evenly distributed." My colleague Danielle Strachman and I came to see this in the starkest terms in our own work. When we met someone like Laura Deming it was as though we'd met the only person on Earth living in a tiny pocket of the future where anti-aging science was real. I suspect hardly anyone had the faintest notion of what she was talking about, much less the patience to take her seriously and to learn from her. But we did, and with Peter Thiel's mentorship and backing, pretty soon it became clear that we'd developed a knack for finding outsiders like Laura who were tinkering away in the hideouts of a hidden future. One of my brothers has taken to calling me Professor X, after the bald telepathic principal who flies around recruiting mutants for his secret school in the *X-Men* comics. Now that I think of it, Professor X *did* go to Oxford before accepting his status as a mutant. But as flattering as the comparison is, what Danielle and I do doesn't require special powers.

At the Thiel Fellowship, we'd been criticizing the "higher education bubble" for years. Google shows a big spike in the phrase's use after the launch of Thiel's program. But there was no direct way to short this bubble in a financial trade. Sadly, third-rate colleges do not offer stock that we could borrow, sell, and then buy back at a future date for a lower price to reap the difference. Nor did we think of inventing arcane financial instruments to short the least credit-worthy loans in the $1.7 trillion of outstanding student debt. Some of those loans would surely default in the years to come, but that was too bleak to try to benefit from.

Instead, in 2015 Danielle and I raised a venture capital fund that would back the wizards *without* credentials, the outsiders who, in the eyes of some authority or other, should not be doing what they're doing. About ninety percent of our investments were and are in companies led by dropouts or people who never set foot on campus. They have no college degree. While the Thiel Fellowship is a non-profit and continues to this day, it is limited to Thiel's generosity. Danielle and I spun out and started our fund because we saw there was the potential for massive upside and the opportunity to expand on what we were doing. If we did our jobs well, we'd be working with way more than twenty people a year. Our hope is that the more successful our founders become, the more others will follow in their footsteps and the more the cracks in the edifice of our shambolic education system will fissure outwards, wider and wider. We envision a future in which all American families can take their children's education into their own hands and chart their own course outside of failing institutions. Learning is important, but fulfilling and rewarding careers are possible without college degrees or even schools. We call our fund 1517, after the year Martin Luther nailed his theses to a church door. We don't believe in indulgences.

But I'm getting ahead of myself. This book is our story, an unlikely account of how two outsiders—a charter school principal and defrocked philosopher—with no experience in finance started a venture capital fund to short the higher educa-tion bubble. *Who would do such a thing?* Pursuing this madcap strategy, we are now fortunate to preside over one of the most successful early-stage funds in the business, having made our investors over $200 million to date, with more to come as our investments continue to mature. If we were a typical upstart venture fund, this performance would be unusual enough. Competition among VCs is brutal: about 80 percent of all funds fail and no one seems able to dislodge the legends from the top of the pyramid.[4] David Swensen is the chief investment officer of Yale University's $31.2 billion endowment. Thanks to Swensen's colossal returns for Yale over two decades, he is the investor all other institutional investors copy and pay heed to, and he emphatically warns everyone to stay away from venture funds unless they can invest in the equivalent of the Yankees for Silicon Valley: Sequoia, Kleiner, Benchmark, Accel, and the like. "Investors providing capital to the venture industry receive returns inadequate to compensate for the high degree of risk,"

Swensen writes in *Pioneering Portfolio Management*, the investment Bible for pension funds, sovereign wealth funds, and endowments. "Only if investors generate top-quartile, or even top-decile, results do returns suffice to compensate for the risks incurred."[5] 1517 Fund's returns place it in the top one or two percent of all funds in its class. So the fact that we perform this well, are a brand new fund competing against the Yankees, and limit ourselves to investing in dropouts or people who never went to college is truly extraordinary. I take particular pleasure knowing that our fund has outperformed MIT's fund of the same vintage—the E14 Fund—which only invests in their grads. Naturally, I am biased about our success. Like a gonzo Hunter S. Thompson I do not write as a disinterested outsider but as a crazed participant gone berserk. Readers, of course, should decide the significance of what we're doing for themselves. There are certainly those who have not wanted me to tell this story.

I can't say I was canceled exactly, but no sooner had I submitted this manuscript for publication than a claque of corpses at famous publishing houses in New York City rejected it because, to quote my favorite, "Peter Thiel is a man with too much power at best, and is a borderline evil conspiracist at worst." Others identified themselves as "educationalists," and doubted the book's central thesis. (I imagine them as prim Ivy League alums, twisting the signet rings on their fingers, head held back, with horror in their eyes, having felt a hairline fracture in their assurance.) "Had some game-changing innovations come out of the Thiel Fellowship or 1517 Fund, I might have been more convinced," one editor grumbled, leaving me to wonder if Vitalik Buterin's $1 billion donation to Covid relief counted as anything in his condescending view.

Then, September 2021 saw the publication of a mendacious book purporting to call itself a biography of Peter Thiel. *The*

Contrarian by Max Chafkin, a reporter for Bloomberg and a Yale graduate, contains so many lies and inaccuracies I don't know where to begin, but the most relevant to me is that Chafkin claims I was fired from my job with Thiel in 2015.[6] Imagine my surprise when I read that! As you will read in these pages, this couldn't be further from the truth.

So we're a joke, but a dangerous one—a joke that throws authority into a panic. Decaying, corrupt institutions—not just higher education but the media, publishers, think tanks, non-profits, city halls, and other government bureaucracies—are crumbling all around us. They are no longer trustworthy. They are failing to achieve their stated purposes. I have taken to calling these institutions, whose center of gravity resides on the East Coast from Washington D.C. to Boston, the Paper Belt. Once challenged, rather than reform, the Paper Belt elite tend to offer only self-serving denials and contempt. Or, for reporters like Chafkin, they lie and fudge. But the problems cracking the foundations of our society cannot be ignored. We live in a turbulent age with no real safe spaces. A social crisis is at hand. I hope our surprising story points one way out.

The genre of our tale is a whydunit. Not a whodunit. After all, I've already spoiled the ending: Danielle and I discovered and backed young people the rest of the world would not take seriously, and then we made our investors more money than the *Ocean's 11* team steals from the Bellagio and MGM Grand casinos. But why we did it, and how we did it, and what it means—that's something I think you'll find entertaining, and perhaps even edifying.

The central thesis of the book has four parts. The first is that science, know-how, and wisdom are the source of almost all that is good: higher living standards; longer, healthier lives; thriving communities; dazzling cities; blue skies; profound philosophies; the flourishing of the arts; and all the rest of it. The fate of all of these depends upon gains in knowledge. The second is that the rate of progress in science, know-how, and wisdom has flatlined for far too long. We have not been making scientific, technological, or philosophical progress at anything close to the rate we've needed to since about 1971. (Computers and smartphones notwithstanding.) The third claim is that the complete and utter failure of our education system, from K-12 up through Harvard, is a case in point of this stagnation. We are not very good at educating people, and we have not improved student learning all that much in more than a generation, despite spending three to four times as much per student at any grade. Our lack of progress in knowing how to improve student outcomes has greatly contributed to the decline of creativity in just about every field. The last, chief point is that the fate of our civilization depends upon replacing or reforming our unreliable and corrupted institutions, which include both the local public school and the entire Ivy League. My colleagues and I are trying to trailblaze one path in the field of education. We might be misguided in our methods, but our diagnosis is correct. I aim to convince you of it along the way. I will lay out the evidence as I discovered it, turning over the cards one by one along the trail. I was changed by what I found. I hope you will be too.

Economists track a bewildering profusion of statistics, but the one stat they do not measure is the rate at which we accomplish what was once thought impossible. The discovery of penicillin has saved many lives, but its economic benefits only show up in the additional spending people undertake later in life. True, average life expectancy goes up, but that aggregate number doesn't tell us why. To track the rate of progress we need to mark discoveries and measure how they make life better. At a minimum, bad things should happen less frequently, to fewer people, and with diminishing effects. And at best, we may achieve goods we cannot now even imagine. I have written a coda at the end of the book that details our stagnation and a handful of unsolved problems we need to figure out to break free from its hold. The first two thirds of the book tell the story of our attempt to liberate the young so they can attack these problems and save us. The coda is certainly not the last word, but it may be the first.

Our community of hackers tells me I have a garage-sale writing style. Odds and ends, bits of memoir, bursts of philosophy, shards of scholarship, vignettes, reportage, untranslatable words, history, shifting points of view—I use every tool I have to try to convey both the intellectual and emotional truth of the matter. For insight and understanding, I turn to poems as often as economics. And if I digress at times, and weave multiple story arcs, I beg you to hold on tight. It's a story set against the backdrop of a rip-roaring ten years in Silicon Valley, which is not so much a place as an ideal, as well an open-air asylum the size of a city. And yet despite the decade-long tech boom, it also takes place during an era of technological and scientific stagnation, which you'd never have guessed was happening if you listened only to the hype gushing from every new startup's press release or the ecstasies of the votaries anticipating the coming "singularity."

In January 2020, the severity of our stagnation and sclerosis became undeniable as the first people infected with Covid-19 spread the virus throughout the United States. By the end of the year, millions had died worldwide, and the entire planet was paralyzed. The crisis exposed the Maginot Line of our brittle status quo: the diagnostic tests we needed were slow and scarce; the treatment options were few; and any hope of a vaccine more than a year off. Our science was inadequate to the challenge and our big public institutions—the governing bodies meant to protect us—had failed. Some lied. The aftershocks from this seismic convulsion will define the next decade. The year 2020 also marks the end of Silicon Valley, as the fires of creation in this once great hub gutter out.

I began writing this in quarantine from a bungalow in Venice Beach, California, where I had lived since the January before the outbreak. I finished it in the Colorado mountains. I'd fled San Francisco after living and working there for a decade cut perfectly at the joints, from 2010 to 2020. The future, I'd come to believe, would be built elsewhere. I knew for sure that the Bay Area was past the parabola's peak when the owner of my building paid me $40,000 to move *out* of my modest one-bedroom apartment, which was rent-stabilized at $3,200 a month. This was sheer madness: people were pouring into the city with nowhere to live because the city authorities had made it impossible to build new housing—yet another sad example of institutional failure. It was high time to get out before the place hit bottom, which it did only three months later.

● ● ●

To give Bill Gates his due, in March 2015, a year after I tangled with him at the Villa Simonyi, he gave a TED talk in which he anticipated the catastrophe of a future pandemic. "If anything kills over ten million people in the next few decades," he said, "it's most likely to be a highly infectious virus, rather than a war." When the contagion came, Gates stepped up big time. He pledged billions to accelerate the development and production of a vaccine. But, as he warned in his prescient talk, "Time is not on our side."

The story that follows describes a fight against time when most thought we had all the time in the world. It's a fight against our standstill. Ours is an age of scrambling for lost time. As nearly all real gains in our living standards come from scientific and technological progress (about 85 percent, according to the standard economic model), there is an even greater moral urgency to discover and develop the talents of the next generation of builders and makers.[7] Gates has his approach to education. We have ours. One of this book's epigraphs comes from Arthur S. Eddington's groundbreaking treatise on how the Sun and other stars generate such powerful energy. Modern science began in the skies, only 450 or so years ago. To my astonishment, we feel less certain about the sources of our own dynamism than we do about the tremendous fire-breathing crucible at the center of our Sun, which Eddington's equations describe. We've come so far, and, still, we're less wise than we are clever.

I hope this book shows that permanent stagnation need not be our destiny. I believe that our greatest inventions and discoveries are still ahead of us. Never has there been such a clear horizon, such an open sea. But we cannot take comfort in passive techno-optimism or press release showmanship, which flourishes in Silicon Valley's fantasyland of denial. Life can be so wonderful, as well as terrible, but we can never forget we have the power to make life good. There's a lot of work to be done to make sure of that: stale institutions to transform; bold ideas to nourish; wildcat inventors to fund. *Will the future be worth it?* Ensuring that it will requires nothing less than transforming ourselves and our society in ways we have yet to fully grasp. "What appliance can pierce through the outer layers of a star and test the conditions within?" Eddington wrote. I hope this book provides a glimpse. It is also an intensely personal book, as all visions of the future must be. Who we might become, after all, begins with who we are.

·1·

LAST NAME FIRST

I interviewed to become a spy with the CIA in the fall of 2007. It started with a phone call. There was a short greeting, some minor chit-chat, and then a disembodied voice said "Michael, we came across your application for the role of political analyst, but we were wondering if you might instead be interested in the clandestine service."

I can't exactly recall what I mumbled right then, partly because I was surprised, but mainly because I had never thought of becoming a spy before this moment. I had no background whatsoever for it, neither in my academic studies nor my employment. My goal in applying was deeply personal and, to tell the truth, a secret. I have spent most of my life wondering who my dad was, searching for clues about Frederick Whittle Smith, whom I last saw when I was sixteen months old, three days before he died. I hoped that if I got the job as a CIA research analyst, I might gain enough security clearance to discover the truth about whether my late father had been an employee, a source, a cut-out, or some kind of paid consultant for the intelligence community.

This is what my dad had told my mom the last time they saw

each other. He was holding me, a toddler, in his arms when he said it. He told her he feared for his life because he was involved in some secretive work unrelated to his career as an engineer at NBC, the television network. He and my mom weren't married yet, nor did they live together, so naturally their separate lives left some room for surprises. But this was astonishing.

"Fred, you're scaring me," she said, as he tried to explain why he was in danger. She couldn't imagine how the things he was saying could be true, but as he spoke, she knew deep down that they were. There was an urgency and clarity behind it. Too many details. "How do you know these things?" she asked.

"I'm an operative," he said.

"What's an operative?"

"I find out information..."

"Are you a spy?"

"...yes." He paused, then looked down at me in his arms and said, "I don't know, Michael—you're so darn cute, if I were Jeffrey, I think I'd hit you too."

Just a minute before I had tussled with my brother, Jeffrey, over a toy car we both wanted to play with. My brother had pushed me hard to get it back. My dad was consoling me.

"You can't mean that," she said.

"I do. I'm a spy."

"No, I mean about Jeffrey and Michael. Jeffrey only pushed him to get back his car."

"I like my version better," he said, laughed, and then continued on with his story.

That conversation was mid-afternoon on Thursday, July 27, 1978, in New York City. We were all on the corner of 55th Street and Sutton Place, outside my dad's apartment building, which overlooked the East River and Roosevelt Island near the Queensboro Bridge. Three days later, on Sunday, after my mom reported him missing, two police officers opened the door to his apartment and found him dead on the floor of his home office. There were no signs of forced entry or of violence. No autopsy was performed, but the New York City coroner said he died of heart failure. To this day, my mom believes he was murdered.

I was so young at the time, a toddler. Saying goodbye for the last time is sorrowful enough as it is. Not remembering your dad is tinged forever with something searching, a longing for someone who will never arrive. There is hardly a day in my life that I don't wish I could say hi, give him a long hug, and hear him say, "I love you." But the past is gone, and it will not answer. What is left in the dust that remains?

● ● ●

So, this was my secret aim in trying to work for the CIA: get in and see what I could find in the archive. It was naive—preposterous even—but it was a plan. At this point, I was renting an attic apartment in a family's colonial home off Brattle Street—"Tory Row"—in Cambridge, Massachusetts. *Technology Review*, MIT's magazine, had hired me as an editorial assistant, with the offer to write stories as well. I covered everything from quantum computing to ultrasonic backscattering for brewing a better beer.

I had first submitted my application for the analyst role while I was still at Oxford a few months back, believing that my hours sitting in the Bodleian Library writing philosophy papers qualified me to sit in Langley, Virginia doing something somewhat similar. But the whole clandestine thing felt beyond me. True, my studies in the UK had given me overseas experience, and I had a facility for foreign languages, at least in the fading syntax of a classical education. I read in French, Ancient Greek, and Latin. But this was not how *Casino Royale* is supposed to begin. I didn't own a suit, much less a tailored one, and I couldn't even pick out a luxury watch. Still, I was tempted to see how far down this clandestine rabbit hole I could go. I made a move.

"Yes," I told the disembodied CIA voice, "I would be interested."

"Great. Let's schedule a preliminary phone call interview for next week."

During the following week, I had no idea what to expect, let alone any clue how to prepare, so I did nothing. It's not like a McKinsey or Bain interview for which you can practice in advance by bullshitting case studies and tumbling through mental math about how many ping pong balls can fit into a 747.

I took the next interview call in the living room of the family I lived with, amid the rubble of children's toys. It was one of those late October afternoons when you first notice the days are getting shorter. The reception was awful in the colonial attic, and I was afraid the call from this unknown, untraceable number would cut out. But being in the living room had its dangers, too. The mom and her children could walk in at any moment.

Then, suddenly, the call came. Short greetings again but a different bureaucratic voice. "I'm going to go through a series of questions and do your best to answer them. O.K.? So…"—recall this was 2007—"In your assessment, what are the main grievances driving sectarian conflict in Iraq between the Sunni, Shi'a, Yazidis, Assyrians, Kurds, and Iraqi Turkmen?"

Yazidis? I pace when I have serious conversations on the phone. Hurdling scattered toys, I said, with great weight and authority, drawing on the classic works of Plato and Aristotle, "Ummmm…"

I did my best to repeat the general analysis I'd gleaned scanning the *New York Times* and the *Wall Street Journal*. I probably sounded like the slouch in class who hadn't done the reading but raised his hand anyway to get credit for attendance.

The voice cut me off. "Michael, what is intelligence? What kind of information does the CIA want? Just any? Is it the kind that you can Google?"

"Ummm, well of course not," I offered. "It's the kind that someone else doesn't want you to have."

"Sometimes. But not always. It's information that is of critical interest to the United States, for its national security, for its foreign policy. That may involve the plans and intentions of high-level foreign government officials. But it may be time-sensitive information that these officials don't even realize is of importance."

I tripped over a stuffed penguin. "I see."

He then went on to explain to me that there are two main entry-level roles in the clandestine service, and that spies typically worked in pairs, one of each role together. On the one hand, there is the "operations officer," who is closer to what you think of when you imagine a spy. In memoirs, movies, and novels, they are more commonly referred to as "case officers." (Heavens help the poor soul who calls a case officer a spy or a secret agent to an employee of the CIA. Only amateurs do that.) Undercover abroad, case officers work to turn non-U.S. citizens who have access to foreign intelligence into sources. This involves building relationships, and also cajoling, persuading, and manipulating. The kind of person who's good at this is someone who can size someone up, build rapport, and make friends quickly. My high school and college friends would be the first to say that I am not that person. Case officers also practice what is known as "tradecraft," which refers to the bug plants, dead drops, car tosses, street surveillance, safe houses, and all the rest of it. Maybe I could do that, I thought. I left a key under a rock outside a friend's house once.

The other spy role is called a "collection management officer." When the operations officer collects the jigsaw pieces, the collection management officer is supposed to consider how they fit together, what picture they form, even though he doesn't yet have the puzzle box that shows the finished product. With a view to looming trends, this person places the information collected into the wider context of events, backed by research and regional expertise. Together the two spooks solve the puzzle of the future.

"So what role would you prefer to apply for?" he asked.

I don't know how I passed this round of the recruiting process, but I did. I told him I'd probably be better suited to the collection management role, only because it felt more academic to me. Next came the second round, which included an IQ test, a personality test, a statement of values, a set of essay questions, and a list of the books I was supposed to use as sources in my answers. I still have the booklist. Here are some of the titles, many deeply critical of the CIA's activities and failures: Steve Coll's *Ghost Wars*, a meticulous history of the Taliban and the rise of Osama Bin Laden in the 1990s; the impassioned *Imperial Hubris* by Michael Scheuer, the former head of the Osama Bin Laden unit at the CIA's counterterrorism center; and strangely, I thought, a spy novel set in Beirut concerning the U.S. Embassy bombing—*Agents of Innocence* by David Ignatius.

I had to print out my essays and send them to an address in Virginia that disappeared a week afterward. One of my favorite details came from a question on the personality test. "On a scale of one to five, with one being 'strongly disagree' and five being 'strongly agree,' this statement is true: When I walk down the street, I feel an aura of power around me."

Aura of power? What the hell were they tracking for? If I had to guess, a grandiose sense of self-importance. In the end, though, I'd never find out, because a week after taking the

CIA's battery of tests, I got a letter saying they had passed on my candidacy. Why they ended up passing on me will forever remain a mystery. But ever since then I have reflected on the nature of intelligence gathering, the difficulty of predicting the future, and the psychology of recruiting sources.

I've since read, for instance, that the CIA's shrinks filter for skilled manipulators.[1] The best case officers are not extroverts, as one might expect for a profession that involves luring foreign friends into committing treason against their country. Just imagine a case officer at an embassy cocktail party—the whole James Bond thing—making the acquaintance of a potential source, exchanging witty banter, trading gossip with the ambassador and his wife. A week later, our case officer goes on a skiing trip with the targeted diplomat, because the ambassador's wife mentioned the target loves it...even though the case officer has been on a mountain only a few times in his teens and now has to lie about his excitement for the trip. This kind of lying and greasing feels extroverted to me, but I would be wrong. Extroverts do this too naturally. They do it without having to notice the character of the people they are getting warm to, which is why it appears that the best spies tend to be "compensated introverts." These introverts use their ambition to overcome their inward turn, which doesn't come easily. They are reserved but not shy. It is by pushing through their discomfort that they come to understand what motivates others, to clearly read a situation, a face, a gesture, or the emotional nuance of a passing comment. As a result, they make great chameleons.

It's no small task to convince people to betray their family, their employer, their native country.[2] It may involve nothing less than a systematic exploitation of a defector's vulnerabilities. According to declassified articles from the CIA's own internal journal, case officers sketch a chart representing the creaky architecture of a target's weaknesses: does this person have loose lips? Does he seem dissatisfied at work? Resentful of his boss and passed over for promotion? Miffed? Humiliated? Is he bitter about his henpecking wife? Lonely? Maybe he has a sick child and can't afford the medical bills. Maybe he can't get his daft son into an Ivy League College. Or maybe he needs money to gamble, drink, and shag two mistresses. To channel and direct the target's will, one must quickly discern flaws of his character—vanity, self-pity, petty self-importance, yearning for his father's approval—and then use them as handholds to maneuver him into compliance. This is the psychology of treason.

Perhaps the CIA passed on me because they did a background check. Perhaps their battery of tests was better than I thought and they saw through to my vulnerabilities. It was only when I was nineteen that I discovered who my real dad was. I'd grown up believing someone else was my father, a very loving and kind man long divorced from my mom. Throughout my teens, however, I'd sensed differences between my three half-siblings and me. I didn't know they were half-siblings, of course. I believed we were fully related. But I intuited enough was off by the time I turned nineteen, so when I had a hunch in the middle of a conversation one day, I asked my mom straight up. I even guessed my dad was this man Fred Smith she talked about from time to time because he was so alive in her heart and conversations. She had kept one or two pictures of him on the walls. And so she told me. "You weren't surprised it was true," she would say. "You were surprised I said it."

Now it all seems so obvious in retrospect. My two half-brothers and half-sister are fair, and what's more, two of them have fine platinum blonde hair. Strangers will tell me I look Basque or Irish: dark disheveled hair, worn penny brown eyes, and sometimes a King of Spades Neanderthal beard. I've always found the differences in disposition and temperament between us most fascinating. For one thing, they all inherited a flash of Viking anger from their father's Danish ancestors. Unimportant small things, like who drank the last of the milk, could irritate them and be blown out of proportion. I love them dearly, but that temper could be explosive in a family fight.

Before I was twenty, however, the contrast between us could still be explained away. It reminds me of the way a counterfeit painting's shoddy defects grow more obvious once art historians have determined the fake's true origins. The Dutch forger Han van Meegeren raked in the equivalent of more than $80 million selling his knockoffs as authentic Vermeers in the 1940s.[3] Seeing the counterfeit van Meegerens now, though, one can't help but wonder how anyone was ever fooled in the first place. The brushwork looks clumsy by comparison: no finesse, no lightness of touch. Even the shadows look clunky. There is a missing radiance. And yet, before van Meegeren's confession, it wasn't so clear cut. He had his buyers.

What I inherited is more of a mystery. My first attempt to learn more information about my dad didn't get very far. Even though I told my mom and step-dad about interviewing with the CIA, I never told my family why I did it. That was too difficult for me to talk about; better to keep it secret and not trouble anybody with my curiosity. Which brings us to the vulnerability a CIA shrink might have glimpsed in my psyche, the invisible scar I live with: my origins have always been something my family felt it had to hide. It was never spoken about openly. For twenty years it was a secret. Then I had to hide who I was even after I'd learned the truth. There were feelings to consider. Differences to explain. Conversations too difficult to bear. Better to avoid the disquieting truth and tip-toe around it quickly and quietly. My last name is Gibson, not Smith.

So I was born. My upbringing was not a hurricane drama—in fact, I was quite content—but I was later told my childhood was a fiction. How do you know who you are? Are you so sure? My identity changed in a shocking instant. All of a sudden I discovered I lived in a lie created by others, which left me holding only a brittle sense of who I truly was.

It could leave me paralyzed. One time, I was with my family for Thanksgiving. My mom and some others at the table wanted to know what last name my then-wife and I might give our child one day, if we had one, since she had kept her maiden name. Defensive and pressed into a corner, my wife said something she would later regret. "His last name doesn't mean anything," she said, no doubt referring to my mysterious origins: "It could be anything." What she said cut deep, but I was silent, dazed. Part of me understood why she might reach for that sharp weapon. I had been so uncertain about my name myself that she clearly picked up on the ambivalence. Even so, our marriage soon collapsed because time and again I chose silence over revelation.

A man's life is shaped to a strong degree by his relationship to his father, if only genetic, though the unspoken debts are usually more oblique, more unpredictable. I know I've lost something. I lost someone. And for the rest of my life, I've been trying to get it back.

● ● ●

The books the CIA told me to read in 2007 detailed the failures of the intelligence community in the Middle East. George Tenet, the director of the agency, had told the president and Congress the evidence for weapons of destruction in Iraq was "a slam dunk case." So formidable in bearing and pedigree at the time—the expert's expert—Tenet now in retrospect looks utterly clueless. At center stage, for the whole world to see, the political elites had failed. It was about to happen again. Sitting at my desk at *Technology Review*, I never would have guessed for a moment that a financial crisis, which would end in an economic catastrophe not seen since the Great Depression, was only months away from its first earth-rattling bankruptcies. It was October 2007. Over the summer, hedge funds run by Bear Stearns, Goldman Sachs, and others had lost billions as more and more people began defaulting on subprime loans. A *Tech Review* editor told me to look into the role computers played in the massive sell-off that had turned into a nosedive. I thought—quite mistakenly—that these banks knew what they were doing. In the story I filed for the magazine, I foolishly wrote, "Once fund managers understood what was happening—too many computers were executing the same types of trades based on the same strategy—the models were altered, and in time, many losses were recovered." How wrong I was!

By March, Bear Stearns lay in ruins. And then in September 2008, less than a year later, Lehman Brothers blew up. The entire world economy ground to a halt. Unemployment levels skyrocketed. The bankers, the regulators, the rating agencies, the faceless bureaucrats at the Fed—all of them were blithely oblivious as they led the world economy off a cliff. All of a sudden we recognized we were not as wealthy as we thought we were. We discovered we lived in an illusion created by others. I had known the feeling.

I had some of the puzzle pieces, but I couldn't see how they fit together. My whiskers twitched, but there was nothing to unify what appeared to me to be unrelated catastrophes. Pick just about any domain of authority, and I could see a chasm widening between the stated purpose of an institution and its actual performance. Then one day, David Rotman, one of the *Tech Review* editors, asked me to interview an entrepreneur for an article, one of the cofounders of PayPal. Rotman thought he'd be a good fit for the Q&A at the back of the magazine. When I talked to him, Max Levchin mentioned a friend of his who, as I would learn, had a theory that could explain our decline and the rumbling beneath the foundations. The dot-com bubble, the Housing Bubble, the coming Sovereign Debt Crisis—Levchin's friend was saying in public speeches that these events were all connected by an underlying trend, which was gathering force. And so it was that I first learned the name of a man who would dramatically change the course of my life. That, too, started with a phone call.

• 2 •

CARDWELL'S LAW

In San Francisco there are no explosions of light. A washed sea light, filtered by vapors off the Pacific, soften the city's colors, so the sun is never blinding and the edges never sharp. It is an enclave of pastel Victorian townhouses floating in the fog, where a gilded youth once gave free rein to animal spirits. A misty chaos bathed in a golden light, it has had its share of roaring noons. Out of an office window, I could see Alcatraz about two miles away. A ferry full of tourists, whipped and battered in the wind, was making its way to the grim little isle. How absurd, I thought, that a city would waste that astonishingly beautiful island to honor the monument of a ghastly prison.

"Hi, I'm Peter," said Peter Thiel, stepping into the room through the door.

A printout of my résumé was in his hand. He was wearing white athletic shorts, a white polo, and sneakers and looked as though he had just returned from a workout. I was surprised by the informality. It was a late afternoon in August of 2010. I was dressed in the only semi-formal attire I owned at that time, the uniform of my bookish life: a drab professorial corduroy blazer too long in the sleeves, a crumpled dress shirt, and jeans. Peter motioned me to sit and, as he took his place at the head of the table, placed my résumé in front of him. I took the seat closest to him on the right-hand side. We were in a conference room in his offices in the Presidio.

He stared for a moment at the résumé. "You've been to a lot of schools."

"I've been to the innermost room of the temple. And I can tell you, it's empty."

Peter laughed. "And grad students can only live on burnt microwave popcorn for so long."

The first time I'd heard Peter's name was on that phone call with Max Levchin I took a couple of years before at *Tech Review*. I interviewed Levchin about what he'd been up to in the five years since selling PayPal to eBay for $1.5 billion.

"I took a year off to travel the world and relax on a beach," Max told me. "It was probably the most miserable year of my life."

I almost blurted out: "What is *wrong* with you?"

"I was consuming things while all my friends were building great companies."

"Who are your friends?" I asked.

I had to look up the names. Remember this was 2007. No one outside tech really knew who these people were. He mentioned Elon Musk, who I discovered was building electric sports cars and rockets; Reid Hoffman, who founded LinkedIn; Chad Hurley, Steven Chen, and Jawed Karim, who founded YouTube and sold it to Google for $1.65 billion in less than two years; Russel Simmons and Jeremy Stoppelman, who founded Yelp; and finally, this one guy who was vaguely like a public intellectual, an outspoken libertarian, except he ran a venture capital fund and hedge fund. His name was Peter Thiel. All of them had come together on PayPal. From out of nowhere this offbeat network of friends was building the future during a digital gold

rush. When the interview finished, I hung up the phone astonished by a feeling of sudden excitement. In my tiny cubicle in
the newsroom bullpen, I felt like Marvin Berry in *Back to the
Future* who hears rock 'n' roll before anyone else and calls his
cousin Chuck, as in Chuck Berry: "You know that new sound
you're looking for? Well, listen to *this*…"

Peter and the rest of them were hardly the first to claim that
the influence of Silicon Valley on the rest of the country—and on
the world for that matter—was immense and profound. Far from
it. Steve Jobs took first prize at the Los Altos Hyperbole Awards
when he said, "We're here to put a dent in the universe." But
Peter was the only one among all of them who said that despite
the rhetoric, we actually weren't making much technological
progress. To put that in perspective, I wasn't in Silicon Valley
for five minutes before hearing people making oaths about the
future, declaring cosmic prophecies, telling big stories about the
brain and computers and inevitable exponential growth. And yet
by the time I met him in 2010, Peter had been giving talks for a
few years on how this account of accelerating change was wrong.

He pointed to three key facts. The first was that median wages
had been stagnant since about 1971.[1] Prior to that era, wages
and productivity gains went hand in hand. Since technological
progress meant doing more with less, people used to see their
paychecks grow alongside those newfound capacities. After 1971,
those gains vanished. The second was that the frequency and
magnitude of manias, booms, and busts were on the rise: Japan
in the '80s, Long Term Capital Management's implosion in '98,
the dot-com boom and bust from 1995 to 2001, and, to top it off,
the 2007–8 financial crisis. There were all sorts of debates about
the origins of these bubbles, but a good analogy was that if doctors were looking at this graph and its increasing amplitudes,
they'd know there was something deeply wrong with the patient's

underlying health. The third fact was the number of failed rosy predictions from the space age of the sixties. Peter loved to cite a French journalist who wrote a bestseller in France in 1967 called *Le Défi Américain* (*The American Challenge*), a delusional book that predicted Americans would be working only fifteen hours a week by the year 2000 due to the abundance created by technology. To add to that, the whole genre of science fiction had degraded from the adventure of *Star Trek* to the terror of the *Terminator*. This crystallized into Thiel's famous aphorism: "We wanted flying cars, instead we got 140 characters." Peter would give versions of this stagnation talk at Silicon Valley conferences to audiences who thought they'd achieve immortality someday soon by uploading their minds into computers. He told them they were in denial.

• • •

Like Peter, I felt that the modern world was becoming increasingly hostile to innovation. I'd been writing about this on a blog called "Let a Thousand Nations Bloom." I'd set myself the task of answering a question that would never get raised in the philosophy department on Merton Street in Oxford: *what if there were no new countries?* Then, as now, there were 193 countries recognized by the United Nations. In 2050, should there be more or fewer than that? Different answers to that question imply different visions of the future. The science writer Robert Wright, for instance, in his book *Non-Zero*, argues the number should be one: all the nations of the world united under a one-world government, the better to handle global existential issues like bioterror or climate change.[2] To the contrary, I thought that would be a total catastrophe. My answer was that the future would be worse and worse the lower the total number of countries sank below 193. History suggests that fragmented governance, as well as new nations with new laws, are a good thing. Without them, social, technological, and scientific stagnation tend to follow. The big question for me was *why*.

Era by era, innovation has been concentrated geographically, like a hive. Since the First World War, America has been the leader, the Bay Area in particular in the latter half of the 20th century. But before that, Victorian Britain led the way, and before that, it may have been the Netherlands, and then earlier, Renaissance Italy, and before that Fujian China, Rome, and Athens. The historical record shows all creative clusters, businesses, and institutions age and then eventually collapse, unless they are renewed by the dynamics of competition and new entry. In my writing, I argued there's no reason to suppose this decline won't happen to laws, social policy, and even the spirit of a culture, as vested interests poison the sources of creativity and thicken the barriers to entry.[3]

This creative life-cycle, this transition from birth to flowering to corruption to decline, from ripeness to decadence, has come to be known as Cardwell's Law, after an idea that the British historian Donald Cardwell hammered home in his classic 1972 book, *Turning Points in Western Technology*: "no nation has been very creative for more than a historically short period. Fortunately, as each leader has flagged there has always been, up to now, a nation or nations to take over the torch."[4] "Up to now" was the key phrase. If the United States stopped innovating, there was no one left to keep the flame burning. China may have begun to quicken its development, but its expansion was merely catch-up growth: it is far easier to copy than to invent. Instead, new nations, like the United States at its founding, offered the most hope because they could experiment with new rules and weren't beholden to the accumulating coalitions that had largely bent the political system to their own selfish ends.

The only problem was, there was no land left on Earth for new nations to sprout from. So we were stuck. Unbeknownst to me, months before I was hired, some of my blog posts explaining the political economy of this dynamic had already made the rounds in Peter's hedge fund office. I'd never have guessed that a few months after I wrote them, I'd be in his conference room discussing my theories, as we were doing now.

This was ostensibly a job interview—that's why my résumé was on the table—although going in, I wasn't sure exactly what the job was. There was no description. Peter's executive team had told me only that they needed a researcher. I had little money; no health care; and was holed up in a tiny apartment in Los Angeles, freelancing and writing stories. When Peter's team told me about the job opening, I was instantly curious about it, despite my inexperience in finance, because I remembered hearing about Peter's contrarian streak during that phone call with Max Levchin. The setting also added a strange allure to the idea: I was standing on the roof of a houseboat in the Sacramento River Delta with a few of Peter's staffers. I recall being mildly awed at having just met the inventor of the Facebook "Like" button. It was after midnight, and we were all watching an acrobat do flips on a trapeze that was hanging off the side of another boat piloted by a Burning Man fanatic named Chicken John. The trapeze artist stuck all her catches, swings, and flips. Amid all that, these two guys had told me about a job opening with Peter Thiel and I said I'd like to pursue it.

● ● ●

Now Peter and I started chatting about the pathologies of dysfunctional universities. He would turn his head and look into the distance out of the window as he thought a question through. Thiel is comfortable with silences in conversation, letting seconds tick by to actually think. Such moments generate suspense, but more often than not, he pops the tension with a wry aphorism or a telling anecdote. People are always surprised at how funny Thiel is in person, chiefly because they expect to meet a Vulcan. He is not that. He has the mischievous smile of an American pirate, but there's also something faintly European about him, even in athletic wear, even in California. He would quote Goethe's *Faust* in German, which he speaks fluently (he was born in Frankfurt), while his intellectual mentor is the French literary theorist René Girard, who rose to prominence in the 1950s and '60s for his work on religion and the madness of crowds.

Though Peter didn't tell me this in our conversation, I would learn later that he had spent the previous year researching universities. He, too, had seen the cracks in the ivory tower. The head of his philanthropic foundation was looking into what it would take to start a new university, gathering a history of schools established over the last 150 years, how they had fared, and what the outcomes were. Peter wondered if a new competitor to all the others would be able to offer something truly different. Perhaps the problems plaguing higher education could be avoided by starting over from scratch. But he and his team had concluded it was impossible and unwise. There were too many regulatory hurdles. Too many issues with prestige.

"When I was eighteen or nineteen," I said, jumping into a moment of silence. "I fell in love with T. S. Eliot, and I was obsessed with the author bio on the back flap of all his books. The little paragraph under his picture. It said Eliot had a Ph.D. in philosophy from Harvard. *Talk about mimetic desire.* I remember thinking I'd need to do the same if I was ever going to write well. I was in the grip of something."

"Well, it's tricky," Peter said. "Don't be too hard on yourself."

"Mimetic desire" was the term René Girard had coined to describe his theory of human motivation. At bottom, Girard believed we didn't want the things we wanted for their own sake. We wanted them because other people wanted them. We imitated their desires, in a way that resembled a contagion. I had no notion of where it came from, but I burned with a longing to become a poet and a philosopher, a writer like Eliot, but I couldn't admit that out loud to anyone. Certainly not in an academic philosophy department. I suppose I was used to hiding sensitive truths. I imagined the Ph.D. credential would be an armor against my insecurities, as well as a way to buy time for reading and writing. It was a way to hedge my true ambition. In the event, though, I didn't even get that. I found I had trapped myself in a cage among academic hairsplitters who believed it was more important to be careful than exciting. The field was creatively exhausted—no new revelations or path-breaking discoveries, only pedantic fine-tuning by imperceptible degrees. Careers were made by pleasing your betters and winning their recommendation, rather than by advancing bold ideas. But worse than that, from top to bottom, I felt that humanities departments suffered from a spiritual sickness.

When I think of my time in grad school, I recall a professor from George Washington University I overheard once at a cocktail party. Walking around a conversation cluster, I heard him giving career advice. He had studied both law and philosophy for joint degrees and was telling a group of grad students with the same credentials that they could improve their chances of being hired by writing a few substandard articles for some second- or third-tier law reviews. It's easier to get published in a law review, he explained, because they're run by law students, not professors.

I was affronted by his candor. It was dishonest to the fight, and dull to the imagination. No doubt, he had his practical problems. He talked about his wife, the kids, the mortgage, the bills, and his Zoloft prescription. But he was so professionalized, so subject to the conforming norms of bureaucratic professorhood, that I wondered whether there was any gap between the floor of his dullness and the height of his imagination. Thinking about him made me want to surface and gasp for air. His story was by no means exceptional. Academic philosophy was like Alcatraz. A museum prison built on a beautiful old island. I chose to escape.

And so, much to my amazement, I found myself sitting across from a man who was the antithesis of that professor. Like me, he had studied philosophy. Unlike me, he did not hide his ambitions. He asserted them with gusto. He possessed the strength I found wanting in myself. The founding vision of PayPal wasn't to argue with the Federal Reserve about the correct rate of inflation. That was for the readers of *Econometrica*. In the 1990s, Peter and the other PayPal founders—Max Levchin, Elon Musk, Luke Nosek, and others—dreamt of escaping that turgid debate by creating a new world currency, free from all government control and dilution. This would be nothing short of the end of monetary sovereignty. Bitcoin before Bitcoin. In the end, they didn't get there, but they did invent a payment system worth billions in the process. For Peter, new technologies and scientific discoveries were primal, fundamental forces shaping human history. Seven billion mouths to feed. One hundred and twenty people dying per minute. Human destiny was perpetually in sudden death overtime and the fate of our world could depend on the efforts of a few friends building the future in a lab or a garage on the hinge of history.

"I know a lot of people who believe the world could come to an end soon," I said. "And yet I find it funny that these same people are all banking their retirements on the price of their homes increasing in value."

Peter expanded on such inconsistencies, the chasm between belief and choice. "This is just crazy at state pension funds," he said. "They're locked into promises with guarantees that their pensions will grow at seven or eight percent annually. But then these same people vote for policies that make it impossible for the economy to grow fast enough for any pension fund to earn anything close to eight percent."

He then launched into a short dissertation on the failure of libertarians to understand that groups, crowds, tribes, and nations all had lives of their own and behaved in distinctive ways. The discipline of economics and the theory of efficient markets were on shaky foundations because they relied on the assumption of methodological individualism, meaning that in building models of social phenomena, economists took prefer- ences as given, and that any differences or changes in behavior could be explained solely by differences in prices or incomes. This assumption could not explain the madness of crowds, however. Nor, according to Peter, could it explain bubbles.

We covered a lot of ground in over an hour. It hadn't felt like a job interview. To wrap it up, Peter said, "I'm teaching a course this winter at Stanford Law School on technology and philosophy. Would you like to help me on that and work on the research team on the fund? We can start there and see where it goes."

It felt like an opportunity I couldn't pass up. Besides, I could work for Peter for a year and then head back to my garret in Los Angeles and return to scribbling. "That sounds fun. I'd love to."

Peter and I walked out of the conference room. He took a

turn into his executive assistant's office, my résumé in his hand, to find out what was up next for him. I made my way across a library full of chess boards to Jim O'Neill's office. He was one of Peter's lieutenants I met on the houseboat.

"How'd it go?" Jim asked.

"I think he likes me. He says he'd like to hire me."

"Great. Did you talk about compensation or the role?"

"Not really. He asked me if I'd help him with the law school class."

"Well, how much do you make now?"

"I make nothing."

Jim laughed. "O.K."

"But I love what I do," I said. I knew I had to think about the details, even though I had already agreed in principle. The truth was, I didn't want to be owned by anybody. My twenties had been spent in a library but that didn't mean I'd wasted them. Many of my friends had established their careers as bankers, management consultants, doctors, and lawyers, but I wouldn't have traded my path for theirs. I was a fledgling writer. It is worthwhile, I've found, even when light is absent, to face in the direction it might emanate from.

•   •   •

It was late in the day. I left Peter's office, which was located in the Letterman Buildings of the Presidio, the same complex that housed Lucas Films. There was a statue of Yoda in a fountain outside. Taxis were hard to find in San Francisco. There was no Uber, no Lyft. My flight time was approaching. I walked into the Marina district to find a cab. From there, the city's disorienting hills rose quickly after Lombard Street into Pacific Heights, which was rich with townhouses and terraced mansions. There were views to the Golden Gate Bridge, the Bay, Alcatraz, and the tony towns to the north. At dusk, the sun reflected off thousands of windows in the East Bay, flaring apricot then red.

As my plane back to Los Angeles banked west over San Bruno Mountain and South San Francisco, I thought about the California light. It was so bright compared to back East. I hoped it was never going to run out. But Cardwell's Law said otherwise. Innovation always dries up. I rested my head against the window and, as I began to doze off, the thoughts of the day came back to me. That sad professor from George Washington University. We were both at a conference about the moral principles that should guide us in no-win scenarios, such as deciding who should live and who would die. I thought of Peter Thiel at a chessboard refusing to lose. To find a route, believing it exists, although it has not yet been found. A philosophy hidden in every action. "In the beginning was the deed," Goethe wrote in *Faust*. "*Im Anfang war die Tat.*"

The next day Jim O'Neill called me. He said they'd like to offer me a job as an analyst at the hedge fund. Starting salary at $75,000. I took an hour or two to mull it over and talk to my mom. I called Jim back. Like Lucretius, I wanted to be a poet-philosopher. But unlike him I was suddenly trying to work at a hedge fund.

"I accept."

He laughed again. "I'm going to pretend you made a counteroffer. We can give you eighty thousand."

There was no denying it, I sucked at negotiating and Jim wanted to help me out. I was greener than a one-dollar bill when it came to business. In preparing for the law school class, however, Peter gave me one request: "We have to make it as subversive as possible." Oh, I may not know business, but I could do that alright...you know that new sound you're looking for?...well, listen to this...

· 3 ·

THE ANTI-RHODES

A burnt hole from a cigarette in a hideous floral duvet. I didn't see it when I went to bed, but here it was staring at me. A leak stain on the ceiling tile. I got in late to the motel, La Luna Inn, on the corner of Lombard and Broderick in the San Francisco Marina. On this stretch, which carries traffic from the city to the Golden Gate Bridge, Lombard Street is a filthy boulevard of diners, dive bars, and seedy motels. Just one block to either the north or south on parallel streets is another world of chic shops and charming apartments. It was my first day of work. I'd picked La Luna because it was cheap, and only three blocks from the Letterman offices in the Presidio. But now I was questioning my judgment as I saw the faded stains from God-knows-what brownish liquid on the bedsheets. It was even on the curtains and the ceiling. I sat down in a chair, which had a gash down its backrest like a knife wound, and opened my email.

Jim O'Neill wrote to me at 10:41 p.m., but I hadn't seen it until now. "There's a good chance you and I will need to leave the office by 9:35 a.m. to meet Peter for a media interview. So go ahead and arrive by 9:20 if you can, and we'll see what happens."

A week before, I'd purchased a gray off-the-rack Banana Republic suit, figuring that if I worked at a hedge fund I'd need it at some point. Should I wear that? It wasn't so much a question of wanting to wear the right thing. It was that I *really* didn't want to wear the wrong thing. I didn't like standing out. I fell back on the corduroy blazer, with no tie, the better to blend into the background. I emailed my mom: "first day, wish me luck!"

Half an hour later I entered the office, my college-ruled notebook in hand, and introduced myself to the sunny Megan Wheeler who greeted me at the Thiel reception room. After a few quick HR formalities, Megan walked me down a corridor towards chattering and keyboards, and then on to the vast trading floor. The room had a high vaulted ceiling and daylight poured in from a long wall of windows looking out to the leafy Presidio and, beyond it, to the enormous classical rotunda of the Palace of Fine Arts. She showed me to my desk on the trading floor. Two monitors. Why would I need two monitors?

No sooner had I put down my notebook than Jim O'Neill appeared at my desk.

"Good to see you. Let's go. We have to get to Peter's house."

Curiosity passed over the faces of some of the traders and the back office ops team. Siu Chang, the CFO, poked her head around her four monitors to size me up, raising a quizzical eyebrow. Who is this guy? The general counsel would meet me later to give me the statutory compliance spiel. But all their final judgments would have to wait, because now Jim and I were walking out of the office to the elevators back down to street level.

As we walked, Jim talked: "On the plane ride back from New York last night, we came up with the idea of paying people to work on stuff outside of school. For now, we're calling it the 'anti-Rhodes Scholarship.'"

I loved the name. The Rhodes Scholarship was a program at Oxford first established in 1902 and dedicated to the idea of empire.[1] But along the way the empire vanished. And its founder, an impassioned imperialist, became a moral disgrace. Nevertheless, in one of the more surprising episodes in the intellectual history of colonialism, the Rhodes Scholarship became the premiere trophy in the English-speaking education of the polished, credentialed elite.

As an American at Oxford, I found the U.S. Rhodies insufferable, always toadying their way to greater prestige. Imagine the very best of the second-rate who contemplate nothing but looking good in the eyes of a committee. Naturally, the most famous of them became politicians or media stars: Bill Clinton, Pete Buttigieg, Rachel Maddow, George Stephanopoulos. I stayed away from them all.

My best friends at Oxford were a Marxist political theorist from Glasgow, a Dutch diplomat, and a devastatingly charming scholar of African American studies from Baltimore. One late, drunken night, the Marxist and I had a fistfight with a group of undergrad snobs by a kebab van. One of the kids knew precisely which working-class neighborhood of Glasgow John the Marxist was from just by hearing his accent alone. He asked John what a poor sod like him was doing in Oxford, and expressed disappointment that the school would admit someone like him. I told the kid to piss off.

He heard my accent. "Ah, a Yank. You have no idea how to run an empire. Your Monroe Doctrine is bullshit."

I threw the kid up against the kebab van and suddenly felt a terrible freedom in the air. Anything goes! It was an overreaction, I admit it, but the next thing I knew his friends were piling on top of me. The brawl was short, I took my licks, and when my friends and I were back in the graduate common room, laughing it off—only in Oxford would the Monroe Doctrine lead to a fight—we asked the Marxist how this little snot knew exactly where in Scotland he was from. John explained to us that the old British, aristocratic hierarchy of social class and status, with its endless gradations from the Queen to the court to the gentry on down, still lingered on in various ways, especially in accents. The British are branded on the tongue. The BBC at that time was extra careful in choosing its broadcasters, so sensitive was this issue of the accent, region, and class. I remember thinking how peculiar that was—that an accent could be a life-long tattoo of social rank. Granted, Americans have regional accents too, and the working class and underclass tend to speak in colorful slang, but for the middle-class on up American-English generally sounds the same. There has always been a determined rejection of formality among Americans. Perhaps this is an ancient relic of life on the frontier, like wagon or horse, but in voice and manner. But I tend to believe it is the vestige of something else, something long forgotten: a profound reaction against the imperial splendors of old Europe.

Though America has always had vast inequalities in wealth, and an appalling past of slavery, Americans have never lived under a hereditary aristocratic class system with titles and orders of nobility. Nevertheless, in recent decades, higher education has begun to create something close to it, as divisions have hardened into a status pyramid with hundreds of gradations, from the Rhodes to the Fulbright to the Marshall Scholarships, to the Ivy League, and so on downwards. Like any aristocratic society, with their obsessive interest in lengthy family trees, the mind of educated America has become dominated by endless conceits of pedigree. The new social pyramid isn't as sharp and steep as the old European aristocracies, but it does appear to be dividing Americans into two broad social classes: those who

have a college degree and those who do not. William Deresiewicz, a professor at Yale, confessed in a popular 2008 essay that
he "never learned that there are smart people who don't go to
college at all."[2] Which was a rather surprising statement, since
as a professor of English literature, he could have started with
William Shakespeare, Jane Austen, Charles Dickens, George
Eliot, Walt Whitman, Emily Dickinson, Ernest Hemingway, or
James Baldwin. Deresiewicz, however, was speaking candidly
to the situation today. Put simply, college graduates earn more
income on average than those who only have a high school
diploma.[3] Since about 1971, the college degree—and particularly
an Ivy League college degree—has become a badge of social and
economic rank, impervious to change and worthy of life-long
respect. In the eyes of the labor market, if someone didn't go
to college, it was as if they had to wear a hat with a D for dunce
on it for the rest of their lives. I had come to feel that view was
misguided from anecdotal observation: the average college grad
has forgotten most of what they've learned in a major they don't
even use. Employers won't hire someone if he failed all of his
classes. On the other hand, forgetting everything in those classes
seems to be fine. Failing and forgetting a class should have the
same consequences. But they don't. That's very peculiar, especially if knowledge is rewarded in the labor market. And where
is the professor who could have taught young Shakespeare? Can
greatness be taught in a classroom? (Funnily enough, Shakespeare's rivals in the theater ridiculed him for not having a college degree.) At any rate, the contemporary mania for obtaining
degrees became so intense that it was harder and harder for
anyone talented to disregard the pressures of family, friends,
and the wider world. Not going to college was unintelligible to
them and, therefore, deranged and mad. My anarchic reflexes
bristled against all of this—the accents, the pecking order, the

unexplained value of a forgotten college degree. Whatever the anti-Rhodes scholarship would be, I was all for it.

• • •

Jim and I exited the Presidio Park and crossed a street to enter the Palace of Fine Arts, a palatial domed rotunda designed by Bernard Maybeck and built for the Panama-Pacific International Exposition in 1915, a World's Fair–type event meant to stoke excitement for the universe of tomorrow. In his classical design, Maybeck wanted to convey a mood of sadness and introspection, which he felt was essential to the experience of art.[4] Around the rotunda, he placed towering Corinthian columns topped off by mysterious crates. At the corner of each crate, high in the air, a sculptured woman is standing, craning her head over the lid to see what's inside. On the ground, we're left to wonder what she sees. Perhaps it is the sight of a future that never was, boxed up and forgotten. (The glittering future of *Star Trek* also hovers about in spirit, as these grounds are also home to Starfleet and its academy for starfaring buccaneers.)

Peter's house was part of a ring of homes that circled the reflecting pond of the rotunda. He lived about 400 yards from the office. He encouraged all of us to do the same. Employees were granted an extra $1,000 per month in rent if they lived within a half-mile radius of the office. It meant we were more likely to come in early, stay late, or take a surprise meeting on the weekends. It had the added effect that we would all show up to the same watering holes after work to knock off a few drinks and gossip, tell war stories, argue over the jukebox, and have a few laughs. As far as employee benefits go, I always thought this was a wise one.

At any rate, Jim and I arrived at Peter's house and were shown to his living room by his executive assistant, where we waited a few moments. Then, bounding down the stairs, Peter suddenly swept into the room. He was in a gray suit, no tie, and a blue dress shirt. I'm no fashion expert, but his suit did not look like something off-the-rack from Banana Republic. He and his assistant debated whether or not he should wear a tie. He decided not to. The schedule for the day was first for Peter to appear on Fox Business for an interview to talk hedge fund finance, and then on to the biggest tech conference of the year, "TechCrunch Disrupt," where Peter would sit down with the reporter Sarah Lacy for an intimate fireside interview in front of several hundred people. On the way over to Peter's, as we walked under Maybeck's columns and dome, Jim told me that they had decided last night that he was going to announce the anti-Rhodes program during his talk with Lacy. The only problems were, we couldn't call it the Anti-Rhodes Scholarship and we didn't know any of the details of the program.

Peter, Jim, and I hopped into a car, and were off to the Fox network studio on Battery Street near the Embarcadero. Peter rode shotgun, with Jim and me in the back. The conversation became a rapid-fire exchange of ideas. Some matters they had discussed on the plane ride the night before, but by the time we reached the studio, we'd settled on calling it the "20 Under 20 Thiel Fellowship." It would be $100,000 for up to twenty people a year. Candidates would have to be aged nineteen or younger when they applied. And it would be a two-year program. In typical Peter fashion, there was also a *Lord of the Rings* allusion: the Fellowship of the Ring was the name given to the nine protagonists in Tolkien's first novel who set out on the quest to destroy the all-powerful evil ring.

The Fox producers brought Peter, Jim, and me to wait in a green room until they were ready to film the segment. We continued our conversation. This was Monday, September 27, 2010, and the movie about Facebook's founding, *The Social Network*, was set to be released nationwide that coming Friday, October 1. Aaron Sorkin's script had been leaked months before, and it was clear that Mark Zuckerberg, Sean Parker, and, in one short scene, Peter, were all being portrayed negatively. On page 135 of the script, we meet Peter, who became the first outside investor into Facebook in 2004:

INT. THIEL'S OUTER OFFICE - DAY
We're in the offices of a guy whose hero is Gordon Gekko. MARK and SEAN are waiting—seated side by side—for a verdict. SEAN's wearing his best Prada, MARK's wearing his hoodie and Adidas flip-flops. After a moment....

SEAN
You know this is where they filmed Towering Inferno.

MARK
That's comforting.

Aaron Sorkin may write dialogue like Gershwin crafting a tune, but he has trouble with the facts. Peter's hero is not Gordon Gekko. But the most egregious fiction in *The Social Network* is that Sorkin tries to pin Zuckerberg's motivations for everything on the resentment he supposedly felt being rejected by a pretty girl. But the truth is Zuckerberg was already dating Priscilla Chan then, and he went on to marry her in 2012. Only Hollywood can build a fiction like this and still tell audiences that the movie is "based on a true story."

As far as this scene goes, the pitch meeting at which Peter decided to invest in Facebook was nothing like Sorkin portrays it. The key player who brought everyone together was Peter's old friend and former Stanford roommate, Reid Hoffman, the founder of LinkedIn.[5] Ever since the early 1990s, when he was reading novels like *Snow Crash* by Neal Stephenson, Hoffman had been forecasting the arrival of virtual networks. He tried to start his own in the late '90s, more or less a dating site, but it failed. He still kept tabs on the landscape, though. Friendster, which Hoffman and Peter invested in, emerged as the market leader in the early 2000s, followed quickly by Myspace. This nascent industry was suddenly lifting off. Hoffman wanted to see the technology deepen and broaden freely, so early on he acquired the patent for the invention of the online social network with Marc Pincus, the founder of Zynga, paying $700,000 to an extinct company called sixdegrees. A virtual social network seems like more of a concept than an object such as a telephone, but there's still a patent on its invention. It was a defensive purchase, because competitors like Yahoo! might have out-bid him for it and then used the patent to shut him and the others down. But since Hoffman and Pincus refused—very generously—to enforce the patent on others, it also meant companies like Myspace and Facebook could grow.

Sean Parker reached out to Hoffman to pitch him Facebook. Parker was eager to have him invest in the company, given his knowledge and reputation, and Hoffman was impressed by what he saw. But he also felt it might present too great a conflict of interest with LinkedIn. So he arranged a meeting with someone he knew who would be the best angel investor for the company: Peter Thiel.

On the day of the meeting back in 2004, it's true that Zuckerberg showed up in a T-shirt, jeans, and his rubber Adidas flip-flops. Sean Parker was there along with Peter, Hoffman, and two others.[6] Zuckerberg showed no impulse to fit in or look professional—he would never wear a tie or gray suit—and

Peter and Hoffman recall that his pitching skills were abysmal. Zuckerberg stared at the conference room desk, not saying much. Ever the showman, Parker led the pitch from the start. Halfway through, Zuckerberg woke up, cut in, and started pitching a totally different idea, a file-sharing company called Wirehog. Alarm bells went off in Hoffman's head, "No! Get rid of that!" Peter wasn't interested in file sharing. They wrangled the conversation back to this cute little company Thefacebook. It was growing at a tremendous rate on college campuses, and its user engagement was unreal. Once it captured a campus, 80 percent of users returned to the site every day, many of them four times a day. There were still big questions about whether the company could grow out of college campuses into the wider world, and there was competition from Myspace and others, but that intense level of engagement impressed Peter. And so it was that a few days later when Peter, Zuckerberg, and Parker agreed on terms, Peter made one of the greatest angel investments in Silicon Valley history: $500,000 for about 10 percent of the company.

There was another fact about Zuckerberg in the 2004 pitch meeting that stood out. He was twenty years-old at the time. By launching a fellowship to support nineteen year-olds five days before the opening night of *The Social Network*, Peter was in effect changing the conversation. Not only were there other people like Zuckerberg out there, but Peter was going to give them no-strings grants to help them get started.

● ● ●

Back in the green room at the Fox Business studio, the producers hadn't come in yet. Jim, Peter, and I were discussing potential answers if he was asked about *The Social Network*. Peter hit it: the Facebook movie is actually an accurate portrayal of how

Hollywood works. Hollywood feeds upon narcissism, syco-
phancy, fragile egos, stolen ideas, and vendettas. Today, its chief
emblem is Harvey Weinstein's heavy-jowled plutocratic sneer.
Hollywood is all about fame, a zero-sum game, where the more
famous you get, the more people try to destroy you. That's not
how Silicon Valley works. Silicon Valley is about positive-sum
games—employees, investors, and customers all win. There is
no limit to discovery and invention, which cannot be faked or
handed out to favorites.

Sure enough, when Peter was on stage being interviewed by
Sarah Lacy at TechCrunch Disrupt, she brought the movie up.
And that was the answer he gave. But then he added something
else. "One very good thing about the movie is the extent that
it encourages young Americans to think that they too can start
great companies—I think that will dominate everything." It was
his hope that even though the movie is full of inaccuracies and
falsehoods, it might still convey some of the allure and excitement of starting a company from nothing.

"How did you get away with being in this movie so little?"
Lacy continued. I was backstage with Jim, peeking from behind
the curtains. Just an hour or so before, the three of us had
been knocking around ideas on the fellowship. Jim and Peter
huddled to discuss things further, and I was playing block and
tackle, as businessmen and women—many of whom paid huge
amounts of money for backstage access—approached Peter to
try to pitch him their big idea. It was unrelenting. My job was
to talk to these people, hear them out, get their business cards,
and politely thank them for their offer. I had no way of telling
if they were visionaries or frauds.

Peter was on a roll answering Lacy's questions. I strolled
from backstage to an area to the side of the auditorium. The
stage was brightly lit, with Peter and Lacy sitting in two large

armchairs, as though their conversation were a cozy tête-à-tête in a weird furniture showroom. The auditorium was dark like a theater. Red diodes moved about. Many faces were lit up by the feeble blue glow of laptop screens.

Then Lacy turned to the crowd. "We only have two and a half minutes left, but Peter has a rather exciting announcement here to make at Disrupt."

I saw some faces look up from their laptops. Peter launched the fellowship.

"We've been brainstorming on how we might break the relative stasis we've been in as a society. With the VC fund, we've been investing in great new technology companies. One of the things we think is very important is to encourage potential young entrepreneurs to get involved in science and technology. And one of the initiatives we're going to start in the next few weeks is a program for offering grants up to a hundred thousand dollars for twenty people under age twenty for starting something new."

"For dropping out of school?"

He laughed. "Ahh, for *stopping out* of school."

Lacy cracked up. "This is every parent's worst nightmare! You're offering kids money to leave school and start companies."

"Well, it depends on what the parents are worried about. Look at all the debt students are accumulating."

As many in the audience knew, but I did not, the term "stopping out" comes from financial trading. If a trader is stopped out, it means he's cutting an existing position that's losing money. If students were going to stop out, it would mean that if they had an idea, they could stop paying $60,000 or $70,000 a year to pursue it. Because the cost of college had skyrocketed more than four hundred percent (not counting inflation) since the 1970s, students and their families were paying extraordinary sums to avoid falling behind. Like the Red Queen says to Alice in Wonderland, you have to run faster and faster just to stay in place. It was increasingly rare for any student to graduate debt-free. The upshot was that instead of pursuing a risky idea or a passion project, many graduates chose to take safe but well-paying jobs. They needed to discharge those debts, even if it cost them their imagination. Thus, the best universities in the world turned many graduates into krill for too-big-to-fail corporate leviathans. That year, in 2010, investment banking and management consulting swallowed up more than *half* of Harvard and Princeton's graduating classes.[7]

As Peter stepped off stage, there were a few chuckles and head-shakes of disbelief in the audience. Another eccentric Silicon Valley absurdity! Immediately, another reporter, Evelyn Rusli, grabbed Peter for an interview. With more time, he expanded on the connection between the monolithic path to college and stagnation.

"Congratulations on the announcement for the Thiel Fellowship. If I have this right, it's roughly hundred thousand dollar grants for twenty people under twenty—"

"—for two years," Peter picked up. "For intense work in a science and technology area, which we'll collaborate with them on to figure out how to do. The basic idea is to try to figure out how we start building the great technological breakthroughs that will take our civilization to the next level. We think that things have stalled out. And we think we need to go back to some of the hard technologies—space, robotics, artificial intelligence, next-generation biotech—that will really make living standards better in the next twenty years."

Why focus on young people? Because no one else was. We were looking for a third way. The first way was the path through the college admissions committee all the way to Goldman Sachs.

Most believe that should be the goal for all. In order to improve the lives of everyone, we need more people going to college, so they say. The other way was the struggle of those without the skills to succeed in the present-day economy. Sure, they didn't have soul-crushing debts and hyper-tracked careers, but, because they were branded as non-graduates, they had to work even harder just to stay afloat. So, what if instead there was a third way that denied the assumptions behind these two paths? We could be *for* learning, but *against* the empty, expensive rituals the world had come to call "higher education."

It's a myth that the elite students of today are all the leaders of tomorrow. The future was built in garages. Jobs and Woz. Gates. Zuckerberg. Hell, let's add Shakespeare. Barely three years of college between them all. Our theory was that these people weren't merely outliers but, with Zuckerberg, the start of something new. Peter had spent the previous year investigating how to start a new university. But somewhere along the way, he learned that competition is for losers, as he'd say many years later. The standard view about competition is that it's the crucible of excellence from which flows all progress and prosperity. The paradoxical thing, however, is that whenever we compete against others very intensely, we get better only at the dimension we're competing on. AP exams, SATs, GPAs, diplomas—what does this system do to children and teenagers? What does it do to society? We've been competing on these dimensions for so long that we forgot to ask whether they were worth pursuing at all. And here we come to the worst consequence of the whole tournament for prestige: if progress had stalled for forty years, then the so-called meritocratic elite were actually failures. The cultivated class had made a mess of things for a generation. So how to avoid this destructive competition altogether? As Emerson wrote in "Self-Reliance," "There is a time in every man's education when he arrives at the conviction that envy is ignorance; that imitation is suicide." Invent your own game.

• • •

When Jim, Peter, and I got back to the hedge fund's office in the Presidio, Peter splintered off to attend to other matters, while Jim and I walked into Jonathan Cain's office. Jonathan was the president of Peter's philanthropic foundation. He had spent the day hashing out with the foundation's attorney how it would work, legally, to run this kind of program. He had also written a draft of a press release that we needed to send out to the media. None of us had eaten all day. We were starving. I ran out across the street to Liverpool Lil's, a famous dumpy pub on the edge of the park. I picked up some grub and met Jim and Jonathan on a balcony outside the trading floor that overlooked the Palace of Fine Arts, Bernard Maybeck's imagined ruins of a lost civilization.

Jonathan got in touch with Elon Musk to get a quote for us to include. We were picking at french fries and scarfing down burgers and then something Jim or Jonathan were discussing made me remember my old friend, John, the Glaswegian Marxist.

"You know it's a superpower," John had said.

"What is?"

We had been eating breakfast, sopping up fried egg yolks with toast at a dingy English diner off St. Giles Street in Oxford. The spring term was over, and we had stayed up all night, first roistering at the pubs and parties, and then binge-watching Aaron Sorkin's *The West Wing* until dawn. Now John was trying to convince me not to drop out, not to quit philosophy.

"To be able to think. To write. To understand the things we study. It's a superpower. And we have an obligation to pass it on to the next generation. You can't leave."

I pawed at what remained of the English breakfast on my plate. Sausage, beans, and runny eggs.

"Superpowers—come *on* man. I'm done. " I dropped out of Oxford a few months later.

There was a famous quote of Marx's that John liked, from Marx's collection of notes on an obscure thinker named Feuerbach. It is also on Marx's gravestone in Highgate Cemetery: "Philosophers have hitherto only interpreted the world in various ways; the point is to change it."

Jim and Jonathan were brainstorming, throwing around potential tag lines for the press release. I surfaced from my daydream and broke in: "Change the world and call it a senior thesis." They loved it. It was my sole contribution in the announcement.

It didn't take long for the media to pick up on the launch. Jacob Weisberg, a former Rhodes Scholar, wrote op-eds denouncing us immediately. He deemed the fellowship an "appalling plan." First in *Slate*, where he was an editor, and then again in his column in *Newsweek*. "His latest crusade is his worst yet," Weisberg wrote. "Thiel Fellows will have the opportunity to emulate their sponsor by halting their intellectual development around the onset of adulthood, maintaining a narrow-minded focus on getting rich as young as possible and thereby avoid the siren lure of helping others or pursuing knowledge for its own sake."[8] Ah, the old American Rhodies coming with the hard zingers. This was only the beginning. In the years ahead, our opponents would include all the bastions of elite higher educational success: the media, universities, and the Treasury Secretary of the United States.

Back at La Luna Inn that night, I turned on the lights and threw my notebook and keys on the desk. I saw the stains on the curtains and the ceiling, the hideous floral duvet, the winking cigarette burn hole, but was too tired to care. I called my mom and step-dad to tell them about my day. "If that was my first day," I told them. "I wonder what tomorrow is going to be like."

There was a lot to do. I'd been hired to help teach a class and do research for the hedge fund. Now I was also part of this new thing. "Applications will be available in October," we announced in the release. "And due later in the fall, with the fellowship beginning in 2011." We were going to have to find someone who had some experience with this kind of thing. Fortunately, she found us first.

· 4 ·

LEAVE THEM KIDS ALONE

In the last week of September 2010, Danielle Strachman watched an online video of Sarah Lacy's interview with Peter Thiel. She thought the fellowship sounded smart and timely, in line with her own ideas about learning-by-doing, but because Peter talked about the program in the present tense, she figured he already had full-time staff working on it.

Danielle was living in Mountain View in an intentional community called Monroe House. The commune had an eco-green ethic and, while she understood that the environment was in peril, her real interest was to experience communal living. Monroe House's soft, laid-back atmosphere was a far cry from the pragmatic, upright Yankee industry of her hometown near Boston, where her dad worked as a mechanic on vintage cars and her mom worked as a carpenter. Danielle may have dressed like a California hippy, but if anyone was late to a House meeting, her blue eyes were as cold as the North Atlantic.

Danielle was also attracted to Monroe House by the commune's large garden. After exhausting years spent educating children, she finally had the freedom to get her hands dirty and, more importantly, reflect on her life's direction. It was all perfect except for one thing. Despite its collective nature, living in an intentional community was pricey. She paid $800 a month for a decent-sized room in Monroe House, to live alongside four other people. It wasn't all that much more expensive than her old place in San Diego, but now she was burning through her savings. Plus, in San Diego, she didn't have housemates who practiced orgasm as a form of meditation.

Danielle had moved up to the Bay Area to be closer to her boyfriend. She was 29-years-old and knew she couldn't tune in, turn on, and drop out forever. One time in the garden, uprooting weeds in the dirt, she cried suddenly, wondering what the hell she was doing in Silicon Valley. She wasn't a coder. She didn't have the technical skills—none that would be valued in the Bay Area, anyways. Back in San Diego, she had founded and run a charter school. What use would that be among all these tech companies?

Then one day in early October, Lindy Fishburne called her, fizzing with excitement. Lindy worked for the Thiel Foundation and had hired Danielle part-time to help her plan and run a philanthropy event. "The Thiel Foundation has lost its mind!" she said. "They started this new program, and they have no one running it. You have to get over here. It's perfect for you." Lindy suggested Danielle meet the foundation's president, Jonathan Cain.

In principle, the fellowship seemed exciting, but Danielle was taking time off from work for a reason. She'd worked eighty-hour weeks for two years straight as an elementary school principal. Four hundred students, aged five-to-thirteen years-old, scream-ing, running around, caroming off walls, ricocheting madly off each other, not washing their hands, getting sick—getting *her* sick! She'd never been sick so often in her life. She felt burnt out. The garden was a respite from all that.

Still, she was curious. She and Jonathan agreed to meet at a Peet's Coffee on University Avenue in Palo Alto, down the street from the entrance to Stanford University's campus, and around the corner from Facebook's (then) headquarters. University Avenue was lined with high-end shops and quirky places like the old-time Mission-style movie theater converted into a Borders Books. As Danielle didn't think it was a formal job interview, she came straight to the Peet's Coffee from the commune, where she had been gardening all day. She wore a green t-shirt with crazy wild floral patterns all over it and ripped jeans covered in dirt stains.

She arrived punctually at the Peet's and saw that Jonathan wasn't there yet. She was sipping on her chai when, from out of nowhere, he arrived in what looked like a *five-piece* suit. He was also wearing a bow tie. The only thing missing was a top hat and a monocle.

Danielle, alarmed, took another sip of her tea, and threw Jonathan some wide-eyes.

"Sorry I'm so dressed up. I have a board meeting later," he apologized.

They started with some small talk, but she couldn't stop thinking about the chasm between the way they were dressed. It was standard deviations apart. Not just two standard deviations, she recalled, because the range wasn't from normal to weird. It was far greater. Huge. Hippy Hobo meets the Monopoly man.

"It's so exciting that the Foundation launched the Thiel Fellowship. What have you got going so far?"

"We've got a website." Jonathan offered.

"O.K. great—do you know what a Thiel Fellow looks like? Who you're looking for?"

He started hemming and hawing, looking down at his polished shoes. The silence went on and on, but Danielle remembered that some people needed a lot of time and space to think. She began counting the seconds in her head. One second, two seconds...she got all the way up to fifteen. A thoughtful silence stretched into one that was awkward. She jumped back in.

"Do you know what you want the fellowship program to look like?"

Dismay crossed Jonathan's face at the mention of the word "program." Another long pause followed.

"You're not actually thinking of writing an eighteen-year-old a one-hundred thousand dollar check and then calling it a day, are you?"

Silence. Maybe that *was* the plan?

"O.K. how about this," she said. "I'm going to write you a needs assessment of all the things I think you're going to need in the next six months. And if you think I'm right about what you need, then you hire me. And if you think I'm wrong, then you can hire someone else."

"That sounds great," he said, with perceptible enthusiasm.

Back home, Danielle opened up her laptop and began to write. She explained what an application process would look like with screening. What the finalist round looks like. What happens after people are on board. She kept going, pouring into the document all the ideas she'd had in the last decade about education. The whole system, from top to bottom, was rotten. It was cathartic.

• • •

Back in 2006, in San Diego, she had confronted head-on the wall of resistance in the education establishment. That year she and her best friend, Christine Kuglen, started a charter school with the hope of testing out all these new theories on how children can learn best. Danielle had already spent five years researching pedagogy, personality, and the brain. She and Christine would meet in a coffee shop every Friday from 3 p.m. to 5 p.m. to brainstorm, get fired up on new ideas, and plan. They entered a program called Charter Launch, which the California Charter School Association put together to help new school creation.

But from the outset, they encountered formidable resistance. To get approval for the school, they'd need buy-in from the local public schools. This is like a Burger King needing permission from McDonald's to open. State funding was allocated according to "butts in the seats"—that is, if the public school lost a student to the charter school, it meant the public school also lost the money for that seat. In practice, this meant that public schools accused charter schools of stealing their funding. The resulting rancor made starting the school even tougher. But Danielle and Christine built up grass-root support by standing in front of neighborhood grocery stores for hours, talking to people in the community. In the end, their hard work paid off: they opened the school and in their first year they had 160 students. Four years and two buildings later, the school was thriving: the grades expanded, and they were up to four hundred students. They named the school "Innovations Academy."

As well as they were doing, though, Danielle felt they could be doing better. Her biggest surprise was that they had to hold off on many of their deeper theories about education. She had a strong hunch she could find a better way to open a child's curiosity, the essence of which came down to a single principle inspired by Maria Montessori: choice and non-coercion. That meant *not* using force to educate people. It meant starting where children are at—their yearnings, their interests and even their stubborn ways. But the population they were serving at Innovations Academy—working-class San Diegans, the children of recent immigrants—had other basic needs to meet first, like

having a hot meal to eat, a good night's sleep, and a stable home
life. There were also all the requirements the state of California
heaped upon them, greatly limiting what any school could do
differently. So she and Christine scrapped a lot of their bolder
plans and went back to basics.

They both worked eighty hours a week, year after year,
doing their best to help their students and manage the school's
operations. Danielle was pretty sure they both lost and gained
fifteen pounds from the stress of it. There were also the challenges she never expected: one family sued the school because
they wanted more than the school could reasonably deliver.
Then there was the problem of parental abuse. Danielle knew
that by state law, a school is categorized as a mandated reporter,
but she never expected that she'd have to call Child Protective
Services. But she did. She saw first-hand some of the dark things
that parents still do to their children. But all in all, as hard as
it was, she knew that she and Christine were doing great work
for the families they served. It warmed and thrilled her to see
the students develop and learn over time. Sure, she wouldn't
wish being a school principal on anybody. It was the most chal-
lenging thing she'd ever done. But it was also one of the best.

By 2010, Danielle needed a break from school leadership.
It had been a tremendous effort to make only incremental
improvements. She was nearly thirty and had fallen in love.
Her boyfriend lived in the Bay Area, so she moved to Mountain
View to take some time off and reflect on what to do next. The
last thing she expected was that her next educational opportunity would come so quickly or be so unusual. Thinking about
what the Thiel Fellowship might look like, she reflected on all
she'd learned about education, as well as the ideas she hadn't
yet been able to implement. It all came back to the principle of
non-coercion.[1] The fellowship would have to be an extension of

the independent, child-directed learning she'd witnessed earlier in her teaching career in homeschooling communities—only for an older age group. The fellowship couldn't be a single program or a startup accelerator, like Y Combinator. Every Thiel Fellow would have to have his or her own program or plan, and one-to-one tutorials as needed.

• • •

She wrote all her thoughts up and emailed them to Jonathan Cain. He liked Danielle's vision and they got on a call. Unlike me, she knew about anchoring in negotiations. In the needs assessment and proposal, she didn't put in anything about payment or title. She wanted to be an independent contractor. It was all so up in the air, she thought it'd be good to maintain some independence. It wasn't even clear if it was a full-time role. On the phone, Jonathan threw out the first number to her for what she'd get paid.

"How does $25 an hour sound?" he asked.

"That sounds really low."

Jesus, she couldn't believe this guy. For part-time, he was proposing to pay her less than she believed interns made.

"I was thinking more like $50 an hour."

Jonathan said he'd have to get back to her. When he did, he agreed to her terms. Given Silicon Valley's reputation for mistreating women, I should explain that Danielle and I had different jobs, and to begin with, she was a part-time contractor. But because of her talent and no-bullshit negotiating skills, within three years Danielle would be making twice what I earned. I'd learn a lot from her about business and negotiating. Many years later, when we were pitching Peter on our second venture fund, the two of us were at his conference room table. I was sitting in the very same seat I'd sat in when I'd first interviewed with

Thiel and could see Alcatraz out the window again. I'd finished explaining how our fund would serve as an indirect way to short the higher education bubble. Peter then turned his head to Danielle. Using his thumb like a hitchhiker to point at me, he said to Danielle: "Well, we know he doesn't like talking business. How much money do you need?"

But that was years later. On her first day of work on the Thiel Fellowship, Danielle wore a brown skirt and a magenta-colored top from a second-hand store. She came to the Letterman office in the Presidio and had a very good opening conversation with me, Jonathan, Jim O'Neill, and Deepali Roy, who was on the ops team at the hedge fund. It was only when Danielle got home back to the community that she saw her magenta top had big, ripped holes in the elbows, hobo style. But no one at the office had said a thing. She was starting to think maybe a former school principal could fit in after all.

·5·

THE DESK

Josh Piestrup knew this was his chance to prank the whole office. As an opening, it was just *too* good.

It was a Saturday, when the Thiel Capital office was usually empty. Piestrup had come in to put together a presentation on emerging market currencies, his assigned topic for the coming week. The research and trade meeting was a weekly gathering that Peter and the hedge fund team held to dig into big-picture themes running through financial markets and then propose trades to express these views. Sometimes it could turn into a freewheeling seminar; others it could heat up into a cross-examination with Peter as lead counsel for the prosecution. On edge at the prospect of a sandbagging in front of a room full of clever contrarians, Josh had a big homework assignment to finish before Monday morning.

Piestrup was at the trading desk, relishing the silence and carefully building his slideshow, when suddenly, the door burst open and the room was filled with thundering country-western music. The racket was followed quickly by a work crew, wearing big leather tool belts and wheeling in crates. Piestrup watched as they unspooled their measuring tapes, found their marks on the walls, and began banging. In an instant, the trading desk was filled with noise: shouting, singing, drilling, hammering, all against a blaring country soundtrack.

From London to Wall Street to Greenwich, Connecticut, the center of every hedge fund around the world is the trading desk: a big, cluttered surface, longer than any dining room table you've ever eaten at, like a banqueting table at a medieval feast. Only the work stations at this feast are overwhelmed by a mass of computer screens—often six monitors to a seat in multi-level triptychs. The mess of this machinery sits at the center of an open-plan room that provides the intellectual focus of the whole enterprise. Here, each day, beneath softly lit, high vaulted ceilings, CNBC would run mutely on television, while stock ticker symbols were on the move across the bottom of the screen. Traders would periodically bark orders into phones and pull up price charts on Bloomberg terminals. But that was where the similarity ended. The Thiel trading desk was less like a frantic pit and more like the reading room of some renegade history faculty.

Around Josh, beyond the clutter of the desk, most of the decor at Thiel Capital was in the familiar modern style, with sleek surfaces, neutral colors and clean lines. More unusual was the tremendously large taupe wall full of protrusions and indentations, like a climbing wall in a gym, that turned to form the right-hand corner of the T-intersection at the heart of things. Its sheer height opened up the space, and made the office feel like a concert hall waiting for an orchestra. Coming from the entrance corridor and taking a right at the end of that enormous wall took visitors towards Peter's corner office, down past the tables set with chess boards and chess timers and behind the mahogany bookcases filled with leather-bound editions of Madame de Sévigné, Charles Dickens and George Eliot (as well as treatises on manias, panics, and esoteric financial instruments). Elsewhere were gestures to the future: the glass doors of most offices slid open by pushing a touch-screen console, like on a starship. As most of the offices also had glass walls, on the occasions when the doors malfunctioned, the occupant was left looking like a despondent animal, trapped in a lab experiment. But for the most part, the whole environment felt polished and flawless.

Nearly every wall was blank and pure white, in keeping with the minimalist design. But this weekend, as Piestrup discovered, that was about to change. As he struggled to focus on the movements of the Peso, the Turkish Lira, the Ruble, and the Rupee amid the din, the crew was working at breakneck speed, hanging photographs and paintings.

The noise soon became too much for Josh. Just as he thought he couldn't feel any more annoyed and distracted, Eric Woersching, one of his teammates on the trading team, entered with his wife, Jessica, who was not an employee. Woersching looked surprised.

"What are *you* doing here?" he asked.

"Presentation for R and T. What are you up to?"

"Got to get my shit done."

Stanford engineer shit done, Josh thought, I know what his shit is. Like a good German obsessed with systems, Woersching always wanted to populate a giant spreadsheet that would incorporate all the data on changes in prices, indices, interest rates, fundamentals, voodoo technical indicators, and who-knows-what-else to create the holy matrix to track market movements. Like me, Woersching fit the mold of a lot of hires to the team—intellectually quick, but with no background in finance. He approached problems in his own way. Before joining Thiel Capital, he'd studied electrical engineering at Stanford and worked at Microsoft.

Josh could only see the top of Woersching's head over the computer monitors on the desk. Woersching was wearing his Stanford hat. And next to the Stanford hat was a blue hat with an American flag on it. After five minutes, the Stanford hat said to the American flag hat, "What are you working on?" And the American hat said, in a woman's voice imitating a man's, "Got to get my shit done."

Josh didn't know what was worse: listening to the maintenance guys' country tunes as they banged stuff into the walls or these two newlyweds spending their weekend cooing over a spreadsheet.

At this point, with the workers on a break, Josh took a tour, pausing in front of each new art piece. He's no art guy, but he once spent a pleasant semester in Rome taking art history classes. It seemed to him that the three collections weren't united as a satisfying whole. The landscape photos were wannabe Ansel Adams. Alongside these were photographs of colossal scientific machinery, like the inner workings of the Large Hadron Collider. Rounding it out were a few forgettable abstract paintings.

A thought hits him, and it becomes a plan. What is art, after all? Do people really judge for themselves? Or do they take someone else's word for it? No one in this office would know if any one of these pieces is good or bad. No one could rank them correctly according to any dimension—quality, monetary value, difficulty, complexity. Josh realized he has his prank: he will hang something here that he drew himself, get it on the wall before the workday begins on Monday morning, and—as long as he adheres to artistic simplicity well inside any Tom Hatten squiggle—no one will be able to tell the difference. It would be a social experiment, a probe into the desire to see what we've been told to see.

But where to hang it?

He played with the idea of hanging it in the Chief Compliance Officer's office. He was an agreeable guy. If he got caught, Josh thought, compliance isn't going to be mad at him. He's going to laugh.

But, then again, there was the Fear of Fitz. Fitzgerald was the General Counsel and in charge of operations, which is to say, he ran the place. He could banish you to a desk in a closet if you got on his wrong side. Worse, he could fire you. Now, the thing was, attire in the office was generally casual: button-down shirts tucked in without ties, jeans, hell, even sneakers. As I mentioned, Peter himself would often show up to meetings in shorts and a polo. But on the days when Fitz had to fire someone, he *always* showed up in a tie. Sometimes even with a blazer. It was a dreadful signal. He would arrive in the morning, tie on, stride down the entrance corridor, and walk by the trading floor on the way to his office. And from that moment, the wheels of anxiety would start turning in everyone's stomachs. Who was getting canned? Sometimes the suspense would last hours.

Josh feared an encounter with Fitz in a tie, even if they had shared the occasional power hour of vodka sodas in the Marina bars. But he also felt the tremors of excitement, at the glory of pulling it off. It was why he wanted this job on the Thiel desk in the first place. Peter was known throughout Wall Street for running a different kind of shop.

• • •

That Peter ran an unusual fund became very clear one time in the first couple of years I worked there, when a portfolio manager formerly of George Soros's office tried to get a job on the Thiel desk. The Soros guy—let's call him Captain Gascan, because he loved oil—knew that Peter has an enormous appetite for risk.

In trading, there's a metric called VAR, short for "value-at-risk." Most hedge funds will limit a portfolio manager's VAR to below one or one-point-five, meaning that if a trader is managing $100 million, based on the historical movements of the assets held, the daily profit or loss swings would be expected to fall within $1 to $1.5 million dollars in any day. Go over your VAR limit, then expect that fund's version of Fitz to show up at your desk in a tie. Now, with respect to VAR, Peter pushed the envelope. His attitude was that if you have conviction, don't come talk to me about it until you have a VAR of four. This was insane to the staid traders in New York City. The only other shop—that's a real shop—where you could run that kind of VAR, was George Soros's office.

Captain Gascan had done well for Soros, but there'd been a big shakeup, and he needed to move on. Drawn by the stories of ambition and appetite for risk, he reached out to some people on the Thiel desk. Eventually, he got on the phone with Josh.

"Listen," Gascan says, after interviewing with some of the other Thiel traders. "I feel like I was talking to the JV team. Who are these guys? They all feel pretty green."

The Soros office was widely known as a blue blood fund: MIT, Caltech, or Ivy League grads who had spent the first half of their careers matriculating up the conventional desks of Wall Street before Soros poached them for the big-time. Gascan had talked to the traders assembled on Peter's macro desk and could tell they were kind of out there.

Josh had to set him straight. As accomplished as Captain Gascan was, he didn't get it.

"Dude, you've been yammering to me about this Colombian oil company you've wanted to buy for months," Josh said. "You've been in due diligence forever. You've tried herding all these different investors on board. You've hustled and hustled and hustled on airplanes everywhere and still haven't closed a deal. But here's what you're missing about sitting on this desk. If you've got a great idea, and your shit is together, and he's grown to trust you and your work, you can walk down the hall to Peter, after sending an email thirty minutes earlier, saying 'I have an idea, here it is,' and there's no, 'I'll get back to you in two weeks' or any of that. If your shit is together and you've got a great idea, you're walking out of Peter's office with the war chest to buy a Colombian oil company. In minutes. There is no other place like that on earth."

Josh had momentum. "And another thing."

"What?"

"These guys you're calling the JV team? There has been a run of people just like these guys. Take all the talent that has filtered through this office, who have walked down past the chess boards to say the holy words, 'Peter, I have an idea.' Add up all they've created from nothing, the market cap of all the companies and funds they've founded, and stack it up against the returns made from all the portfolio managers at Soros going back as far as you want. The numbers here will dwarf it. If you think Peter assembled this so-called JV-team with the long-term objective of finding directional edge in dollar-yen, then you don't have a clue what's going on here."

There was a long silence on the phone. Perhaps Gascan was doing the sums. In 2004, almost as a side project, Peter, Stephen Cohen, Joe Lonsdale, and Nathan Gettings created Palantir from this very trading desk. At the time there were other companies incubating in the fund offices as well. The joke was no one knew which one was craziest: a NASCAR magazine called *American Thunder*; a line of food for yogis; or a startup building software for the CIA. Today Palantir provides its services to counter-terrorism analysts in the U.S. intelligence community as well as the Department of Defense. As of April 2022, it's valued at $24.5 billion.

More recently, Erin Collard, a head trader of the fund, had peeled off the desk and co-founded a financial services company called Blend that is now worth close to a billion dollars. And only a few months before, a portfolio manager sitting right next to Josh walked into Peter's office with the sacred words, "Peter, I have an idea." He pitched Peter an idea for a biotech startup: "My dad is dying of brain cancer and out of a large number of potential treatments, the doctors only have time to try one. They've only got one shot on goal. But what if I built a way for doctors to know in advance which cancer treatments were best based on genetic data on tumors and blood work?" He walked out with Peter as his first angel investor.

Enough time on the phone had passed. "Ok, I gotta go." Gascan said. Josh never heard back from him. He figured the Gascan was empty.

● ● ●

The media consistently gets Peter wrong, but in a revealing way, even on the topic of hires. The *Atlantic*'s George Packer, in his book *The Unwinding*—which won the National Book Award for non-fiction in 2013—wrote that Peter's hedge fund had the reputation of being a "Thiel cult," that was "staffed by young libertarian brains who were in awe of their boss, emulating his work habits, chess-playing, and aversion to sports."[1] Packer is a great writer, but in this he was dead wrong, as anyone actually working on the desk knew. Sure, Patrick "the Wolf Man" Wolff was technically a chess grandmaster, ranked higher than Peter, but hardly anyone else ever played. More importantly, the Wolf Man was a diehard Krugman Keynesian. Woersching was a lefty, too, an ardent fan of the egalitarian philosophy of

John Rawls. And Josh, he was a dirt-road California Democrat who was a downhill ski junkie. Peter was never interested in building a cult around himself, much as it makes a neat story for the legacy media to suggest otherwise. This became even clearer as the years passed and the team was joined by people like the mathematician Eric Weinstein, a minor public figure with his own independent notoriety, who was known to sit squarely on the left. Invariably, all of this was overlooked in the reporting.

The French philosopher Jean Baudrillard once wrote that Americans had built fanciful theme parks like Disneyland to convince themselves that the insane world outside the park was solid and stable—if this is fake, ran his argument, all that is beyond it must be real. "[Disneyland] is meant to be an infantile world," Baudrillard speculated, "in order to make us believe that the adults are elsewhere, in the 'real' world, and to conceal the fact that real childishness is everywhere."[2] In essence, this was the role Peter played in the media: he was the Disneyland that reassured the commentariat about its sanity. His views and interests were always described as fun to hear, but relegated to mad minority positions, ultimately kooky and fringe. The implicit assumption throughout the press was that elite opinion in New York or Washington was rational, sane, real—and not at all childish.

In truth, Peter didn't just hire libertarians. He hired scape-goats who'd survived a mob. People who felt comfortable being a minority of one. There *were* some libertarians, certainly more than the average office. But what Peter prized most about them was that they were used to being the only people in a room to believe in something and defend it. There were also mon-archists and conservative anarchists like me. (I believe in the most irrational form of romantic anarchism.) There were a lot of oddballs, but the last thing Thiel wanted was to be around someone who was in awe of him. His most famous interview question is, "What's something you believe to be true that the rest of the world thinks is false?" It isn't: "tell me something we both agree on." Peter loathes sycophants and obsequious cronies. If he sometimes struggled as a manager, I felt it came in part from his fear of people imitating him. If his language could sometimes be enigmatic and oracular, that was because he didn't want people to parrot what he said to suck up to him. In interviews, you can see him squirm whenever he's asked for a formula on how he invests. He wants more people, even his employees taking his orders, to think for themselves. Of course, this can be confusing. His is a profoundly unusual genius. I defy anyone to tell me exactly what his political essay "The Straussian Moment" really says.[3]

Thiel's sensitivity to imitation and groupthink grew out of his undergraduate study at Stanford under René Girard. Nothing in Girard's work is straightforward, but the principle at play in Peter's office was to see the wellspring of creativity and dynamism in the unity of extreme opposites, the tension of polarity. Now, to say people united opposites is not to say that it was done in harmony or in balance or in some synthesis. Quite the opposite. The point was to spit and spark lightning by attempting to fuse contradictions. In some cases, the results were reckless, incorrigible, and maddening hires who could not be managed, like kites cut from a string. In others, a strange tensive brilliance. Girard came to this insight into personality and character from a literary angle. He had examined the world's mythologies and found that the line between the scapegoat and the hero could be very fuzzy indeed. "Extreme characteristics ultimately attract collective destruction," Girard wrote in his monograph on the violence of crowds towards their victims.[4] The perfect scapegoat for the crowd, Girard found, represents a paradox, someone who improbably unites two extremes. In the words of the Talking Heads' David Byrne, they tend to be strange, but not a stranger. Both insiders and outsiders at once: close enough to bear some resemblance to the community, but also distant enough to have caused a social crisis. Oedipus, to take a famous example, rules in Thebes, but believes—mistakenly—that he is from Corinth. He is both familiar and foreign. And he is the cause of the plague that ravages Thebes. In a similar vein, I recall Oxford University used to have an examination grade that captured this type of thinking about tensive characteristics: the alpha-gamma.[5] The Oxford grading system was similar to that of the United States, with alphas and betas instead of As and Bs. Gamma was the equivalent of an F. The old alpha-gamma grade meant that there were both astonishing, brilliant things in an exam paper, but also idiotic and stupid things. The joke was that the examiners couldn't decide which ones were which. Peter developed this alpha-gamma attribute, this unity of opposites, into a heuristic to think about the types of people who founded companies and whom he wanted to hire. His office and the companies he backed were full of them.

At the hedge fund, there were nuclear engineers, computer scientists, statisticians, and literature scholars, but hardly anyone who'd studied finance in school. All of them were insiders, in the sense of having obtained some level of rigor in a scientific field or achievement in an academic subject. But they were also outsiders in terms of being dropouts or in coming to finance with fresh eyes and quirky theories, like the peak oil fanatics or the gold bugs. Having an MBA—the ultimate insider badge—was a huge negative.

Of course, there were good hires and bad hires over the years. That's true of anywhere. But the really suspect employees were the ones who stayed too long, who wanted to make a career on the desk. It meant they had no ideas, no sparks. The worst thing you could ever do was grind your way up the corporate ladder, show fanaticism for title bumps like "Vice President" or "Partner," and elbow your way into a corner office. In most companies, it's a grave error, a serious breach of decorum, to go over the head of a superior and break the chain of command. Not here. If you had an idea, you pitched Peter directly. It was like flopping the nuts in No-Limit Texas Hold'em poker.

• • •

After a stroll around the office, Josh was back at the desk. He wasn't thinking about currencies. He was thinking about philosophy. What is real? What is fake? Do people notice? Josh decided he didn't take this job at the Thiel desk to fret over Fitz showing up in a tie. He wanted to put this philosophical question to the test. He left the office, headed to the shops on Chestnut Street outside the Presidio, and bought two art frames. Back at his apartment, he drew two pictures using a magic marker from his junk drawer and two sheets of paper retrieved from his computer's printer. The first drawing is of a man in a boat. He's fishing and the line from his pole descends all the way to the bottom of the frame. The second drawing picks up where the first left off. A fishing line comes down from the top of the frame, falling down to the seafloor. There is a hook on the end of it. A fish looks on.

Monday morning, Josh woke up excited. He clocked in at the office fifteen minutes earlier than he normally did, which means 4:45 a.m. because San Francisco global macro funds operate during New York hours. He brought a hammer and some nails.

Josh walked around the office looking for the perfect spot, somewhere people would notice, but not a place that increased Fitz-in-the-tie danger. It couldn't stand out too far from the rest of the photographs and art. Weighing his options, he stared at the coffee machine as it dribbled out its first espresso of the day. The kitchen would be perfect.

Bang, bang, bang. The first nail was in, but before he could hammer in the second, he felt a strong sensation of being stared at. David Kalk stood stock still right behind him, coffee cup in hand, with a look that says: "why would you nail anything to a wall in the office at 5 a.m.?"

Kalk: "What the fuck are you doing?"

"This huge art collection showed up this weekend." Josh shrugged. "I made something. I want to put it there and mix it in."

Kalk put it together in two seconds. "Fucking awesome," he said, refilling his coffee, and heading back to the trading desk.

All day Josh couldn't hold back. He asked everyone, fellow traders, the executive assistants, anyone in the office: "What's your favorite new art piece? And why?"

Annie Le, one of the assistants on the trading floor, took the bait. "That weird one near the kitchen with the fisherman!"

By the end he was satisfied. His piece didn't get the majority vote for the best. But it got the most mentions by far.

Eventually, little cards were stuck to the walls under all the artworks, listing the artist's name and the title of the piece. Josh needed a name. He wanted it to reflect the question he was posing. At first, he considered *Will They Bite?*, but that was too on the nose. Might as well call it *Do They Think It's Real?* Instead, he settled on *Baitless Hook* by Yoshito Ranago. Charcoal on rice paper. 1945.

Josh then found a website that posts notices for art lost or looted during the Second World War. He used Google translate and in mangled Japanese wrote a notice with a picture of *Baitless Hook* that said: "The piece is missing, but we're optimistic we have a chance at recovery because some of the other artworks that were looted from the collection in the aftermath of World War II have recently surfaced." He double-checked the translation by going from English to Japanese to English. It was awful, he knew, but by being garbled, it was oddly perfect.

In time, Josh let a few people in on his ruse. It's hard to keep secrets. One of the few people he told was Belgo, another trader on the desk. Belgo was a fiery Belgian statistician and Ph.D. dropout who could multiply five-digit numbers in his head.

One night, after a few drinks at a happy hour, Belgo told Annie Le. She couldn't believe Josh drew it. She *refused* to believe.

"He's not an artist!" she protested.

All Belgo could say was "No shit."

• • •

When I arrived on the Thiel trading floor for my first day of work on September 27, 2010, I didn't know any of this. Coming out of the entrance corridor, I saw the enormous wall, the open space, and CNBC on flatscreen TVs with the ticker tape of prices scrolling along the bottom. The trading floor was full of men and women staring at their triptych of computer monitors and punching at keyboards. I figured they were like any other hedge fund employees around the world. What the hell was I doing there? I felt the temperature drop, a chill that I always get when I'm afraid and about to speak in public. I had no background in finance. I studied Ancient Greek and philosophy. It took weeks and weeks for me to shake the feeling whenever I arrived for work that I was an imposter.

In those first few months in 2010, I also didn't know anything about walking into Peter's office to pitch him, let alone leading a presentation for a research and trade meeting. I'd begun sketching out the initial outline for the Stanford Law School class. It required a ton of research, and the books began piling up on my workspace on the trading floor. There was no shelf so they would accumulate back to back in a long domino line. I spent my days reading silently, while financial activity swirled all around me. After withstanding some hazing, I earned a new name. The trading team began to call me "the philosopher," which was OK as far as nicknames go. It was better than Batman, which they called the guy who showed up to work so tired every day that he fell asleep, head sagging down in front of his computer monitors. The joke was that the only reason Batman could possibly be staying up so late was to fight crime. What citizens of mischief! And how odd! In time, I came to appreciate and then grok Peter's method of hiring. I wouldn't have had a chance at a job here if he'd hired like any other hedge fund manager. What we were doing was potentially lucrative and definitely mad, but if that wasn't your brand of bourbon, I understand why you might want to order a weaker drink at the bar. Eventually, my books piled too high on my desk, and Fitz came by, not wearing a tie (much to my relief).

"Alright," he said, "We have got to find you a better desk off the trading floor."

· 6 ·

INTELLIGENCE REDEFINED

Sometime into 2013, three years into the Thiel Fellowship, I picked up a call on my office phone from a New York City real estate agent.

"I have some twenty-year-old kid here who wants to rent this penthouse apartment," she said in disbelief.

"He has no income. No credit history. He's not American. But he says he has the cash to pay for the year's rent upfront. He gave me your name saying he's part of some grant program. I don't know who you are, but what kind of grant is this?"

I guessed whom she was talking about even before she told me his name. I'll call him Cipher because he's the best hacker I've ever met to this day. Cipher was an expert in cybersecurity—in fact, he looked and talked like the main character in *Mr. Robot*, except he always wore a black leather motorcycle jacket. To show off and razz you, Cipher could hack into your phone and mess around with the settings if you made one mistake and pressed on the wrong link. I'd first met Cipher at Defcon, the annual cybersecurity conference in Las Vegas, where the good guys (NSA, FBI, CIA) and the bad guys (Anonymous) put down their weapons, get together, and trade stories about hacking and being hacked.

I recruited Cipher into the Thiel Fellowship, and only months later he was doing extraordinary things. Cipher could monkey around with the lowest levels of code in a system, the code closest to the hardware. It was the equivalent of accessing a secure property through the basement. This was his sales pitch, because he also built the security to protect businesses from this type of attack. It's easy to sell the solution when the problem is vividly demonstrated. In one weekend hackathon contest at Facebook, he was so adept at coding in low-level programming languages that he demonstrated how Facebook could port their entire website to servers using different processors than the ones they were currently using. Apparently, this was a project Facebook thought would take at least a month. Cipher did it in hours.

Soon after that, he started licensing his security software to a big player. He earned a $2 million contract that paid five hundred grand upfront, which is why I knew this call from the NYC real estate agent was about him. It fitted his personality. The day before he had posted pictures of himself on Facebook taking his girlfriend on a helicopter ride out to the Hamptons in Long Island. Later that night, he had rink-side seats at the New York Rangers hockey game at Madison Square Garden. He posted pictures of that, too. So I wasn't all that surprised to hear he was looking into renting a penthouse apartment.

"He earned that money. It's not from a grant," I tried to explain.

"Well without a steady income, I can't rent it to him."

"He has the money. Take the rent upfront."

"This is the strangest charity organization I've ever heard of. I'm sorry, I can't."

Cipher caused me many headaches. He put the disruption

into disruptive innovation. It was not a question of his technical chops, which were formidable and allowed him to make
imaginative advances in computer security. It was that he was
wild and unruly, possessed by some spirit of speed, swagger,
and commotion, the volume turned up to eleven, a vandalizing
velocity of code. We would hold monthly catch-up meetings with
each Thiel Fellow in order to give advice, provide feedback, or
point their way to resources. As time went on, whenever Cipher
showed up to these meetings, he would invariably flirt with the
new administrative assistant and ask her out to dinner, despite
being seven or eight years younger than she was. One time he
even showed up with an open beer in his hand. He was still not
twenty-one.

But Cipher was no slouch. He made more money in that
first year than many successful people make in a decade. But
he was incapable of working with other people. In the end, he
became something of a blunder for me. His ferocious creative
energy would quickly turn into combative frustration in the face
of questions or objections. It soon became clear that he would
be a one-man shop forever. No one would ever work for him.
He could never build a company. The idea of the lone genius,
the heroic individualist toiling away in obscurity, isn't a myth.
It just doesn't work.

Cipher crystallizes a devilish problem that we'd been trying to
solve since we began taking applications in the fall of 2010: what
makes a great entrepreneur? It's easy enough to look at someone
who's already successful—like Elon Musk or Jack Dorsey—and
break it down into parts, inserting the appropriate platitudes
like "resourceful" or "relentless." But this method is hazy at best
because of survivorship bias. We never get to hear about people
who had those traits but still failed and disappeared. Moreover,
we were trying to do something much more difficult. Take a

look at Elon Musk right now, and what you see is someone at the height of his powers after years of experience. What's missing is the untested twenty-something founder who once had a lot to learn. Who was *that* person? That's who we were looking for. We were searching for potential, not accomplishment. Someone like Cipher clearly had the technical brilliance to build, but I'd erred in recruiting a person who was so disagreeable he could never make a hire or work with an investor.

Throughout the first few years, the press always characterized our program as a search for the next Mark Zuckerberg. In one sense, this is the job of every early-stage venture capitalist, and therefore nothing special. All investors want to be the first to back the next billion-dollar company. Welcome to Silicon Valley. But the greatest challenge with thinking about the "next" anyone is that the next great company won't be a social network or an electric car maker. It very well might be something long dreamt of, like a cure for cancer. But most likely this new company would offer something practically no one had thought of before. We realized that pattern-matching to previous examples would quickly lead us astray if the new idea was in a far different domain. More troublesome still were the founders who imitated the previous Greats to try to pass off as great themselves. Suddenly, we were infested with mimics in black mock turtlenecks or hoodies and flip-flops. "Many of the people who want to be like Steve [Jobs] have the asshole part down," Bill Gates said once. "What they're missing is the genius."

The second challenge we faced, which conventional investors avoid by letting startups mature, is that our grants supported individuals, not companies. Zuckerberg had thousands of intensely engaged daily users on "The Facebook" by the time he pitched Peter. He had cofounders. They had incorporated. All that would mean he was further along than most of the young people applying to our program. The more traction a company's product has, the less risky the bet. What makes the term "tech startup" confusing is that it's often used to describe any company that is private and less than five years old. But a company worth billions, with 1,000 employees, and hundreds of millions in revenue is a very different animal—not just in degree, but in kind—from a team of three people in a garage pitching an idea to a skeptical investor. That billion-dollar company a day before its IPO? That's not a startup. The young people we were looking for weren't even at the garage stage yet.

In short, we had to (1) find innovators before they invented anything, and (2) look for this person while restricting ourselves to people who could barely vote and who couldn't legally order a beer at a bar. Yeah, piece of cake, all right.

If we failed, we would be a laughingstock of the press and the establishment. Larry Summers, the irascible former president of Harvard and erstwhile Treasury Secretary of the United States, came out punching in a 2013 interview. He scoffed at our program, saying it was "meretricious in its impact" and—my favorite—the "single most misdirected philanthropy of the decade."[1] He continued, "if any significant number of intellectually able people, of the kind that would have the opportunity to attend top schools are dropping out, I think it's tragic."

Of course, despite the distortions and caricature by our antagonists, we were not telling all—or even many—students to drop out. What we *were* doing was telling young people to push out to the frontiers of knowledge as fast as possible. If that meant getting started on an idea today instead of attending classes, so be it. Some ideas can't wait. Many creative college students were sitting on their hands in classrooms because they had been convinced by America's credentialist elite that it was the only path to a fulfilling career. Our grant program was a wake-up call to a small but important group of young people to get moving. No one else anywhere was saying anything like this.

But the ultimate stakes are far higher than a tarnished reputation or being ridiculed by Larry Summers. American ingenuity was—*and is*—running dry. It cannot be repeated enough: the idea that we're experiencing rapid, inevitable technological progress is a myth. By any metric, if we want the next generation to be better off than the last, we have to invent and discover the means to raise living standards to new highs. Sustained progress—life expectancy, quality of life, clean air, you name it—all depend upon the contributions of millions of innovators finding new ways of doing things. To be sure, entrepreneurs can't solve all the world's problems—government-funded basic science has its role—but America is heading for a precipice unless it can wake up from its sleepwalk. The credentialist impulse to keep every talented young person in a classroom for seventeen years is holding our society back.

The looming threat of open-ended stagnation is difficult to convey in feeling. Imagine life under Covid lockdowns, but for decades—the shortages, the loneliness, the narrowness of activity, the sameness of our days, the worst in us exposed by our desperation. But perhaps I can be more direct about its appearance: if in the near future, in fifteen or twenty years, Harvard still sits at the apex of all opportunity and learning, if all of our Supreme Court Justices, Cabinet members, and Presidents come only from the Ivy League, as they almost all do now, if the markets continue to skew freakishly towards the same few gargantuan companies, then the bogus, delusional elite will have won, our institutions will have failed, and we will be left ruminating upon our keenly felt regret in front of the fading fires of a lost civilization. If you think that political polarization is bad now, wait till we have twenty more years of shrinking budgets, stagnant wages, higher debts, and greater catastrophes. There really isn't time to be polite or patient with figures like Larry Summers and his theories about what young people should do.

•   •   •

One day early on, while we were collecting applications for the first batch of fellows, Jim O'Neill asked me to dig into some research about age, inventions, and scientific discoveries. He mentioned an economist from Northwestern University, Benjamin Jones, who had written a series of papers on the subject.[2] Jones looked back over the previous one hundred years and created some interesting data sets on Nobel Prizes, patent filings, biographies, and almanac entries. He collected information on the age at which an inventor brought forth his or her first discovery; the average age of a scientist's greatest accomplishment (including their age when they published the paper that won them the Nobel Prize); and the productivity lifespan of innovators and scientists (namely, how long did they work across their lifetime and how many discoveries did they make over their career?).

What I discovered in Jones's research was striking. There were multiple arrows on the chart, and all were moving in the wrong direction. One key to seeing the trend was to think of inventors and scientists like painters and novelists. Most of the greats produce multiple works over their lifetimes with a three-act structure. In a rough outline, there is the first breakout, then the masterpiece, and finally the late work of accomplished maturity. Ernest Hemingway storms onto the scene with *In Our Time* and *The Sun Also Rises*, secures his reputation with *A Farewell to Arms*, and rounds out his career with *Old Man and the*

Sea. The careers of great scientists and inventors follow a similar arc, but Jones found a worrisome change over the last century:

- ACT I: Inventors and scientists are getting started later than they used to. The average age at which innovators launch their first inventions increased by eight years over the course of the previous century, rising from a mean age of about 23 in 1900 to approximately 31 in the year 2000.
- ACT II: Innovators today are older than they used to be when they achieve their greatest accomplishments, on average by about six years. Scientists are now closer to forty years old when they conduct the experiment that wins them the Nobel Prize. Earlier last century, they were closer to thirty.
- ACT III: Scientists and inventors are slowing down in their later years despite living longer. As a consequence, the late start in Act I is truncating the length of their whole career. That is, there has been no compensating shift in the productivity of innovators beyond middle age. Very few, if any, innovators increase output into their fifties and sixties. The window for creativity has narrowed.
- Because scientists start Act I so late in their lives, Jones estimates a 30 percent decline in the number of inventions and discoveries we would have seen had these scientists started their careers in their early twenties instead. By analogy, imagine how short careers in baseball would be, how unimpressive total career stats would be, if the Major League said no one could play until they were thirty. Those lost years represent a portion of what we're missing compared to the past.

- Lastly, Jones announced the death of the renaissance inventor. In other words, specialization has increased in patent filing; it's now rare to see a single name as the sole author of a scientific paper. More people are working in teams that require a division of intellectual labor. And very few inventors make jumps from one patent category to another, meaning that it's rare to see one inventor make multiple discoveries across different fields. Compare that with Benjamin Franklin, who invented a stove, bifocals, and the lightning rod.

"The shorter the period that innovators spend innovating," Jones writes, "the less their output as individuals over their lifetime. If innovation is central to technological progress, then forces that reduce the length of active innovative careers will reduce the rate of technological progress. This effect will be particularly strong if innovators do their best work when they are young."[3]

Benjamin Jones has his own explanation for why it's taking longer for people to reach the frontiers of knowledge. His answer is that the burden is heavier than it used to be: more books to read, more papers to master, more hours in the lab. Ph.D.s now take upwards of seven or eight years to complete. There is also the increasing complexity and difficulty of science: the peaks of the most recent achievements are far higher, and, with every fresh attack upon a new ascent, the angle of the mountain gets steeper. Newton is easier to comprehend than Schrödinger; it's easier to cure an infection than to treat dementia. Specialization also now requires an intense, if narrow, focus. According to Jones, the young must spend more years training and acquiring knowledge of tinier niches only to reach the cutting edge well into their thirties.

I found Jones's history compelling, but I wasn't convinced by his explanations. Granted, quantum mechanics is baffling even to a genius and requires knowledge of more complicated math than the inverse square law, but I had seen the academy's chamber of inertia for myself, while I studied philosophy, and I knew that schools and universities wasted a lot of time across the board, from undergraduates to Ph.D.s. Our education system takes its sweet time pushing students out to the frontier in any subject, not because it's difficult, but because there's no urgency to get them there. The final, damning point is that our institutions simply don't trust younger scientists and inventors. Grant-making bodies cover their ass by awarding research funding only to the established over the new, the prestigious over the experimental. The National Institute for Health, for example, allocates just two percent of its funding to scientists younger than thirty-five, while 98 percent of its money goes to scientists older than thirty-six. If scientists and inventors are more creative in their twenties and thirties, then this funding policy has things completely backward.

So, despite what Larry Summers says, there's a lot of potential being squandered by having only one sclerotic path to success: the college degree. As Jones's research shows, in the past, scientists and inventors started their careers much earlier than they do now. I'm certain that Jones would not endorse our program: in one of his later papers, he slights us in a footnote. Nevertheless, the fellowship was a bet that we could get a few young people out to the cutting edge quicker where they could take risks and do things differently. At a minimum, they would learn as much as they would in college. And at best, they would launch a career that embraced the strangeness, uniqueness, brilliance, and intensity that is at the heart of any innovation.

• • •

The first applications to our program trickled in throughout November and December of 2010. We didn't do much to promote the fellowship. Peter gave talks at Stanford and at MIT. But beyond that, the biggest boost was the attention the media gave to us for our radical proposal. As Jim O'Neill would say, "There's no need to buy advertising when scandal is free." Still, we hadn't expected the storm of coverage. It began as soon as we announced and didn't stop for the next three years. At the end of every week, the PR agency we'd hired would send us a document accumulating all the news stories from around the world. This document grew so long it would cause our computers to freeze while downloading it. But if a program had that kind of attention and notoriety, we realized that the answer to our search problem was to let the "next Mark Zuckerberg" come find us. Our job was to recognize him if he did.

By the deadline at midnight on January 1, 2011, we'd received 438 applications, many of them coming on that last day in a rush. We spent the next three months sorting through them, winnowing them down. My mind was blown by some of the things I read: "I founded Scanboy when I was nine, and I ran it as a sole proprietorship until I graduated high school." Or: "I've educated myself since I was seven, reading textbooks and independently researching what I was interested in. When I was fourteen, I applied to MIT and got in." Danielle had pulled together a number of veteran startup founders and experts from the Thiel Foundation's network to help us with phone interviews. By March, we had narrowed the pile down to forty candidates, whom we flew into San Francisco for two rounds of interviews: one with us, the core team, and one with that community of mentors Danielle had brought together.

Over the years, the finalist weekend became tremendously busy. There were a lot of moving pieces: interviews, talks, catch-up conversations. The first year we had no idea what to expect, but there was a fear it would be too competitive. With forty people vying for twenty spots, an intense rivalry might develop among the young candidates. That could be mitigated if they never interacted with each other. But we weren't sure about that either, because we also knew there was a chance for friendships and community to form. In the event, we ended up rolling the dice and brought them together from the get-go, right in the hotel lobby on day one.

I can still hear the buzz that day as the first forty rolled into the Hyatt Regency on the Embarcadero in downtown San Francisco. They were like manic puppies running free in a park for the first time, and their laughter and chatter bubbled up and echoed throughout the hotel's cavernous atrium. The staid guests in the lobby bar turned their heads, stared, and had this look of…Are those *teenagers*? But this wasn't a debate tournament or a spelling bee or a meeting of class presidents. They were talking about working on problems normally only tackled by top-tier scientists and business people. It wasn't unusual for finalists to tell us that at first, they felt intimidated by the intelligence and confidence of the other candidates. But then one of them would ease into a conversation cluster and announce, nonchalantly, that they were planning to mine asteroids for precious metals. All of a sudden, the fears would fall away, and a detailed discussion would begin in earnest on the challenges of asteroid-mining. None of these young people had ever met anyone else who, like them, was intensely curious about such things. One young man told me it felt like he had won the *Charlie and the Chocolate Factory* golden ticket. And that was for just being at the finalist round.

First up, the candidates interviewed with us. On our end, the questions were pretty standard. It was on the other side of the table where things got interesting fast. Laura Deming: "I believe that aging is a curable disease and that we can achieve an indefinite lifespan within the 21st century. Most people do not know that this is scientifically feasible." Taylor Wilson began his interview: "When I was fourteen years old I became the youngest person in history to produce nuclear fusion."

The next thing for the crew was the lightning pitch. Each finalist would have two minutes to present their ideas to a room full of investors, operators, veteran founders, and other pros. To ramp up the dread, Peter would grab a seat in the back. Over the years this became a pivotal moment for finalists. The pressure would build all weekend to this event. In the first year, it was in the Hyatt's ballroom. The next, we held it in a theater.

Backstage the finalists were always restless. They rehearsed. They pitched to walls. They paced. They double-checked note cards. Pulses pounded. They wrung their arms and hands, took deep breaths, checked their outfits. Right before stepping onto the stage, they'd take a second to collect themselves in the wings. Once out into the open, their eyes would dart around the auditorium. Some would grip the lectern. Others would let it rip and gabble like country auctioneers, cramming as much into two minutes as they could. One guy threw on mirrored sunglasses and rapped his pitch about using 3-D printing to make a cellular matrix for a new heart. Another delivered a pitch on chemistry and light in the form of spoken word poetry. Over and over we had to remind ourselves that all these brilliant people were teenagers.

After a minute forty-five, a red light on the lectern warned them that in fifteen seconds they'd be cut off. It threw a few people off at the end. Others would stumble all on their own, forgetting their pitch in mid-sentence. Nerves would sabotage them. I remember one young woman in particular who went blank on stage, completely losing the thread of her speech after her first sentence. Her silence hung in the air for one mortifying minute. When I think of her now, I still want to reach out to tell her it's going to be O.K.

Then we'd have what we called the Mentor Match. This combined the finalists with Silicon Valley insiders—successful technologists, scientists, and business people—who might help them along the way. It was also a way for us to have some experts dig into the viability of some of the ideas. These mentors had launched their own businesses worth hundreds of millions, if not billions of dollars. Finalists were all assigned to their own table in an enormous room, where they'd wait for the mentors from the auditorium to pour in. For the first five minutes, before anyone sat down at their table, they looked so lonely, like kindergarteners hoping to make friends on the first day of term. If the tables were empty for too long, Danielle and I would fill in and make small talk. Gradually the conversations with the mentors would pick up, the din eventually rising to the volume of a packed cafe. The whole grueling thing lasted maybe two hours.

The finalist weekend always ended on a Sunday, and we'd start our deliberations first thing Monday morning. Danielle had Kinko's make us fifteen-pound binders full of information. Each one contained the candidate's application, updates, notes from the finalist interviews, notes from all the technical experts, and so on. The first year, we holed up in the conference room at the Letterman Building in the Presidio. Jim went to the whiteboard and drew an x-axis and a y-axis. The x-axis represented the likelihood of success: the further out to the right, the better the chances were that the person's idea would work. The y-axis was the magnitude of the idea. The higher, the greater the consequences of success. Then we wrote the names of each of the forty candidates on Post-it notes and we'd position them on the board according to where we thought they fell according to those two dimensions. We'd argue it out, digging through the materials to support our case for where the Post-it should go on the board. That might mean making phone calls for references or asking a mentor to go deeper on technical diligence. Seeing the board filled like this gave us a sense of the shape of the batch. The whole process often took a week.

Over the years, we'd disappear to different places instead of the conference room. We'd find a house on Airbnb in an isolated beach town up on the coast in Marin, a tiny place surrounded by Eucalyptus trees tucked away in the tawny hills of Northern California. The debates became a lot of fun, particularly over the borderline candidates. At the end of our deliberations, we'd go to Peter's house to show him who we were picking and why. The first year, we were in his dining room, standing around the table. Peter was looking down at a sheet of photographs of the twenty we'd chosen. Danielle remembers thinking, "Are we really doing this?" Peter scanned the photos in silence, nodded, and gave his customary approval: "Ok, looks good."

The notification video calls were the most thrilling part of the whole thing. Finalists would always answer the call with a sense of foreboding, fearing that they were going to be cut. After the second year, we'd have a little fun with this, drawing out the beginning of our call to heighten the suspense. It would get sharp. Jim in particular would really ham it up: "We really enjoyed meeting you last week...I'm so grateful you were a finalist...it was a really tough decision...there was a lot of stiff competition." Here, he'd throw in a long, excruciating pause. "It

was very hard for us to narrow it down…you have a big imagination…you have great potential…and…"—for the love of
god man, *just say it!*—"We'd love to have you as a Thiel Fellow!"

Their reactions were wonderful. Their eyes would open—
thwok!—like umbrellas in the rain, their eyebrows arches of
surprise. A thousand-watt smile would break, waves of joy and
relief passing over the face. Some would cover their faces with
their hands in shock and then lean backward in their chairs,
almost tipping over. There was always a lot of laughter.

A few parents would take convincing. They were not thrilled
about their children leaving school. This was particularly acute
for the children of first-generation immigrants who had moved
to the United States so their children could attend college. We
lost a couple of finalists because they or their parents couldn't
get comfortable with the stopout. But as exciting as it was for
the rest, winning a fellowship was only the beginning. It wasn't
supposed to be an award, but the resources to get started on
something meaningful, which meant the hardest part for all of
them was ahead. The failure rate among startups is brutal. To
top it off, the whole world was watching. The pressure on our
fellows was enormous.

•   •   •

What did we learn from reviewing ten thousand applications
and picking one hundred fellows over the next five years? These
people are way more dynamic in person than they are on paper.
If anything, the biggest mistake we made at the beginning is
that we started too close to the university model. Our application asked for things like SAT scores, GPAs, and what schools
a candidate had applied to. Rather quickly, even into the first
year, we learned that raw intelligence and technical know-how
only go so far before other forces must come into play. Some

people who looked great on paper—high test scores, numerous science awards—failed to transition to life in the wild, outside of institutions, where time is unstructured and goals must emerge from self-directed exploration. Young men and women in thrall to rectitude tended to languish as they waited for someone or something in the world to tell them what to do. I came to see that the types of people who are good at pleasing admissions committees are not the types of people who are good at founding companies. A stripped bolt is tough to wrench out of the machine.

In our second year in 2012, Dylan Field, one of our most promising candidates, called us out on it. He wrote to us about why he omitted his test scores from his application:

> I am intentionally choosing not to submit my SAT scores as part of this application. It is my belief that the SAT is a poor reflection of aptitude and can easily be gamed. The concept of standardized testing is contradictory to two values the Thiel Fellowship supports: lifelong learning and independent thought. I hope this choice does not disqualify my application.

It did not. We awarded him a fellowship and nine years later he is leading the top design startup in the country. At the time of its last round of venture financing in 2021, Dylan's company was valued at $10 billion. This is what I take Peter meant when, throughout our first year, he told us: "We're not looking for Einstein. We're looking for Howard Hughes."

Confusion abounds in America on the question of talent. *Webster's Ninth Collegiate Dictionary* defines genius as an "extraordinary intellectual power especially as manifested in creative activity" or, alternatively, as a "person with a very high intelligence quotient." That second definition became the dominant one in the early 20th century, after the invention of the IQ test.[4] At Stanford University in 1916, the psychologist Lewis M. Terman created what is known as the Stanford-Binet Intelligence Scale. This is what Mensa uses, for example, requiring a minimum of a 132 IQ for entry into its society of "geniuses." Terman was the first psychologist to study a large sample of high-IQ people from childhood to middle age. He tested thousands of young children with his new Stanford-Binet test and identified a subgroup of 1,528 extremely brilliant boys and girls. Their average IQ was 151; seventy-seven of them had IQs between 177 and 200. He then followed this group, retesting them and getting life updates from 1925 to 1959. The end result was the staggering five-volume *Genetic Studies of Genius*. And what were the results? Well, many had successful careers in the professions, becoming doctors, lawyers, and professors. A high IQ does correlate with a good income, and high-prestige jobs are often filled by smart people. But then a curious thing happened.

There were two young boys Terman had tested but excluded from his study because their IQs weren't high enough to count as "genius." One, Luis Walter Alvarez, won the Nobel Prize in Physics in 1968 for his work in particle physics. Alvarez and his geologist son Walter were also the first to advance the theory that the extinction of the dinosaurs was caused by an asteroid hitting the Earth. The second young boy Terman excluded was William Shockley. Shockley won the Nobel Prize in Physics in 1956 for inventing the transistor. His effort to commercialize his invention, the Shockley Semiconductor Laboratory, was located in Mountain View, one town over from Palo Alto. Take any history of Silicon Valley, or the biographies of the men and women who built the region into what it is, and all of them begin at Shockley's lab. (One ironic twist to the story is that Shockley alienated his employees by making them all take psychological tests. They left to found what eventually became Intel.)

No one in Terman's genius group won a Nobel Prize. No one wrote the Great American Novel. This is peculiar to me. Why do we call these people geniuses? Marilyn Vos Savant is listed as having the highest recorded IQ, and what does she do? She writes a column for a Sunday supplement in the newspaper. Why do we care so much about test scores and other supposed signs of potential? It's as if we've stopped caring about outputs and only care about inputs. IQ scores, GPAs, college degrees, Ph.D.s—hell, even new patents—are all only inputs. As a society, we're so obsessed with them that we've stopped paying attention to whether anything was coming out of the other side. This is why the "meritocratic elite" is bunk. Smart America isn't so smart. What's come out of it is not impressive. The thing that matters is actual creation, as the first part of the *Webster's* definition says. I don't care what your score is and where you went to school, if your ability doesn't manifest itself in some creative activity...well, you might be smart, but you're not a genius.

But this was something I had to learn over the coming years. I had recruited Cipher, but at the beginning, I was still too biased towards technical brilliance alone. What, then, is the difference between the ones that make it and the ones that don't? What is that ineffable combination of qualities that amounts to the right stuff?

• • •

Sometimes, when Peter was passing on a potential investment, or hire, or fellowship finalist, he would say, "it doesn't match my pattern recognition." If you asked him to elaborate, he might point to one or two red flags, but it was obvious there was more going on. He had met with thousands of entrepreneurs over the

years and had worked alongside some of the best of a generation—Elon Musk and Mark Zuckerberg, to name only two. All
of them had come to inform the unconscious intelligence behind
his judgment. In the jargon of computer science, it was a form
of object recognition refined by training on a set of previous
examples. Working with Peter, at first Danielle and I would feel
a beginner's frustration, since we thought it should be pretty
easy to state what exactly didn't fit the pattern in Peter's judgment. But in time we saw that learning would proceed from
rules, features, and facts to these expert, tacit assessments of
unique cases. All masterful judgment becomes situational.[5] Its
answer to any query is, "It depends." By contrast, learning in this
trade would never move in the opposite direction, from a set of
examples to clear, crisp general rules. There is no manual. No
checklist. No playbook. If someone successful starts speaking to
you in rules, that may well be what they were taught when they
were beginners, but as pros they've moved beyond them. This
is the point of apprenticeship and why most "How-to" books
are worthless beyond the basics: understanding something or
being an expert at it does not require being able to state your
knowledge in explicit facts, rules, recipes, or procedures. Crafts-
manship is leaving your initial awareness of the rules behind
for a sixth sense that cannot be explained and to which words
cannot do justice.

But, the faithless may ask, if we can't trust his theories
and what he says, how do we know if a person's judgment is
not just good, but great? To which the Bible replies, "Ye shall
know them by their fruits." It's an investor's track record
and, to show that luck can't explain it, persistent success over
time.[6] To work alongside Peter was to apprentice with the best
angel investor of all time. This is not to say that he actively
coached us. He didn't listen compassionately to our frustra-

tions and then offer encouragement and tips for improvement. A master craftsman doesn't dumb down his craft. Either you learned from Peter on the fly, or you bought a return flight home to Wichita.

Over five years of the Thiel Fellowship—after reviewing more than ten thousand applications; after conducting thousands of phone interviews, hundreds of in-person interviews, and five finalist weekends; after advising one hundred Thiel Fellows through the program—Danielle and I had stocked our memories and honed our judgment. That ineffable quality we were trained to ferret out? The right stuff for startups? It wasn't the so-called "reality distortion field" Steve Jobs was said to have possessed. Or, as one of our great female founders put it, "assertive male narcissism." No, I came to think it was something I'd studied in another world, belonging more to poetry than to engineering. It is not to be found in any English dictionary. No test exists for it. I have not come across a quick process to screen for it. And it expresses itself in each person somewhat differently every time, though they all bear a family resemblance. This virtue isn't so much about knowing the right way versus the wrong way, or the light versus the dark side of the force, but about two dark ends and a thin light wedge opening in the middle, which the very best shot through repeatedly to hit the mark. It is all about character.

There is no consensus on an English equivalent of the ancient Greek word πολύτροπον, or "*polytropon.*" Funny enough, the Greeks still argue about its elusive meaning themselves. The fifth word of the first line of Homer's *Odyssey* is hard to pin down. Going back to the late 1500s, there have been about sixty published translations of the *Odyssey* into English, and all of them translate it differently. A literal translation breaks the word into two: "*poly*" meaning many, and "*tropos*" meaning a turn, a course, a way. It is Odysseus's signature—the many-wayed man. But that's a simple gloss. The word is richer and far more allusive, suggesting movement along a twisting path *and* the character of mind that allowed a man to find his way back home on that path after twenty years abroad. Some of the best poets over the centuries have attempted to capture that deeper two-sided meaning in translation. They offer "cunning" or "never at a loss." But my favorite is Amadis Jamyn's 1579 French translation, "*ce rusé personnage*," which literally means "that wily character," but which in the flavor of our own times might read "that tricky bastard."[7] My own translation of the first line of Homer's epic poem would run: "That man, remember him, the tricky bastard who always found a way."

The great founders are the ones who always find a way. This is their highest virtue. And like the word *polytropon* itself, this chemistry of cunning is elusive. How someone comes to have it will forever involve a dash of mystery, but we have found that beyond the obvious virtues of brainpower and grit, there are overlooked subordinate character traits and personality styles that comprise different facets of this overarching virtue and that contribute to the success of the crafty and resourceful. To lay these sub-traits out with some degree of admiration is not to say that a startup founder is a morally superior person, let alone some kind of raving Nietzschean Übermensch. Like you, Nietzsche, and me, they are all too human. Nevertheless, they do exhibit traits that work to a company's advantage in getting things off the ground.

In some cases, we had to invent names for sub-traits because we couldn't find any examples in the literature on personality and psychology.[8] I should emphasize again that this is not a checklist that guarantees anything. These traits may be necessary for success, but they are nowhere close to being sufficient. Time and chance happeneth to all. Still, we have found great success honing our pattern recognition to spot them and in coaching novices to gain greater mastery of them. In no particular order, they are "edge control," "crawl-walk-run," "hyperfluency," "emotional depth & resilience," "a sustaining motivation," "the alpha-gamma tensive brilliance," "egoless ambition," and, Danielle's favorite, "Friday-night-Dyson-sphere."

Edge control: The best possess something we call "edge control," which isn't so much about thrill-seeking, as it is about a willingness, day after day, to defy the boundary between the known and unknown, order and disorder, vision and hubris. It is the rare person who can handle and even relish the skid and spark of being ever-so-slightly out of control.[9] Most are either too tentative or too deluded and reckless. On the one hand, a new business can never grow if it makes a comfortable home within the safety of the tried and true. Only by setting forth into the unknown can anyone make new discoveries. On the flip side, however, experiments probing that dark territory can prove too costly. Bankrupt, a team may return with nothing. Maybe they were deluded all along. Others with high pedigree and vast wealth—see, for instance, Quibi and Magic Leap—light a billion dollars on fire and never make a single product. The knowledge found at the edge of experience is not easily won. The only way to discover the limits of what a company can build and sell is to test those limits. It takes edgework to chart that barrier, to test it, to respect it. To venture back and forth from the known to the unknown in an ascending S-curve of real growth, up and to the right on a graph, and to do it in a way that doesn't destroy the company, but rather punches a hole in the sky—this is to carve the edge. It takes a tricky bastard to do it.

Crawl-walk-run: If it is working in high technology, a founding team needs to have the smarts to build what they say they're going to build. Maybe a psychologist can test for that in a single sitting. But the most important things that matter at the birth of a startup, none of them can be communicated credibly in a one-off meeting as on *Shark Tank* or in reading a transcript. Like baseball scouts, we think the best way to screen for these traits is to see them at play in the wild. It takes some time to see their evolution. Moreover, the person on the way up is not the same person ten years later when the company has scaled to dominate an industry. The best have to know how to crawl, walk, and then run. (Danielle will sometimes call this "acorn to oak.") What this means is they have a knack for learning the different skills required to meet the different challenges at each stage of a company's life as it grows up. From a startup with five employees to a corporate giant with ten thousand employees and five product divisions—it is difficult to find people who can hit the mark at each growth phase. In the past, Silicon Valley investors simply assumed these stages had to be managed by two different people. The founders were often removed from the company and a seasoned CEO was brought in, as John Scully was brought in to replace Steve Jobs at Apple in 1983. Even Larry Page and Sergei Brin were not able to escape this dogma and settled on a compromise with their investors. They agreed to bring "adult supervision" into the CEO role at Google, which is why Eric Schmidt was hired. Whether the founders are the best at running a company, in the long run, remains a hotly contested debate. Perhaps Sundar Pichai and Eric Schmidt have managed Google better than Larry Page ever could have. The company's competitive advantage still looks invincible. But when Steve Jobs returned to Apple in 1997, the company was near bankruptcy and on life support. It is now worth more than $1 trillion thanks to his leadership. Schmidt and Pichai both inherited an unassailable monopoly on cruise control. Jobs built the future from a wreck. We side with the founders.

Hyperfluency: The best founders have the charm of a huckster and the rigor of a physicist. There is often a strong, even uncanny sense of fit between founders and the market they're operating in. They speak with fluent competence about why past efforts in an industry have failed; what the competition doesn't know now; and how they're going to move from a few customers to thousands. This we call "hyperfluency." It's like hearing the crackle and pop of a fastball hitting a catcher's mitt. The whole experience is animated by a love and infectious excitement which we can detect in their voice and speech patterns. They are thrilled to explain the intricacies of complex technologies to experts and newcomers alike. (Sometimes, if it's a particularly formidable subject, we pause our meetings by saying, "Please speak to us as you might the dumbest golden labrador you've ever met.") The ability to scaffold information so as to communicate it clearly to everyone, no matter who they are, is one of the unconscious tells of a great leader.

Emotional depth & resilience: They don't have to be the life of the party or a compassionate therapist, but the founders of a company have to have the social and emotional intelligence to make hires, work with customers, raise money from investors, and gel with co-founders. The complexity of this total effort is incredibly demanding and emotionally exhausting. It is a job that involves engaging with a variety of different people, undertaking uncertain goals, and having no rule book for how to achieve them. It requires a constant stream of decisions on matters of life and death for the company, putting the livelihoods of employees at risk and leaving investors' capital hanging in the balance. Sometimes these decisions must be made in minutes. To say that all of this is emotionally taxing is an understatement. The base rate for mental health issues for founders is higher than the average for the wider population, so attention and care for their emotional life is of paramount importance.[10]

Sustaining motivation: Above all, the best work for neither fame nor fortune. Greed is not good.[11] We look for what we call the sustaining motivation. The initial motivation for starting a company is often the excitement of doing something new and risky, which might bear some resemblance to the thrill of sky-diving, but the sustaining motivation to keep going year after year, through all the twists and turns, has to be tied to something deeper, something richer in meaning. It can be a sense of mission about a cause or pure intellectual curiosity or even about pulling off a caper with a few best friends. In some cases, it is the awe felt before a private vision of a future that might be. But what it can't be is money, thrills, or fame, because that garbage won't carry anyone through a dark night of the soul at 2 a.m. when the doubts creep in. Pressure is hellfire. As Elon Musk told CNBC when they interviewed him during our 2012 finalist round for the fellowship, "Starting a company is like eating glass and staring into the abyss. If you feel like you're up for that, start a company." All the talk in pop psychology books about the importance of grit is meaningless unless you can find the reason to persevere. Grit is merely the surface of a soul committed to meaning.

Tensive brilliance: Remember that girl in high school whom the schoolmarm would pick on because she was daydreaming a lot? Or the otherworldly geeky guy who was obviously smart but never got good grades? That's the person we're looking for. (Psychologists have found that teachers are more likely to identify as "gifted" those students who are achievers and teacher-pleasers than those who are creative.)[12] Raw high IQ, straight As, and perfect test scores are the tokens of a cardboard elite. It is true, they are strong predictors of future success, but from our point of view, it is a rather conventional success. To invent new things, some kind of creative dynamism is required beyond the expected. What we've noticed, inspired by Thiel's observations, is that creative people tend to have a unity born of variety. That unity may have a strong tension to it, as it tries to reconcile opposites. Insider yet outsider, familiar yet foreign, strange, but not a stranger, young in age but older in mind, a member of an institution but a social outcast—all kinds of polarities lend themselves to dynamism. This is in part, I believe, why immigrants and first-generation citizens show a strong proclivity for entrepreneurship. They are the same, but different.

One of the strongest findings in the psychology of personality is a link between openness to new experience and higher levels of creativity.[13] A wandering, free spirit is advantageous for creativity, as discovery requires the exploration of novel ideas, feelings, and sensations. It is also true that many inventions are the result of combining elements from two or more domains that no one had thought to connect before. But a tornado can't stack two dimes. While we see this openness in great founders as well—they have a wide set of interests, some that appear irrelevant to their main research—we'd add a twist in that most combine two personality traits that tend to be inversely correlated. Many would score high on openness to new experience, but also high in conscientiousness. A rare combo in the wider population.

Egoless ambition: This is another instance of a dynamic contradiction, a perpetual tension between antithetical attitudes. It has a Zen-like nature to it in that it embodies and expresses a paradox. On the one side, there is an intense commitment to doing great things. There is a sincere dream and a plan for making history, a gusto for being a star player in a larger arena of ambition. But on the other side is an element of detachment, a footloose, untroubled attitude that treats triumph and disaster just the same. The team's conviction is strong, but the startup does not define their life. If the whole enterprise ends in failure or must change course, it is not a soul-crushing matter. This should by no means be interpreted as an acceptance of failure or a stoic refusal to feel grief and sadness. Failure shouldn't be celebrated for its own sake. While great founders learn from their losses and mistakes, they tend to learn even more from their wins. Nor should this be mistaken for simple adaptability or equanimity. It's different because the best teams have simultaneously an emotional commitment to the greatness of the goal, and the ability to put the thought of achieving it out of their minds. One encounter in literature that beautifully captures the spirit of the paradox is when Krishna admonishes Arjuna on the field of battle in the epic *Bhagavad Gita*:

> You have a right to your actions,
> But never to your actions' fruits.
> Act for the action's sake.
> And do not be attached to inaction.[14]

Or, as T. S. Eliot famously condensed it, "Not fare well, but fare forward."[15] What most people overlook is the last line. They tend to think the paragon of detachment is an ascetic sage who lives in a cave in the mountains. A wise monk with no possessions. No, Krishna commands, do not be attached to renouncing life. The epic battle must be joined. Act for the love of the game, and only for the love of the game, but also acknowledge that the game must be played and is worth playing. And, maybe, have some fun doing it.

Friday Night Dyson Sphere: The physicist Freeman Dyson once imagined a sphere of light-absorbing material surrounding our entire solar system on its periphery.[16] In science fiction these power systems have come to be known as "Dyson Spheres," and they represent a civilization's ability to harness all the energy of a star. Practically every photon. Certainly not your typical science fair project. One of the most electrifying moments for us is when a team convinces us, through a series of plausible steps backed by evidence, that they are capable of growing a lemonade stand into a company that builds Dyson Spheres. What's more, it's clear this is the thing they'd rather be tinkering on during a Friday night when all the cool kids are out partying. Now, that nutty ambition may sound deluded, like someone climbing a palm tree and saying they're on their way to a moon landing. But it happens. Think of Facebook starting at Harvard, moving on to the whole Ivy League, then all colleges, then all high schools, then the planet, influencing elections and undermining democracy (according to some). The best teams can tell these kinds of gripping stories, not as pure fantasy, but as a series of steps anchored in reality, which it is our job during the vetting process to assess. Some people fall short on vision. We often work with great teams who have a solid business model: a niche of customers love the product; revenue starts to accumulate. But then the team stalls because they don't know how to connect that initial stream of revenue to a sweeping vision that will fundamentally change an industry.

The other extreme is represented by Adam Neumann, the founder of WeWork. He convinced many investors that WeWork, a mere real estate company, was capable of changing consciousness, the future of work, and the way people relate to each other. Like a conman, Neumann appears to have been a masterful storyteller. But storytelling without evidence is as fragile as glass cracked into a spiderweb—difficult to see through and fragile to the slightest touch. Investors were foolish not to test the veracity of Neumann's claims or to put them in the proper context. WeWork was always going to be a real estate company. But I digress. To tie it up then, the best founders do have a chess master's ability to plan six moves ahead, and to weave credible claims into a story about how each move will take the company from the small to the great. This is the Friday Night Dyson Sphere. It's about those who dare to be unrealistic.

Schools, sadly, have no idea how to impart these virtues. They don't even know they exist. So it is no surprise that the twenty-year-olds who belong in the Venn diagram overlap between having the technical chops, the know-how, the edge control, the emotional intelligence, and all the rest of it is a vanishingly small group. As with all virtues, there are mistakes of too little, mistakes of too much. The perfect founding team would be perfectly balanced everlastingly on the golden hinge between each extreme. But no one can achieve that balance all the time. We exist—all of us, most of the time—in a state of perpetual aim. Back and forth we go, learning to be less, learning to be more. We can only hope that the days are not rare when we hit the mark.

• • •

It took some time for me to understand that character is best revealed in action. I came to hate applications and forms because the information in them is like fruit: it starts out fresh but quickly goes rotten. The status of a company could change in a month. As the years passed, I wanted to meet potential candidates earlier and track them over time. The more data points I could collect, the better sense I'd have of their character. The whole drama of our finalist weekend started to feel cumbersome. I hated that we followed the school year calendar. We needed to rely less on people finding us and more on us finding them first. It hit me one day when I was on the Thiel Capital trading floor near the desk making photocopies. I looked pretty slovenly. My beard had grown to the length of Dostoevsky's. My personal life was falling apart. One of the traders yelled across the trading floor to me: "Yo, John Walker Lindh, what are you doing tonight?"

John Walker Lindh, you may recall, was the bedraggled American who was captured as an enemy combatant in Afghanistan in November 2001. He looked terrible when U.S. forces found him aiding the Taliban, like a ball of fur and dust pulled from a vacuum bag. If I looked like Lindh, I must have looked awful. Later that night at the Final Final, our favorite dive bar in the Marina District, where my colleagues busted each other's chops at happy hour, I had a beer-soaked thought as I stared at the bottom of my empty pint glass (which I always get to too quickly). There was a lesson U.S. intelligence agencies didn't seem to have learned from John Walker Lindh. *He* found Osama Bin Laden before the CIA did. Lindh had gone to high school in San Anselmo, just over the Golden Gate Bridge and not far from the Thiel Capital office. At sixteen Lindh converted to Islam, and by twenty he had found his way to a secret al-Qaeda training camp in Afghanistan where he had a face-to-face meeting with Osama Bin Laden before 9/11. This teenage zealot had managed to do what billions of dollars' worth of spies, satellites, phone taps, and data collection could not. He found the leader of a small terrorist organization capable of delivering global mayhem. The key for Lindh was to share and then tap into Bin Laden's deepest beliefs and philosophy. "What is intelligence?," I remember the CIA officer asking me. Standing in the dive bar, I realized that this was the inverse of my task. Lindh found destruction; I had to find creation: a small band of unknown people capable of generating things of great future value. Like Lindh, the key for me was to tap into their deepest beliefs.

Cipher represented one kind of progress for me. I found him at an underground hacker conference. I'd begun to spend more and more time on university campuses. Sometimes I'd crash in hacker houses. I'd take midnight phone calls from Bitcoin fanatics to meet up for moonlit walks to discuss cryptoanarchy and the intellectual legacy of the cypherpunks from the 1990s. I hung about in overlooked places like Waterloo, Canada, and Champaign, Illinois. I was starting to live the lesson of John Walker Lindh. In the end, that lesson led us to many of the most dynamic people we'd ever work with. I'd find them in places where no one else was looking.

Major League Baseball, the National Football League, the NBA, the English Premier League—all of them use scouts who scour remote villages, forgotten islands, dusty podunk towns, and faraway favelas, hoping to identify promising talent before their rivals. Record labels also used to have scouts who rocked up at bars and clubs to search for the new sound that was different. Unlike pro sports and record labels, our talent scouting team comprised only five people, operating with a modest budget. But we were getting good. And we were about to get a whole lot better.

·7·

THE CLOCK TOWER

I was banned from MIT in the Fall of 2013. Jonathan and Danielle, too. Bill Aulet was miffed by how brazen he thought we were. He was and still is the head of MIT's entrepreneurship center and a professor in MIT's business school. He's the one who banned us. We're not allowed to sponsor or attend any events on campus. What happened was a reporter for the *Boston Globe* noticed Danielle, Jonathan, and me at a hackathon that a few students had organized on campus. The reporter filed the story in the *Globe* the next day:

> Under the noses of school officials, a group started by PayPal co-founder Peter Thiel used an event last weekend at the Massachusetts Institute of Technology to try to persuade budding entrepreneurs that college is a waste of money and [that] they should drop out and start businesses instead.[1]

HackMIT was one of the biggest hackathons in the country. It drew more than one thousand students, mostly from MIT and other Boston schools, but also from elsewhere, in some cases even abroad. A hackathon is typically a thirty-six-hour sleep-deprived contest in which teams compete to build the coolest thing they can dream up on short notice. Naturally, we'd want to recruit at this type of event—it was a gravity well of talent. But that didn't make Aulet happy. He told the *Globe*, "They are taking advantage of the very institution that they are saying you don't need."

Seeing that, I couldn't help but think of the famous Willie Sutton quote (one the legendary bank robber denied ever saying). Asked by a reporter why he robbed banks, Sutton said "Because that's where the money is."

If every talented young person went to college, not because they needed to, but because they had to due to social pressures, then of course we'd try finding people on campuses. That's where the money is.

Aulet's ban didn't keep me from MIT, however. I just had to be sneakier about it. The next year, Dylan Field, one of our 2012 fellows, introduced me over email to Ari Weinstein, after which I met Ari at a Starbucks next to MIT's campus. Alarmingly gifted and lithe as a triathlete, Ari was a programming phenom, arguably one of the best iOS developers in the world even at the age of nineteen. When he was six years old, Ari disassembled a computer and then reassembled it, and to his amazement, the computer still worked. By eleven, he began hacking into systems. And when he was fifteen, just after finishing the ninth grade, he and some friends pissed off Steve Jobs by "jailbreaking" the newest iPhone only two weeks after its release. Jobs was adamant that only Apple-approved software could be downloaded onto the iPhone through the company's app store. But Ari and his buddies discovered a way to circumvent Jobs's restrictions and then posted their program on a website. Anyone who wanted to modify their iPhone could download their program for free. The *Wall Street*

Journal profiled Ari under the headline, "How I Spent My Summer: Hacking into iPhones with Friends."[2]

At Starbucks, Ari gave me a demo of the latest idea he had. He called it Deskconnect. It was a program that let users move files back and forth from iPhones and iPads to desktop computers seamlessly. With his index finger, he was touching files on the screen of his iPad and moving them over to his laptop as if the two devices were connected on one virtual plane. Tens of thousands of Apple customers were already using Deskconnect. Ari was weighing whether to stay in school or stop out and devote himself full time to growing the company. He'd already deferred college a year to work at a startup in Silicon Valley. He wasn't sure he should do that again so soon.

"Well, what's going on at MIT?" I asked.

He expressed frustration with his coursework. In order to major in computer science, you had to take all these low-level course requirements. The problem was that the required courses were covering stuff he already learned on his own in his early teens.

That got me thinking. He was paying fifty thousand or sixty thousand dollars a year to take courses covering ground he already knew. But he had to take the credits to earn the major. It didn't make sense, this time spent sitting in class covering things a student already knew. Why couldn't Ari demonstrate his competence independently of the coursework? It wasn't simply that he was wasting time, it was that he had to pay a fortune to do it too. Shouldn't the college degree communicate mastery of knowledge in a subject and not the amount of time someone sat in a classroom? And right there it dawned on me that colleges are obsessed with time. Course credits are measured in hours per week. A term lasts twelve to fifteen weeks. Students sit for hour-long final exams. A degree is a four-year accumulation of

120 hours of credits. What the hell is going on with this focus on the hour?

• • •

Along with the plow, the stirrup, the crusade, cathedrals, and parliaments, the medieval era gave birth to universities. Plato may have established the Academy in Athens, but he awarded no diplomas. His best student, Aristotle, received no certificate. Everything we associate with a university—faculties, colleges, courses, final exams, commencement, and degrees—all emerged over nine hundred years ago first in Bologna, then in Paris and Oxford. No form of government on earth has lasted as long. Only religions surpass it in endurance. Granted, the university still had some way to grow from its infancy. The medieval university did not yet have libraries, labs, or endowments, but there was one building even then that stood out—it was the tallest structure for miles—and to this day can still be found on nearly every campus as the most noticeable architectural feature. That building is the bell tower clock. And every hour, every bell carves out the time, to remind us also that we are heirs to the movements of a distant past.

As I traveled to so many university campuses, it struck me as curious that the invention of the mechanical clock and sandglass just about coincided with the emergence of the university. I believe this is no accident. The widespread adoption of clock tower technology and other reliable time-keeping devices had profound consequences in the Middle Ages. They fundamentally altered social activities. Belltower clocks partition the day into uniform smaller chunks that everybody can agree on, broadcasting it out for miles. Prior to that, people relied on rough guesses or approximate measures, which would lead to all sorts of disagreements. For example, time spent working was measured in whole days or by shadows and the sun. But what happens when it's cloudy? Or in the Northern reaches of Europe, how do you handle the differing lengths of the day across the seasons? What happens when a landholder accuses a peasant farmer of not working the fields long enough? It's no surprise that these vagaries caused disputes among people. One historian of time, Gerhard Dohrn-van Rossum, has documented 14th-century French legal cases between vineyard owners and workers where the trial is about defining the workday and when it was supposed to end. In one such case in the town of Auxerre, the workers noticed the untrustworthy human-powered bell was ringing the ninth hour too late, "between the fourth and fifth hour of the afternoon instead of the third."[3] The invention and widespread diffusion of the mechanical clock in a public tower eliminated all of these disputes. It had two properties that made this possible: accuracy and integrity. It was precise and it couldn't be tampered with. There are bell clock towers throughout European towns with dedications celebrating the transformation they wrought. The city of Caen in 1314 built a clock tower with the inscription: "I give the hours voice, to make the common folk rejoice."[4] One 14th-century chronicler took the cult of the clock as a sign of absolute authority: "whoever controls this palace and can ring the bells at will can easily rule over the city." By the 16th century, we have Rabelais musing upon clock time as a communal sense-perception: "a city without bells is like a blind man without a stick."[5]

Accuracy and fair broadcast of time enhanced relationships that could benefit from coordination. The nature of work fundamentally changed, as workers could earn wages based on a mutually agreed-upon time rate. Time became a measure of sacrifice, of how much someone was willing to give up in order to complete a task. Keeping the promise of time demonstrated how reliable a person was. And in turn, on university campuses, time sacrificed became an indirect measurement for commitment and knowledge acquisition. Centuries later, it is still with us today. Every diploma is mostly a time rate diploma demonstrating the faithfulness of the graduate in keeping promises across four years. It signals a major sacrifice. Four years spent in school marching around a clock tower is four years not doing something else—partying, traveling, being idle and so on. Or let's hope, in any case.

There is a puzzle in the economics of higher education called the "sheepskin effect." (Sheepskin, because diplomas used to be made of sheepskin back in the Middle Ages.) When economists look at wage boosts for each additional year of education, it turns out not all years of education are equal in terms of payoffs. Graduation is a sacred rite of passage. It is also lucrative; there is quite a large pay spike for earning a diploma in the fourth year. The average study finds that completing senior year in college pays out two times more than completing the first three years combined.[6] That is extremely odd, if you believe college grads are paid more because they have learned more. Why would finishing that last semester improve someone's skill set by double over what they learned as freshmen, sophomores, and juniors combined? That just doesn't jibe with the facts. I remember people coasting and partying in their last semester.

Let's sharpen that puzzle even more. Suppose that a student drops out one class shy of graduating. That dropout still possesses 99 percent of all the skills the degree boasts, right? 119 out of 120 credits completed. We can even say that the missing credit is an elective, the most outrageous credit hour imaginable. The Social Justice of Basket-weaving. Lady Gaga and the Sociology of Fame. Demystifying the Hipster, as taught at Tufts University.[7] If employers value skills, and not diplomas, then our dropout should make about as much in the labor market as the person who crossed the finish line, because they both have the same skill set. But the truth is our dropout doesn't make the same amount. The student who finishes that last credit makes 29.8 percent more on average.[8] This is true even if they both become bartenders. Mastering the concepts in Demystifying the Hipster may be useless, but the payoff is big.

Education pays. Even useless education pays. We have never denied that. Those who have a college degree make on average about 70 percent more than those who only have a high school diploma.[9] The question is *why*. The clock tower offers an explanation. A college degree signals information about its holder, but not what most people think. It doesn't say all that much about the skills they acquired or what they learned. Instead, it's telling employers information about a graduate's ability to keep the promises of time, the willingness to sacrifice four years in the pursuit of a grueling, even if useless, series of tasks and projects. It should be said that only university bell tower clocks have this magical property. A hopeful student cannot study on his own in the vicinity of Big Ben and expect the same result. No one would take his word for it. The sacrifice of time must be made by students before trusted authorities and towards a socially approved goal.

Many college professors—especially those in the liberal arts—even brag about *not* teaching any job-related skills. Instead, they make public-spirited claims about critical thinking (whatever that means) and preparing citizens for membership in a democracy. These professors don't teach students what to think, so they tell us, but how to think. If that leads to higher incomes for graduates, so be it, but that's not the point. It's about having a well-furnished mind, a skeptical attitude, and a rich inner life. Louis Menand, staff writer at the *New Yorker* and professor of English at Harvard, argues in *The Marketplace of Ideas* that an education in the liberal arts "encourages students to think for themselves."[10] Andrew Delbanco, a professor at Columbia University and author of *College: What It Was, Is, And Should Be*, asserts that "the most important thing one can acquire in college is a well-functioning bullshit meter."[11] The stakes are quite high, too, for being able to detect this malodorous excrement for oneself. As the philosopher Martha Nussbaum pleads in her book *Not for Profit: Why Democracy Needs the Humanities*, "cultivated capacities for critical thinking and reflection are crucial in keeping democracies alive and awake."[12]

Given the importance these professors place on critical thinking and independent thought, one might expect them to use those skills for themselves and give greater scrutiny to the effects of what they think they're teaching. Sadly, neither Nussbaum, Delbanco, Menand, nor any other liberal arts professor for that matter, has shown any inclination to test their claims. Quite the opposite. All we find in their writing is evasive sophistry. Blithely and piously across hundreds and hundreds of pages, they all make the case for studying the liberal arts as a way to learn critical thinking skills and even to become a more caring and compassionate person, but they do so without presenting any evidence to support their views. Not one shred.

This may appear to be a harsh, sweeping statement on my part, but colleges do not measure for improved student performance on such noble topics as how to think or how to ask the "right" questions. It is revealing that, despite this being the stated purpose of college, professors are not evaluated for how well they teach these subtle skills, nor are they rewarded for doing it better or criticized for doing it worse. Next, perhaps more tellingly, university presidents are neither ranked nor rewarded for how well they improve student achievement in critical thinking at their respective schools. The best-paid university presidents are not those who are best at improving learning outcomes or advancing science. They are those who raise the most money from alumni.

Of all the radical ideas I have, these findings provoke the strongest resistance, but there is little data to support the view that colleges teach students how to think. In fact, the research points the other way. Contrary to Nussbaum, Delbanco, Menand, and hundreds of other defenders of the faith, there is an avalanche of accumulated evidence that finds studying the liberal arts does not improve a student's ability to think.[13] For nearly one hundred years, educational psychologists have been investigating what they call transfer of learning—that is, the ability to take an insight from one domain and then apply it to something new. Does learning how to take apart Plato's arguments or to deconstruct a poem also help you take apart arguments in the Op-Ed section of the newspaper? Unfortunately, no. In hundreds of experiments, students fail to apply what they learned in one context and then apply it in another. The educational psychologist Robert Haskell sums up the dismal conclusion of this vast body of research: "Despite the importance of transfer of learning, research findings over the past nine decades clearly show that as individuals, and as educational institutions, we have failed to achieve transfer of learning on any significant level."[14]

It gets worse. Go to Harvard College's mission statement:

"The mission of Harvard College is to educate the citizens and citizen-leaders for our society. We do this through our commitment to the transformative power of a liberal arts and sciences education."

Transformation is a sacred idea for universities. So is service to humanity, as Princeton claims:

"A liberal arts education challenges you to consider not only how to solve problems, but also trains you to ask which problems to solve and why, preparing you for positions of leadership and a life of service to the nation and all of humanity."

I could go on through the mission statements from every school listed in the *U.S. News & World Report* college rankings. They all make these same grandiose, hyperbolic claims. The fraudulent joke is that there is scant evidence universities succeed in doing any of the things they claim. Even at Harvard and Princeton. Universities simply do not measure the supposed benefits they impart to graduates. How good are they at preparing the leaders of tomorrow in problem-solving? Beats them. Despite what they boast in marketing material, universities don't bother to investigate. To be at all credible, universities would have to measure the ability of students on day one, measure those same students on the day of graduation, and then perhaps measure them again five, ten, and twenty years after graduation to test for fade out, and then compare the differences. Not one university does this! What a scandal! To borrow a joke from the philosopher Jason Brennan, this is the same as assuming a new drug treatment works with no evidence.[15] If diplomas were a drug—just imagine the slick cheerfulness in commercials for Diplomatis or Universimectin—the FDA would ban them for lack of randomized controlled trials demonstrating their benefits.

More broadly, does higher ed deliver on any of its promised goods? The plain yet disturbing fact is that most students do not improve much, and they rapidly forget what little they learn.[16] Two sociologists, Richard Arum and Josipa Roksa, took up the task that universities do not attempt for themselves: a long-term comprehensive study.[17] From more than 2,300 undergraduates of different backgrounds at twenty-four schools, Arum and Roksa examined students' grades, survey responses, and performances on the Collegiate Learning Assessment, a standardized test designed to measure skills in critical thinking, reasoning, problem-solving, and writing. The researchers looked at students in their first semester, again at the end of their second year, and then at the end of four years. They published their sobering results in their 2011 book *Academically Adrift*, where they find that "at least 45 percent of students in our sample did not demonstrate any statistically significant improvement in CLA performance during the first two years of college."[18] After four years, 36 percent show no gains. For the students who show some improvement, the amount they improved requires a microscope to see. Only 10 percent show strong gains.

Americans spend somewhere on the order of $500 billion per year on higher education.[19] To beat a loud drum louder: tuition has screamed skywards, quadrupling in real terms over forty years; there is $1.7 trillion in outstanding student debt. Never has so much been spent by so many to learn so little. A large fraction of students who enroll never graduate. Those who barely pass and graduate near the bottom of their class do not see a boost in wages. If pharmaceutical companies are required to show their drugs work, then at this cost, it's outrageous that we don't ask the same of our colleges. The current situation is fraudulent and immoral.

To return to the beginning—why are college grads paid more on average? The four-year march around the clock tower is a big part of the answer. The next troublesome fact is that schools like Harvard and Princeton attract young people who are *already* talented when they are accepted. Before they even show up to orientation, they are already the types of people who rip apart arguments and interrogate assumptions. In short, they are smart workhorses wherever you place them. One famous study by the economists Stacy Dale and Alan Kruger looked at students who were accepted to Ivy League schools, but who then chose instead to attend the less expensive local state university.[20] It turned out the grads who got into the Ivies and then didn't go earned just as much money over the next twenty years as those who did. As one prominent economist summarized the findings, "In other words, the student, not the school, was responsible for the success."[21]

Beyond cementing prestige and social status, we also now see why schools crave exclusivity. By narrowing the variance of the incoming class, universities shrink the variance in the perceived outcome at graduation. If freshmen aren't all that different from one another, then—ta-da!—neither will graduating seniors be that far apart. No one will have reason to question the efficacy of the Ivy League's teaching methods when the variance has shrunk to the size of a hairline fracture. Whereas if Harvard expanded enrollment by fifty thousand, would its world-class professors be able to improve the abilities of the bottom third of that class? I very much doubt it.

Employers rarely pay graduates for what they studied over four years. No, what employers pay for are the preexisting traits students reveal by sacrificing the time and showing they can master the—oftentimes—useless coursework. There are many different types of people in this world. But who we are is not obvious, and people lie. Character is revealed in action. The clock tower is a sorting mechanism that tells employers the differences among those who can circle it and those who can't.

It is also worth noting that I am not making the facile criticism of universities that state governors make when they disparage anthropology or the arts and praise engineering and math. Both the arts and sciences are important, but people get it backward. They think poetry and philosophy are for understanding what it means to be human, while the sciences are for discovery and truth. But that's not right; it's the other way around. Science lets us know who we are, and the arts lead us into discovery and truth. Poetry and philosophy can serve as the spark of soul craft; we should all learn to grapple with the great ideas as embodied in great works, but the evidence shows that the way universities teach these subjects is not having the effect they think it is.

Even STEM suffers from much of what I say: the highest paying majors attract people who are already smart, and, while many technical fields appear vocational, there is often a weak link between what is taught and what is later needed in a long career. Most STEM majors pursue non-STEM jobs. As I hardly need to elaborate, having the government forgive student loan debt or cover the cost of tuition does nothing to dismantle the clock tower either. Government largesse will do nothing to ensure the last chime of these bells.

Now, there is one experiment that economists, sociologists, educational psychologists, and other researchers have yet to perform. They have never identified a group of eighteen-year-olds who are already intelligent enough to get into top universities, conscientious enough to finish, but who then decide to forgo that path. By 2013, we had been running that experiment for three years. Most of our fellows' incomes were far higher than the typical college grad's. And, most importantly in terms of the labor market, the founder of a company doesn't have to signal anything about being a dedicated workhorse to a potential boss. They are the boss.

• • •

Back at Starbucks, I told Ari he didn't have to make a decision about leaving MIT now. He could apply to the Thiel Fellowship and then if he got accepted in the Spring, he could decide then what he wanted to do. A few months passed. In the meantime, Ari teamed up with Conrad Kramer and Nick Frey at a hackathon hosted by the University of Michigan at Ann Arbor. Conrad and Nick were also both iOS programming phenoms. Together, over thirty-six hours, they came up with a program that could automate a chain of apps across all Apple devices. Hit one button to order an Uber, put the dinner order in, and text your friend you're on your way. They called their program Workflow. Hardcore Apple users loved it as soon as the team released it. In the first few months, they had about 200,000 downloads at $2.99 each. Of the three, only Ari and Conrad were eligible for our fellowship. And both were tempted to leave MIT to grow Workflow.

But Bill Aulet got wind of our offer. He wouldn't have it. Banning us wasn't enough. According to Ari and Conrad, Aulet persuaded Paul English, one of the cofounders of Kayak.com, to offer Ari and Conrad $100,000 each to stay at MIT and not take a Thiel Fellowship. (English was a co-lecturer in Aulet's entrepreneurship class at MIT that year.)

In the end, Ari and Conrad dropped out, accepted the fellowship, and put their heads down on Workflow. By 2015, Workflow had won an Apple Design Award and was voted one of the best apps of the year. Apple loved the team and the product, so much so, that in 2017 it acquired Workflow for $20 million. If you have an iPhone, open it—there is an app preinstalled on every iPhone sold, all 200 million of them in 2020—and tap on "shortcuts." This is Workflow. Not a bad accomplishment for a few dropouts before the age of twenty-two. Aulet shouldn't have started a fight he couldn't finish.

The truth is Ari, Conrad, and the others were learning a lot. It just didn't look like education in the traditional sense. It obeyed no calendar or clock and didn't require exams. I began to see the fellowship as a way to undermine the notion that centralized, synchronized time should structure the learning process. The more precisely we can measure skill and knowledge acquisition, and the more reliably we can establish our reputations, then the less dependent we are on time as a proxy measurement for intangible character traits. Education should not be based on how much time a student spent in the vicinity of a clock tower. No clock can count this. It should be based on knowledge of what is timeless: continuous edge control along the boundary of knowledge and ignorance, from light out into the darkness, from darkness back into the light, discovering and refining whatever virtues and crafts lie quietly within us. Let the clocks march on with their tick-tock steps. We cannot squander the Earth and stars by mistaking time for learning.

·8·

THE NAKAMOTO CONSENSUS

On July 23, 2014, I made what turned out to be the absolute worst financial decision of my life. Much to my eternal embarrassment. Worse, I could have rectified that mistake over the following year or two with some course-correcting prudence, but I did not. I have no excuse. All told, this infernal lapse has probably meant losing out on tens of millions of dollars. The final number is hard to calculate, but it is colossal.

What happened was that across a handful of meetings and phone calls in the winter and spring of 2014, I'd been advising Vitalik Buterin, the inventor of the Ethereum blockchain. In the early days, there were tensions between members of the Ethereum leadership team, and I was a sounding board for Vitalik to talk through the issues and help him work the kinks out. We'd recruited Vitalik into the Thiel Fellowship earlier that year, not long after he had written his white paper first describing the Ethereum network. Then in July, the Ethereum organization launched the initial sale of its first coins. As an advisor, I marketed the sale to everyone I could. This included a now immortal Facebook post, which I've printed out to remind myself of my foolishness. "Get 'em fresh off the crypto printing press," I wrote all over social media, with a link to the website where visitors could buy some. "Ether, a new currency for the distributed application platform from Thiel Fellow Vitalik Buterin and others at Ethereum." The embarrassing mistake I made was that, despite being involved at the moment of creation—the let-there-be-light moment of a blockchain—I did not buy a single Ether. Seeing my Facebook post, one of my best friends bought one Bitcoin worth of Ether, which was exchanged for 2000 of the new coins (about $1000 at the time). As of December 2021, his holdings are worth about $4 million.

Truth be told, at the time I didn't have a lot of personal savings to place in risky endeavors. My savings when I started working for Peter were zero. I was an out-of-work poet-philosopher. On top of that, the IRS doesn't look too fondly on non-profit officers making money off their grantees. Nevertheless, we'd been at the forefront long before most knew what a blockchain was. That was exciting. One of our Thiel Fellows, Chris Olah, had sent an email to Danielle on November 9, 2013: "Vitalik Buterin is one of my friends from high school. He was an applicant to the [Thiel] fellowship last year. He's spent the last year or so traveling around the world doing Bitcoin stuff. I haven't seen him since, but it's been super interesting to follow his adventures. And now he's visiting the Bay Area!"

It's surprising in retrospect, given his genius, but we'd rejected Vitalik's application the previous year because he pitched us some ideas about improving education with technology. EdTech as a trend always turned us off for a variety of reasons, but mainly because it didn't improve outcomes in learning. But in the year after he first applied, Vitalik had discovered another ace up his sleeve. He'd been quite productive hatching some new ideas for repurposing the blockchain technology that underlies Bitcoin. He told us all about it on December 2, during lunch in the Letterman cafeteria, which we shared with the animators and special effects wizards from Lucas Films. The classical rotunda of the Palace of Fine Arts, with its radiant sandy and copper patina, glowed as always in the sun outside the window as we ate. Vitalik sketched out for us what a "distributed application" might look like, what it might do, what it might replace. He called them "Dapps" for short. His rough draft of the concept was an extension of the decentralizing aspect of Bitcoin's mysterious, but infallible ledger.

Vitalik was only nineteen years old in 2013, but he spoke to us as an authority on mathematics, computer programming, and game theory. His IQ could very well be 200. I have no idea. But at a later meeting over dinner, I saw him texting on his phone in Mandarin with Ethereum developers in China. I asked him how he knew Mandarin and he told me he taught himself. His Russian accent and the cadences of his sentences lend his voice a Stephen Hawking-like, robo-synth quality, though Vitalik speaks quickly and has a slight lisp. But where Hawking was grave and donnish, Vitalik is ironic and playful. He often wears t-shirts colored with defiant go-to-hell pastel gradients, from fawn lust pink to Malibu Barbi teal. The shirts are usually cluttered with graphics pulled from Internet memes, like kittens riding on llamacorns. (That's a llama with a unicorn horn.) He wears t-shirts to the most formal conferences anywhere in the world. His is an affectionate, but self-satirical view of the Internet and its carnival of garish and childish humor. If you saw him on the street, you would think he was a throwback teen who'd fit right in at a 1980s arcade blasting British new wave pop. Skinny kid, gaunt face, black jeans, Vaporwave tee, an Eastern European vibe grounded by homespun Canadian kindness. You would never guess for a moment that this nineteen-year-old would become the architect of a multi-billion dollar international project to overthrow the money-gods of Wall Street, Silicon Valley, and all of its big tech companies that exploit their users like feudal lords and their digital serfs.

But at lunch that day, the vision began much more modestly. I asked him what possible uses a distributed application on Ethereum might have. He mentioned a string of concepts I had heard of but did not fully grasp. Unique digital assets. Smart contracts. Digital registries of personal identity. All of these things, while confusing in detail, were going to open a new frontier in the way people could coordinate and interact on the Internet. Vitalik had flown around the world that year—he listed his home as Cathay Pacific Airlines—to meet with Bitcoin developers in different ecosystems. He found there were pockets in the different places where people were starting to think about how crypto could be used for single-purpose applications beyond money. One prominent one, Namecoin, positioned itself as a domain name system built on Bitcoin's code. But that was all it could do. None of these efforts were thinking in broader, more ambitious terms. During his travels, Vitalik began to conceive of a decentralized system that was general and flexible enough to handle any new use case, not just one application. The functionality of Bitcoin's code could be extended, made more versatile, like moving from a phone to the iPhone. Nevertheless, it all depended on the technological discovery that Bitcoin made possible. Vitalik wrote up his ideas in a research paper that he first sent to a trusted group of fifteen people on November 27, only five days before sitting down for lunch with us. Not too soon after that, we awarded Vitalik a Thiel Fellowship without him even having filled out an application. I ran point on the Fellowship team for helping him out, an experience that converted me entirely over to an unusual, experimental philosophy that I began to sketch out.

Though it offered an analytical framework, which I borrowed from Ethereum's and Bitcoin's designs, it was less a set of principles than an ethos and sensibility. I called it the Nakamoto Consensus. It addressed a general problem of which decadent universities were but one specific instance. Vitalik's expansion of the Bitcoin protocol was the inspiration at the heart of my framework for thinking about institutions and their repertoire of dysfunctional behaviors. Once I had understood Vitalik's and Nakamoto's insights into institutions, I became a bomb fizzing at the fuse.

• • •

The invention of Bitcoin is arguably the greatest unsolved mystery of this century. It may well prove to be the most influential invention as well. Its inventor is on the way to becoming the richest human who ever lived. Only time will tell if one day it replaces the dollar as the world's reserve currency. But whatever its ultimate fate as a currency, it represents a tremendous breakthrough in computer science with profound philosophical implications that will continue to play out in the decades ahead. That story began, fittingly enough, on Halloween in 2008—at 2:10 p.m., New York time to be exact—when a dry, unassuming apparition appeared from out of the Internet mists on an obscure email list composed of cypherpunks and other cryptography enthusiasts. He called himself Satoshi Nakamoto. He used an untraceable email account.

"I've been working on a new electronic cash system that's fully peer-to-peer, with no trusted third party," Nakamoto announces without fire or poetry.[1] He then directs everyone to a nine-page research paper hosted on a Website—bitcoin. org—which he'd registered two months earlier, again using an untraceable account.

The key electrifying term in his announcement is "no trusted third party." It was as if this practical joker was claiming he found a way to generate a working paradox. He was saying, in effect, that he'd invented a form of trustworthy bookkeeping that required no bookkeeper, an unerring ledger that required no certified accountant, or, to bring back the coordinating technology from the last chapter, a tamper-proof public clock with no timekeeper. How would that paradox even be possible?

The experts on the cryptography mailing list were not impressed with Nakamoto. Versions of electronic cash and e-gold had been invented before, but the problem was that they all relied on someone in the middle of transactions to verify them and to keep track of them. That man in the middle—a "trusted third party"—was, in the end, a vulnerability for security, because a guardian or institution could become corrupted over time or grow lax in its protection of data. The weak man in the middle also represented a target for any use-of-force monopolies (the rather charming term cypherpunks use for governments), should any government decide to shut the system down by decapitating its center. Recall Napster, the pirate file sharing service for music that was shut down in 2001, after pissing off anyone who ever won a Grammy and destroying the entire music industry's business model. It was easy for the Justice Department and the FBI to thwart Napster because it was a corporation with a CEO and other officers. Because of such vulnerabilities, a mantra had emerged in the 2000s among many cryptography geeks: "trusted third parties are security holes." So it's not surprising that the initial response to Satoshi Nakamoto from the email list ranged from ho-hum to skepticism. No one had invented an electronic cash system without trusted third parties before. It didn't seem possible. The doubts started coming in right away in replies to Nakamoto's Halloween email. Nakamoto parries them all as they come in, which anyone can read in the email record, but by the lack of enthusiasm, it's clear he hasn't won any believers.

Then on January 3, 2009, two months after his initial email to the group, Nakamoto fired up his new system on his computer and mined the very first Bitcoin. To make a point about corruption in the financial system, he tucked a reference into the data underlying the coin, a headline ripped from the *Times* of London that day:

> The Times 03/Jan/2009 Chancellor
> on brink of second bailout for banks

Over the next six days, he continued to tinker with the software and created more Bitcoins. By January 10, Nakamoto found his first believer on the cryptography email list. Hal Finney, a member of the cypherpunks since the earliest days, stepped forward. Finney had already tried his own hand at creating an electronic currency a few years before. As soon as Nakamoto made the Bitcoin software available, Finney downloaded it. There followed a flurry of matter-of-fact emails between the two as Finney points out bugs in the software and Nakamoto corrects them. Then, two weeks later, Nakamoto sent Finney 10 Bitcoin in the first-ever transaction verified and secured by a blockchain. Bitcoin was born.

● ● ●

Institutions are fuzzy concepts. Marriage is an institution. Baseball is too. But so is a gargantuan administrative body like the Federal Reserve. One researcher on the subject lists twenty-one different definitions for institutions drawing examples from economics, sociology, anthropology, and other redoubts of obscure scholarship.[2] Each has a different emphasis, but a general feature of institutions is that they are the durable forms of our common life, to borrow a phrase from the political scientist Yuval Levin.[3] Institutions structure what we do together in the pursuit of social goals. To see the far-reaching implications underlying crypto, it's important to see that Bitcoin and Ethereum are not just computer networks, and certainly not startups, but whole new institutions meant to surpass the performance of decaying old ones. They are tools for structuring what we do together in the pursuit of common goals. They do this through an intricate set of incentives and rules, which display a workmanship, precision, and interlocking machinery so unbreakable, so startling in ingenuity, that even the greatest of Swiss horologists would be astonished.

Let's return to the advent of the mechanical bell tower clock in the medieval European era. Like the Federal Reserve, this was a public institution serving the common good. Practically all relationships benefit from coordination in time. There are two essential aspects of the bell tower clock that make it a good public institution: it is reliable and trustworthy. Reliability means that the clock is accurate. As far as the technology is concerned, it does what it's supposed to do. The intent of the engineering matches the sweep of its hands. (More formally, we can define reliability as the closeness that repeated actions have to desired results over time. Hitting a bull's eye over and over is the sign of a reliable archer.) That effectiveness leads to a wider social function, which is to tell the time for a medieval town. It provides a measure for when and for how long shared events should occur. At first blush, this may appear to be of little consequence, but, as we have seen, the tower clock makes all the difference when it comes to settling disputes between laborers and owners about how long anyone has worked in a day. It also allows anyone within earshot to coordinate activities in ways that just weren't possible when no one knew what time it was. Suddenly time could become a measure of the sacrifice made in any undertaking. The idea of wage-rate labor became intelligible and workable for the first time. A trustworthy answer to the question, "how much time did you devote to this?," became a rough indirect measure for how much anyone should be paid for completing a task.

As useful as that may be, however, citizens can rely on that first property, and the social benefits it brings, only if the second property can be relied upon as well: the bell tower must be secure from human manipulation. It must be trustworthy. If neither laborers, nor shop owners can trust the time, they simply would cease to use it to forge agreements. Systems of coordination would fall apart. For this reason, the clock's inner workings must be tamper-proof. Some security to prevent this can be structural. The fact that the clock is the tallest building in town makes it difficult to access. Its height also makes it highly visible and therefore easier for anyone in town to detect abnormal change. Monitoring costs are low. A second tower clock in town may reinforce the trustworthiness of the public time, since whenever there is a lack of synchronization, all will know something is off in the tolling of the bells. Tamper-proofing also relies on trust in humans, sadly but not surprisingly a weaker solution than engineering. Here we run into the cypherpunk complaint: trusted third parties are security holes. But the only people who might be able to shave or add minutes to an hour are a small number of insiders, the guards, the clock-maker, or any other authorized person with a key to the bell tower. Collusion is difficult.

These two properties of the mechanical medieval clock tower—reliable performance and resistance to tampering—led to a massive change in medieval social interactions. Nick

Szabo, an eclectic polymath and cryptographer, wrote an essay in 2005 on the invention of mechanical clocks and how their advent helped end feudalism.[4] Szabo credits more precise and trustworthy time-keeping technologies as a decisive factor in the decline of serfdom and the rise of wage-rate free labor in Europe. So far as I can tell, Szabo coined the phrase "trusted third parties are security holes" in a 2001 essay on computer security.[5] There is also something else of interest about Szabo. He is on every expert's shortlist as the man behind Satoshi Nakamoto.

There is a famous problem in computer science that goes back to the 1970s.[6] It is often illustrated with a story about a group of generals who must attack a Byzantine city. The problem is that these generals need to send messages to each other and agree on a time to attack. The circumstances of the battle are such that the generals can only achieve victory if their armies all attack the city at the same time. If any single one of the generals retreats while the others attack, then all are defeated. So it's of the utmost importance that each general receives a reliable message with the correct time of the attack. But there is trouble. The conditions around the city make communication unreliable. Night has fallen. Spies are everywhere. Sent messages can be lost, or enemies can intercept the messages and tamper with them, providing an incorrect time of attack. Perhaps even one of the generals himself is inclined to treason and is tempted to send false information. So, a computer scientist asks, how do you invent a reliable and trustworthy system of communication that ensures the generals attack at the same time? In other words, is it possible to build a tamper-proof bell tower clock with no clock tower? Ever since the problem was first proposed forty years before, the computer science community thought it was unsolvable.

Whoever Nakamoto is, on November 13, 2008, he announced to the email list of cypherpunks that his blockchain framework solves the Byzantine Generals problem. The ingenious technique behind his solution has come to be known as Nakamoto Consensus. It's what prevents the counterfeiting of Bitcoin or the double spending of the same Bitcoin. It's the bookkeeping without the bookkeeper. It also allows the generals to attack the city at the same time.

Again, without fire, poetry, or swagger, Nakamoto tells the email list how ten generals will coordinate using his system. "They use a proof-of-work chain to solve the problem," he begins. He goes on to explain the technical details behind what a proof-of-work chain is. Essentially each computer in a network has to race to solve a difficult math problem, the problem being different for each computer but similar in nature. It takes time, energy, and computational processing to solve the problem. Millions of attempted answers must be processed to find one that works. Today, this number is in the trillions. As a result, to participate at all, every computer must make a sacrifice in order to contribute information. (A second consequence: cheaters, fraudsters, and spies are deterred from bad behavior. Collusion is costly. They would have to expend vast amounts of time, electricity, and computational power to try to spoof the others with false information.)

In any event, the first computer to solve the math problem in the race, which takes about ten minutes on average, broadcasts its answer to the group of other computers. One of the peculiar characteristics of Nakamoto's math problems is that they are difficult to solve but easy to verify. The other computers quickly verify if the first computer's solution is correct. If so, the winning computer is awarded a jackpot: newly minted Bitcoin and transaction fees, both as an incentive for maintaining and securing the system. Then, at that very moment, the other computers take the information the first computer broadcast out and they build upon it. The first one of them to solve the next math problem gets to be the one who builds the next information block and then adds that block to the first. A chain begins to form. Every computer has a copy of it. Over time, these blocks of information on the chain keep an immutable historical record: time-stamped receipts of every past transaction, current account balances, and verification of all current transactions. No single computer can cheat or change the record because its fraudulent blocks would be rejected by the other computers in the network. But more to the point, the incentives to maintain the truth and integrity of the ledger only get stronger in time. If the system were to fail even once—one counterfeit block, one rewrite of the past—then the entire value of the system would collapse, and all previous sacrifices would have been made in vain. That's not so bad if Bitcoins are worth pennies. But it's a catastrophe to be avoided with great vigilance when they are nearly $30,000 apiece with millions of Bitcoins in circulation. As of May 2022, that loss would be $600 billion. What a thief counterfeits would be worthless, too, since his fraud is only valuable if the whole system is working. Self-interest, channeled into this system of interlocking checks and balances, stands as a sentinel overall.

The earlier the block in that chain, the more credible its information is. It has been verified and built upon by all participants. A consensus has been reached—by whom? No, by what—a distributed system of computers acting in the interest of their owners. That consensus keeps the ledger reliable and tamper-proof, like a good mechanical bell tower clock. Every Bitcoin in every account on that ledger represents everything at stake should its integrity be broken. They also signal the value all of the computers have sacrificed to make the system work.

I believe it is no coincidence that the title of Nick Szabo's essay on the invention of the medieval clock tower is "A Measure of Sacrifice." The invention of Bitcoin is the invention of a new way to measure and preserve sacrifice in time. In the words of one investor, In Math We Trust.

After walking the cryptography group through a concise version of this, Nakamoto delivers the coup de grâce. He tells the email list that after using his software for about two hours there would be a chain composed of at least one block from each of the ten Byzantine Generals. One by one, each general can then verify each of the other blocks created in the proof-of-work chain. Each can also measure the sacrifice needed to create those blocks, thereby establishing common knowledge. The time of the attack is embedded in the first block, which has been verified and secured by the Nakamoto Consensus. "The proof-of-work chain is how all the synchronization, distributed database and global view problems you've asked about are solved," he concludes, without so much as an added peep to his interlocutor that he has just earned the equivalent of a Nobel Prize in computer science in incidental remarks and passing observations.

• • •

From its beginning to today, Bitcoin has been condemned by many serious theorists as unworkable. By all the rules and precedents of Princeton and Harvard economists, Bitcoin should not exist. Yet, here it stands, stronger than ever. Some wiseacre at the Nakamoto Institute website has collected many of the skeptics' comments over the years and has listed the quotes next to the price of Bitcoin at the time it was said, and then next to that, how much a dollar invested every day in Bitcoin since that time would be worth today. That number is staggering, in the millions for some and hundreds of thousands for others more recent. Some of the great ones:

> Paul Krugman, Nobel Prize-winning economist, September 7, 2011: "So to the extent that the [Bitcoin] experiment tells us anything about monetary regimes, it reinforces the case against anything like a new gold standard — because it shows just how vulnerable such a standard would be to money-hoarding, deflation, and depression."

Krugman's daily one-dollar buy would be worth just over $6 million in December of 2021. More:

> Justin Wolfers, University of Michigan economist, April 11, 2013: "Money is: (1) a unit of account, (2) a store of value, (3) a medium of exchange. Right now Bitcoin is none of those things (in any serious sense)."
>
> Ian Bremmer, political scientist, foreign policy expert, and author, May 14, 2013: "I would be very surprised if Bitcoin is still around in 10 years."
>
> Brad Delong, University of California, Berkeley economist, December 28, 2013: "unless BitCoin can somehow successfully differentiate itself from the latecomers who are about to emerge, the money supply of BitCoin-like things is infinite because the cost of production of them is infinitesimal."
>
> Jamie Dimon, CEO and President JPMorgan & Chase, January 23, 2014: "It's a terrible store of value. It could be replicated over and over."

What is this devilish Bitcoin good for? What are these egg-heads missing? Throughout history, many different kinds of things have served as money—gold and silver—to name some obvious ones, but also even weird things like seashells, beads, cattle, and, in prisoner of war camps, cigarettes. Money, like the public bell tower clock, is a social technology and is best understood by examining the problems it's intended to solve. Professor Wolfers' comment above is correct in outlining the three things money has to do to be useful. First, it's got to be a medium of exchange, meaning people acquire it not to consume it, but to use it to buy something else (which is why cigarettes might work alright as money in a prison but nowhere else). That function has a network effect to it, where the more people accept something as money, the more useful the good becomes to its holder. One other single person doesn't just want it; everyone in the network wants it. Next, to serve as money, a good's got to be a unit of account, meaning its value is stable enough for people to form judgments and make long-term plans with it. Think about the Metric and Imperial systems for units of weights and measures. People shopping at Home Depot can estimate what they need to build a house based on that system. Money is no different. As a measure of the value of our time, people make career decisions based on a feel for compensation. They have a sense of how much rent and groceries should cost and how that relates to their income. The difference between inches and miles, on the one hand, and dollars and cents on the other, is that inches and miles don't change lengths over time. But the value of money shifts. It can expand or shrink. For it to work as a unit of account, though, it must be relatively stable across time. Lastly, and perhaps most importantly of all, money must be a store of value. People have to have confidence that their money will hold its value well into the future. Grain, cigarettes, and cattle may serve as a form of money in the short run, but they rot, fall apart, or grow old and die. Good money must have integrity through time, which is why gold has been prized so highly since the dawn of civilization. It's tough to destroy, it never rusts, it never corrodes, it never disintegrates. Gold is also extremely scarce, not just here on earth, but throughout the galaxy. Its creation required the rare collision of two neutron stars to generate the unimaginable power necessary to fuse its subatomic particles into place.[7] (Whereas copper and silver required the explosion of supernovae, a more common occurrence, which is why there is more of both to mine.)

And here we come to the nut of it. For a good to maintain its value through time, the supply of it cannot increase too rapidly during the time someone owns it. The value of a single cigarette in a prisoner of war camp decreases dramatically as soon as the prisoners are freed. The value of a dollar decreases the more dollars are printed. The relative difficulty of producing new units of a good that serves as money determines the hardness of that money. Easy money, like dollars, is easy to make more of. New hard money requires tremendous effort and cost.

Gold is great hard money because it's so scarce.[8] If the price of gold kicks up, the miners start digging deeper for more. But it's not easy work. Even at record high prices, the amount of new gold has always accounted for only a tiny fraction of the total stock of gold. That means it's hard to devalue. Over the last seventy years, for instance, despite prices spiking, the growth rate of newly mined gold has never gone higher than 2 percent. That explains why gold has always retained its allure as a store of value. There are natural, physical limits that prevent dramatic increases in its supply. But, even so, it is not without its problems. As rare as it is, the supply of undiscovered gold is theoretically unlimited. Governments can easily prohibit people from buying gold. It is difficult to hide should governments want to seize it as well. To take one underappreciated historical example, President Roosevelt signed Executive Order 6102 in 1933, which banned anyone from owning gold in the United States, a law that lasted until 1975. Americans were forced to sell their gold to the government at a rate of $20.26 an ounce. Then Roosevelt turned around and sold that gold on the international market at $35 per ounce. (Now there's a new deal!) In light of these vulnerabilities, as impressive as gold is as a primordial element for the store of value, it has its limitations.

Bitcoin, however, is the hardest money ever invented.[9] It is the ultimate store of value. Because of Nakamoto's math problems, which increase in difficulty over time, the rate of new Bitcoin creation decreases no matter how high the price of Bitcoin rises. Nakamoto has also placed a hard cap on the total stock. There will only ever be 21 million total Bitcoins. 18.7 million are in circulation now and it's getting harder and harder to make them. It is the first money in human history that there will never be more of.

The Bitcoin network has been in operation for eleven years now without so much as a single hiccup. It is more reliable than any central bank. More trustworthy, too. Unlike gold, it can't be seized, it doesn't need a vault, a life's savings could fit on a memory stick, and its integrity gets stronger every ten minutes. And it never ever fails. A use-of-force monopoly would have to destroy every computer in the network, which now spans the globe and whose nodes number in the millions. Bitcoin is the height of monetary design and technology. No wonder academics hate it so much.

• • •

Now, I don't mean for this to sound like I had an "aha!" moment or anything, but by 2015 a trend had begun to emerge, and so I had written up my ideas on it to be included as a chapter in a book of academic philosophy that I assure you no one has read.

(It is ranked #29,000 on Amazon's bestseller list for political philosophy.)[10] What did catch the attention of some geeks back then was the distillation of a key idea from the essay that I posted as my personal mission on LinkedIn, which I still hold today:

> If the Rust Belt has come to define the hollowed-out industries of the Midwest, in the next ten years the Paper Belt will come to define the paper-based industries from Washington, D.C., to Boston. In D.C., they print money, visas, and laws on paper. In Delaware, companies incorporate on paper. In NYC, they print media on paper. And in Boston, Harvard, and MIT print diplomas on paper. I am dedicated to lighting the Paper Belt on fire.

I make no apologies for this statement. Hyperbolic, to be sure, perhaps a weak match struck in the wind, but a fire has to start somewhere. The whole thing bubbled out of conversations I had with another person I met about the same time I first met Vitalik. There are only two people in this world who call me after 10 p.m.: my mom and Balaji Srinivasan. If my mom calls that late, there's trouble in the family or she wants me to recite her a poem. If Balaji calls, he's about to light a powder-keg of iconoclastic fun underneath some dreary sacred cow. Such ideas simply cannot wait. (Quite charmingly, Balaji pronounces ideas as "idears" in his thick Plainview, Long Island, accent.) He is an idear-sparker of unyielding intellectual ferocity who looks a lot like an Indian Stanley Tucci. His mind will pour itself out in a three-minute torrent, which he'll abruptly screech to a halt by saying, "Let me pause here to hear your thoughts." His list of accomplishments is long for someone under forty—multiple graduate degrees from Stanford, multiple companies founded, partner at a top venture capital fund, awards from MIT—it all reminds me of those Soviet generals who'd have an outrageous raft of ribbons, medals, and chest candy pinned to their left breast. In fact, I sometimes used to tease and call him the Libertarian Lenin. It helped that he was bald. In 2013, I lived near the Presidio at the northern tip of San Francisco and Balaji lived in San Bruno, about thirty minutes south by car near the San Francisco International Airport. The only 24-hour Starbucks in town was in a desolate suburban strip mall near Balaji, so I'd drive down, we'd grab a coffee, and then we'd walk the streets of San Bruno, darkly conspiring and debating the future of technology like drunken poets arguing about art in some Parisian cafe.

A constellation of ideas emerged from these conversations. The first was that progress in America—or the entire West for that matter—had stalled sometime around 1971.[11] The Thiel stagnation thesis. The next was to track the erosion of America's core institutions over the same time period. Sandcastles in a rising tide. To name a handful: the media, Wall Street & the Fed, non-profits, the military, the universities, NASA, the administrative alphabet soup (CIA, FDA, CDC, and the rest), Congress, academic science, and more. All of them were becoming less reliable and less trustworthy than they used to be. Our trusted third parties had become security holes, prone to insider collusion, bureaucratic bloat, cronyism, no accountability, and a proliferation of credentialed dimwits out of their depth. Since many of these institutions depend on paper and are located on the I-95 corridor running from Washington to Boston, Balaji called it the Paper Belt. Then we hypothesized a key driver for this recent history. The stagnation trap. A lack of progress was causing the decline of institutional performance. But, as those institutions became less reliable and less trustworthy, that caused progress to slow down even more. With progress faltering, institutions performed even worse and then distrust began to build even higher. The less progress we made, the worse our institutions performed; the worse our institutions performed, the less progress we made. And so it would go in a vicious circle, spinning into a crisis of authority. And yet, no one was addressing the root problem: stagnation. Instead, these two interacting trends have propelled America into a fifty-year downward spiral. It was not all bad, to be sure, but the scandals and catastrophes were becoming ubiquitous enough to trace a clear course of perilous decline.

Take the Financial Crisis of 2007–8. On the left, the blowup is portrayed as the result of greedy bankers and unbridled, unregulated capitalism. On the right, the culprits are easy money, the implicit bailouts Wall Street counted on, and the government extending loans to people not equipped to pay them off. And there is some truth to both sides when it comes to proximate causes and a list of villains. However, what neither side really acknowledges is that the chief failure here was the failure to innovate. Starting in 1971, the American middle class had seen their paychecks begin to stagnate. That's been relatively constant for about fifty years now. Congress, the Fed, and various presidents have felt their pain, but rather than address the problem—that Americans weren't picking up the skills needed in the labor market—the government papered over it with the greatest expansion of credit in human history.[12] Let them eat debt! Populist credit expansion allowed people to spend in ways far beyond what their stagnant incomes could support. Because we didn't discover better ways to educate Americans, these people languished without the skills they needed, and without progress in science and technology, worker productivity nearly flatlined. If the advances in education and other sectors never came, the Fed and the rest of the government worked hard to generate the illusion that they did. How did the United States deal with the waning of the American Dream? It looked for ways to hide the stagnation. It took on debt, it printed money, it extended loans. Better to have citizens who feel wealthier than to actually be wealthier. The bill could be paid in a tomorrow that never comes.

But debt-fueled consumption has a limit. True progress can never be achieved by cheap credit. Subprime borrowers were subprime because our schools educate the ignorant with ignorance. The American education system is a failure and, despite the government pouring money into schools, huge swaths of the population—especially marginalized groups—have been hit hard by the system's inability to discover new and better ways of imparting the skills and virtues necessary to find success and fulfillment in life. In 2008, the Fed failed. Congress failed. Presidents failed. Fannie Mae and Freddie Mac failed. Wall Street took the upside and socialized the losses. No one went to jail. There is distrust all around. It's rightly deserved, but it starts with the failure to innovate.

Something unexplained happened in 1971, and America hasn't been the same since. Stagnation—whatever its origin in that decade—has now spread and rotted the hull of every institution over the past fifty years. The seals have burst, and the compartments are flooding. America is coming apart—why? My money is that stagnation shapes everything: politics, culture, the national mood. All that is worst in man is exposed in the harsh floodlight of stagnation. Festering resentments erupt. We yearn for belonging and confidence. Instead, we're dazed and broken, demoralized by addled politics and deluded by false finance. But we're lost not because we're polarized. We're polarized because the fires of creation have guttered out.

The upshot of the midnight conversations between Balaji and me was the stirring of a crusade. We needed to renew the dynamism of the West. To do it, we'd have to retire and replace the core institutions. It wasn't going to be easy because the sclerotic corrupt institutions weren't going away. But it was worth the fight. This whole package I dubbed the Nakamoto Consensus. I was drawing on the nature of Satoshi Nakamoto's consensus protocol, but more symbolically, I wanted it to stand in contrast both to the Washington Consensus and the Beijing Consensus, two terms bookish pundits had been tossing around to describe the economic ideologies of the world's two great superpowers. What they both have in common is centralized power. The Nakamoto Consensus seeks to disperse it.

Nakamoto and Vitalik were showing the way. They were in the business of institutional demolition and renovation. As a store of value, Bitcoin was becoming a serious competitor to central banking and fiat currency, both of whose reliability and trustworthiness had been discredited by the Great Depression, the double-digit inflation of 1960–80, and the 2008 financial crisis and its sad, sorry bailouts.[13] Ethereum was beginning to demonstrate how it could revive an ancient aspect of individualism, namely the ability to impose obligations on ourselves where none existed before. Incredibly, Vitalik's invention could let people form contractual agreements without the law or government. For the first time, people could create unique digital assets and trade them, artifacts that no bank, corporation, or government could destroy. They could form organizations with governance structures of their own choosing. The Ethereum blockchain is so flexible that it can serve as the backend to a whole new breed of Internet services to rival those of the big tech companies. Except, in this case, the users would be rewarded and empowered. They would have both a stake and a say in the governance. There would be no man in the middle—no Facebook, no Google—to harvest data and sell it. The world could stop giving away its most precious thoughts and creations for free in exchange for likes, hearts, thumbs-up, and enraging comments.

• • •

So, by the middle of the decade, the hopes of decentralization were in the air. We needed to raise an army to turn the tide on progress. We wanted to start a movement to repair or replace institutions. Balaji had his ideas; Danielle and I would have our own. For his part, Balaji told me about one of his heroes as a kid growing up. There was a man who was born in the southernmost region of India in 1887. Srinivasa Ramanujan.[14] As a teenager, Ramanujan excelled in mathematics, but when he got his hands on a book that was a collection of five thousand theorems, his genius caught fire. For years he toiled on his own, reinventing mathematical concepts others had discovered in Europe but that he had never encountered before. Then he also broke new ground entirely. Eventually, he wrote letters to a few leading mathematicians in the U.K wondering if they might guide him. Only one of them responded. In Ramanujan's work, the great mathematician G. H. Hardy recognized some formulas as already having been discovered, but others he wrote, "seemed scarcely possible to believe."

Hardy brought Ramanujan to Cambridge University, where he went on to make many important contributions to the field in a short time. Balaji marveled at Ramanujan's story; it showed genius could come from the most unexpected places in the world. With nearly 8 billion people in the world, how many Ramanujans are out there today? We were riffing one night on one of our midnight walks through San Bruno; Balaji came up with a plan that was only half-serious. Smartphones were spreading around the world, even to the poorest regions.

What if, Balaji asked, we were to broadcast simple math problems as texts out to a billion of these phones? And if someone answers the first problem correctly, then we send them a more difficult problem. And if they get that right, then we increase the difficulty again. At some point, if they've answered the most difficult problems, we locate this person, airlift them out from wherever they are, bring them to a school, and give them a scholarship. Balaji called this idea 1729, after a number Ramanujan made famous. It's now the $E = mc^2$ of India. Back in Cambridge, Ramanujan had caught tuberculosis and lay dying in bed. One day his mentor Hardy came to visit him. The taxi on the ride over had been numbered 1729. So, Hardy said to Ramanujan, my cab was 1729, a rather dull number. He hoped that such a dull number wouldn't mean a bad omen. To which Ramanujan replied in a flash, "No, it is a very interesting number; it is the smallest number expressible as the sum of two cubes in two different ways."[15]

There must be other Ramanujans out there. There is too much talent in the world languishing in dead institutions. Balaji had 1729. Danielle and I lamented that the Thiel Fellowship was given out to only twenty people a year. In just five years, we had seen how powerful the freedom to pursue ideas could be for young people. How could we expand on it? What would it mean to replace universities with something more renegade, more decentralized?

Balaji was too busy running two companies at that time to get started on 1729. After Coinbase went public, he came back to it in 2020. As for Satoshi Nakamoto, his apparition disappeared back into the mists. The last email he ever sent was on April 11, 2011. Despite a decade-long manhunt, no one has ever been able to find him. Today, Vitalik Buterin is a billionaire.

Meantime, back in 2015, Danielle and I had come to an

idea of our own. I'd landed on my own number that I thought expressed the spirit of the times. We'd seen the success of the early Thiel Fellows, yet the world refused to believe it. But we knew otherwise. Danielle and I were about to walk into Peter's dining room to say the magic words: "We have an idea."

•9•

1517

Every region has its style of rejection. In Moscow, they say "Nyet!" In Madrid, "mañana." In London, "Sorry luv." For the Berliners, it's "Nein!" And in Los Angeles, they say "You're amazing."

Silicon Valley likes to discourage newcomers too, of course, but not completely. Everyone wants to leave a little crack open for the future in case the unexpected happens. Instead of a flat "no," Silicon Valley has evolved an entire language and ritual of false kindness. Silicon Valley says, "It's a little early. Come back to me when you've raised a Series A." Or, "come back when you have a million in revenue." Or, most brazenly of all, "after you've IPO'ed."

Yeah, right. Danielle was lying face down on the carpet of my living room. She was exhausted. It was March 24, 2015. We had arrived at a strong idea behind raising a venture capital fund, but we knew the path ahead was full of daunting obstacles. There would be a thousand and one emails and conversations that ended with "come back to me when." Though we had run the Thiel Fellowship for five years, neither of us had any experience in venture capital. And by 2015, skepticism about the Thiel Fellowship had hardened into wide-eyed terror in the press. What few positive stories there were had dried up entirely, and the only things left were sulfuric vapors of hate. Meanwhile, it felt like we were operating in a completely different universe from whatever the media tried to portray. Danielle and I knew that as a team we both were becoming formidable talent scouts and recruiters. The press simply did not want to believe our success. But by 2015 we'd found Vitalik. Dylan Field. Austin Russell. Laura Deming. Paul Gu. All of these people in the years ahead would be involved in enterprises worth more than $1 billion. To be fair, it was still early in 2015. The endeavors started by our fellows were only a couple of years old, if that. They were all still in their early twenties. So it may have been easier for the media to mistake seedlings for weeds. But Danielle and I were running the numbers, and we calculated what our returns might look like if we had invested in the Thiel Fellows in addition to giving them grants. The number was impressive to us. A series of hypothetical $250,000 angel investments in the thirty-five or so fellows who'd started companies would be worth somewhere between $30 to $40 million by our count in the spring of 2015—three to four times the initial money invested. We didn't even include Ethereum.

"What is this, IKEA?" Danielle was toying at the shag rug in front of her eyes on the floor. I was pacing.

"I'm not sure if people are going to get 1517."

"Did they make you put the rug together too?"

"It's a pretty obscure reference."

"We do what we always tell our fellows. We test the idea out cheaply."

"I'm at UCLA's hackathon in a few days."

"Great. Instead of showing up as part of the Thiel Fellowship, pretend you're from 1517 and act as if it exists. See how people react."

"Not bad. I have a 1517 t-shirt I could wear."

"You really need to vacuum your rug."

I flew down to Los Angeles. A group of students had rented out the Pauley Pavilion, the immense arena where UCLA's basketball team plays. The scoreboards and jumbotron were lit up: Welcome to L.A. Hacks 2015! Pop music boomed over the arena's sound system. From all over the country, but mainly from the western states, 1,400 student engineers poured in and descended upon the basketball court for thirty-six hours of straight hacking. There were sleeping bags, pillows, junk food, miles of red licorice, disgusting energy drinks, and roller-suitcases burst open, their contents thrown about everywhere, on the seats, tucked into every crevice, cramping the aisles, strewn across every table. It was dorm room squalor elevated to an arena spectacle.

The organizers had set up a stage at one end of the floor where one of the basketball hoops would normally be. All of the behind-the-basket seats were full, with 1,400 students waiting for the event to begin. Hackathons always start with an opening ceremony on Friday night, where some grandee from the tech world delivers an inspiring keynote address. After that, a few sponsors pay to address the crowd for two to three minutes to tell them about the prizes for the best hacks. As a minor sponsor, I was slated to speak after Microsoft and before IBM.

I was in my 1517 t-shirt. All black with white numbers on the chest in Goudy Old Style font. I knew I had to express what 1517 was about, but with so little time, I wasn't sure how I was going to communicate it. It's an obscure, geeky reference. I was suddenly nervous that I hadn't prepared a speech.

The Microsoft guy finished his spiel about the company's cloud computing services. "The best hack using Microsoft's

Azure will win four Surface Pros!" I felt sorry for the guy.
His enthusiasm, as though pumped full of amphetamines,
felt insincere and ridiculous against the silence of the crowd.
He exited stage left to crickets. I was up. A mad monk in his
black t-shirt. The girls in the crowd were giggling. The boys
clowning about. No one was really paying attention. I took
the microphone.

"Hi, I'm Michael. I'm from 1517." I had to clear my throat.
The fear of public speaking was clogging my windpipe.

"We're named after the year Martin Luther nailed his ninety-
five theses to a church door in a tiny German town. That began a
revolution, the Protestant Reformation. But it all started because
he was protesting against the sale of a piece of paper called an
indulgence. In 1517, the church was saying this expensive piece
of paper could save your soul. In 2015, universities are selling
another expensive piece of paper, the diploma, saying it's the
only way to save your soul. Well, it was bullshit then. And it's
bullshit now."

Hoots and claps erupted from the crowd.

"You don't want to be a faceless cog in a corporate machine.
You want to do your own thing and you want to do it now. You
don't want to hack your way into an internship. You don't need
a diploma. You want to keep building what you start tonight.
We're giving out $1,000 no-string grants to the top three teams
that want to keep building after this weekend. I'm up in section
106. Come find me."

Then the crowd went nuts. As I walked off stage, I pointed
up to section 106 in the stands where I'd be stationed. I felt like
I had hit a buzzer-winning shot and, walking off, suddenly I
didn't know where I was backstage. I got lost in the rabbit war-
ren of hallways behind the arena seats. It took me some time,
but I finally made it up to the hallway outside section 106. It

was quieter up there near the rafters, but I could still faintly hear the next speakers on the stage down below.

A shrine to John Wooden's greatness caught my eye in the hallway. The Wizard of Westwood. He won ten championships in twelve years as head coach for UCLA in the 1960s and '70s. I'll forever have a love-hate relationship with college sports. I can't stand that kids get exploited while coaches enrich themselves on million dollar shoe deals and sponsorships. But John Wooden was from another era, before all that. He was a master talent scout and the best at bringing the best out in his team. I was studying his version of the right stuff, what he called the "pyramid of success," which outlined the fifteen character traits Wooden identified in great players—when a young man sheepishly walked up to me.

"Hey, are you the 1517 guy who was on stage?"

"Yeah."

A smile broke across his face. "Can I have one of your t-shirts? That talk was freaking awesome!"

I had made a few extra t-shirts and tossed him one. Other people started showing up in section 106. A young woman in the crowd had tweeted a picture of me with a quote from my speech. Beneath it in the comments, a guy wrote "Love it! Any chance I can get my hands on a 1517 t-shirt?" He came and got one. Another young lady, a self-taught programmer from South Central L.A., came by and she also posted on social media. "Yesssss!!! S/o to Michael Gibson for the awesomest shirt ever!! The message behind this shirt couldn't apply more directly to my life and what I stand for! Keep inspiring!! I'm officially part of the movement bro!"

One two-minute speech and she was calling it a movement. I must have called Danielle that night to tell her the story. We were now ready to tell Peter we were going to leave the Thiel

Fellowship. We had a name for our fund—1517. Now we had to try to raise money for it. I emailed Peter's assistant to set up a breakfast meeting. I didn't say what the agenda was.

• • •

The morning of our meeting, which may have been a week later, Danielle came to my apartment first so we could go over what we were planning to say to Peter. I lived five blocks or so from Peter's house in the Marina. Danielle and I were both nervous. We didn't know how Peter would react to our quitting to start a fund. Would he try to change our minds? It wasn't so much that he'd get upset, but that we had worked together for five years on an extraordinary project. Any other manager on the planet wouldn't have hired Danielle or me. But if Peter was anything, he was an expert at finding diamonds in the rough. For us, saying farewell carried a nostalgic gratitude with it—memories tinged with fun, an appreciation for the break he'd given us, the thrill of mischief we had wrought.

All the same, moving on was also something the two of us felt we were ready for. We wanted to reach more people than the fellowship could, which is limited to grants for about twenty people a year. By contrast, a venture capital fund, if successful, could continue to grow, funding more people in more places around the world. There was certainly the potential for massive financial upside, too. We had an edge that no one in the normal world wanted to believe was real. But more than any of this, the plain fact was that Danielle and I had this goal, somewhat vague, but still commanding, to start an alternative educational institution. The heart of our idea was that we would discover the world's best talent as early as possible. We couldn't trust the cultivation of extraordinary talent to the traditional institutions of learning any longer. They were no longer reliable or trustworthy. We'd start with investments in startups because by then we'd become experts at finding and supporting brilliant young people who were pushing the technological frontiers outward. By exclusively backing dropouts or people who never went to college, we'd show that credentials were no substitute for real progress. In time, we could expand from there into backing unorthodox scientific research, the arts, you name it. We were going to take the Great Stagnation head-on with a whole new kind of institution.

There would never be a campus. It would be decentralized, like a republic of letters. Venture capital would merely be the means, the vehicle to accomplish our mission, much in the way that universities have multi-billion-dollar endowments to sustain their operations. Harvard's endowment in 2015 was $37.6 billion. (It stands at a monstrous $53 billion as of 2021.) Against that, Danielle and I were setting out to raise $10 million, a rounding error compared to even the smallest of university endowments. So as ambitious as we were, we were starting out small. Our critics might say quixotic. But that was our long-term goal: create an endowment to back creative genius and set it free.

Before leaving my apartment to walk to Peter's, I took a shot of bourbon to take the edge off. Danielle did some yoga stretches. It was 7:30 am. We headed out through the edge of the Presidio, over into the Palace of Fine Arts, and under its rotunda, where the sculptures look into their mystery boxes, and then on up to Peter's front door. We were on time. I rang the doorbell.

• • •

There was a lot going against us. It is extremely difficult for a new venture capital fund to break into the industry and become successful. For one thing, most venture capital funds fail. Blind-folded monkeys throwing darts to pick stocks would perform better than the investor who picked the average venture capital fund. The median VC firm returns about 1.6 percent less than if someone just put their money in an index-tracking mutual fund.[1] Worse yet, that money invested in a venture fund is locked up for ten years. There is no easy way to cash out. Those monkeys who invested in the S&P 500 can at least sell their stock any day they need cash at the zoo.

The risk of venture capital is so high that investors have to be rewarded in proportion to that risk, vastly more than the nice 5–7 percent return they might get by parking their money in the S&P 500. At a bare minimum, VC fund managers have to triple or quadruple their investor's money, usually over a 7–10 year time period. If Danielle and I managed to raise our $10 million fund, our investors would have to see us return $40 million to make it worth their while. It's a high bar. Most funds don't clear it.

The next problem facing a new fund is that the returns in venture are massively skewed to the established funds. It's not random who wins and who loses in any year. In many other fields, mediocrity is quite acceptable—the average lawyer still does useful work—but neither men nor gods nor retirement funds can abide the mediocre VC. Only a few venture firms make fortunes, while the rest make nothing and go out of business. That means averages can be deceptive. As in *Glengarry Glen Ross*, David Mamet's play about desperate real estate agents, first place in venture capital is a Cadillac El Dorado. Second place is a set of steak knives. Third place is you're fired. Most of the winners park their Cadillacs—now Teslas—at their headquarters on Sand Hill Road in Menlo Park, the Wall Street of Silicon Valley. Along this strip, which starts at the edge of Stanford University and continues west to the last hills before the Pacific shore, there is a long stretch of offices that look nothing like offices but more like well-preserved, private bungalows tucked back behind the conifers and eucalyptus trees. Here and there, a scattering of funds have taken home in grandiose office buildings of uncompromising modernity, something more predictable given the industry. But what strikes most visitors the first time they see Menlo Park is a spiritual letdown: how could this flashpoint of American innovation look exactly like any other humdrum suburb? For my money though, once you walk inside, these offices still manage to evoke an air of mystery and consequence. Sequoia Capital. Kleiner Perkins. Greylock Partners. Accel. And later, Benchmark and Andreessen-Horowitz. This is the Murderers' Row of venture capital, all lined up on a three-mile stretch. These were and still are the winners. Starting in the 1970s, the established order of Silicon Valley was set firmly in place here on this spot. The winners built a cycle of perpetual enrichment for themselves. If an upstart fund tries to enter the game, entrepreneurs tend not to want to work with it because it has no track record. Instead, founders want to collect the magic pixie dust of success by association. They would prefer to work with the legendary fund on Sand Hill Road that backed Apple or Google in the hopes of signaling to other investors and future employees that they are indeed the next Apple or Google. For this reason, those who invest in funds are wise to avoid the upstart firm. Better to stick with the winners on Sand Hill Road who continue to win because they already won.

The next problem was that neither Danielle nor I look like the typical venture capitalist. In 2008, at the end of his storied career, Tom Perkins of Kleiner Perkins wrote a memoir called *Valley Boy: The Education of Tom Perkins.*[2] The book's cover features a picture of Perkins in a navy blue yachting blazer, which is emblazoned with the crest of his prize-winning, 289-foot-yacht named the *Maltese Falcon.* Perkins is leaning proudly on his ship's polished bell, armed with a devilish playboy grin. The boat cost him more than $150 million to build. Perkins belongs on this yacht, and for that matter, at a golf course, a polo field, or at the club trading wit over cocktails by the swimming pool. With only a little exaggeration, Danielle and I would be identified as gatecrashers at any of these places. Neither of us knows the difference between port and starboard. Security would kindly ask Danielle to leave, while I would be mistaken for the groundskeeper or escorted off the premises posthaste.

Some old smoothies like Perkins are still around on Sand Hill Road, but if the next generation of VCs aren't so country clubby, they retain the glow of prestige and grooming. I'm not quite sure when this began, but sometime around 2010 or so the mid-level employees at many of the top funds began wearing a uniform in the corporate casual fashion—khaki pants, forgettable button-down shirts, and zipped-up Patagonia vests made of synthetic fleece. At first, the vests made sense in the Bay Area, since with its variable weather, it would be nice to have that extra layer when the fog rolled in and temperatures dropped. But by 2015, every single Ivy League grad that was shipped out to California came pre-packaged in a Patagonia vest. The manufacturer simply refused to produce a different model Ivy Bot. As a result, a vested army of the flawless and efficient brought an unassailable professionalism to the VC landscape. Though originally founded by bon vivants like Perkins, many of the older funds now secure their dominance with a phalanx of Stanford Business School grads and Harvard Law alums. As I need hardly elaborate, established funds do not look to hire former school principals and recusant philosophers.

The next wave of successful VCs are mostly former entrepreneurs who first made a fortune starting their own thing and now who want to invest. Some of them like Reid Hoffman, the

founder of LinkedIn, have taken a perch at old firms like Greylock. Others, like Thiel, Paul Graham, and Marc Andreessen,
were able to start their own firms. It helped that they were angel
investors to begin with. By successfully staking their own money
first—as Peter did with Facebook—they were able to build an
impressive track record that they then rolled into bigger funds.
Founders Fund, Andreessen-Horowitz—these are the relatively
recent winning entries in the venture capital landscape. In fact,
both old and new VC funds overwhelmingly love to hire previ-
ously successful entrepreneurs. There is the widespread belief
among former founders that it takes one to know one. Only by
actually possessing the right stuff can you identify it in others.
No doubt that may be true to some degree, but more importantly,
by having served time in the trenches, veteran founders can offer
credible advice and strategic tips to newcomers. They also have a
large Rolodex of contacts who might make for great hires, board
members, or co-investors. While Danielle and I had certainly
built up a strong list of contacts through the Thiel Fellowship,
we were not wildly successful entrepreneurs who wanted to
switch sides at the table after having had a billion-dollar IPO.

One final point I'll make here is that only 7 percent of the
partners at the top 100 venture funds in 2015 were women.[3] The
number of *founding* partners you could count on one hand.
Not that being the rare female among men was totally new to
Danielle. "That's been my existence forever," she told me once
when I asked her about it. "I hang out with libertarians. How
many tits are in those groups? Not many."

So, in sum, Danielle and I don't look like traditional VCs,
we don't have the educational background or work experience
of most VCs, we never started a billion-dollar company like
the more recent VCs, and as a spanking new fund, the odds
were massively against us. Oh yeah, and we were only going to

invest in people without college degrees. Most investors would be foolish to invest in us. At first glance. Fortunately, however, there are risk-takers in this world. Peter's chef opened the front door, let us in, and showed us into Peter's dining room.

Danielle and I sat quietly, sipping coffee. Eventually Peter came downstairs in workout clothing, looking like he just woke up, as he normally does in breakfast meetings. Sometimes I swear he would clear sleepies out of his eyes. Peter poked his head into his kitchen and told his chef we were ready to eat.

We didn't have a pitch deck because we weren't pitching Peter. We were there to tell him we were leaving to do our own thing. We did write up a simple one-pager that listed the top eight companies founded by Thiel Fellows, how much those companies were worth as of their last round of venture financing, and how much a five percent stake in those companies would be worth today.

I slid the one-pager across the table. Peter studied it.

"There's a contrarian truth we believe in," I began, referencing Peter's favorite interview question. "The fellowship is way more successful than the world thinks it is."

"We've done some analysis on the fellowship," Danielle jumped in. "And it's done really well. If we had been making $250k investments in these companies at the seed round, we'd have a strong start to a fund."

As we talked, Peter was taking turns looking down at the paper and then back up to the two of us. At first, he wasn't sure why we were telling him this.

"So we're going to leave the fellowship to set up a fund."

Peter was Peter. He did the thing he does where he turns his head, looks out the window, and thinks for a second but it feels like a long minute.

"Ok, how much are you guys raising?" he asked.

"We're raising ten million."

"You should raise fifteen. And I'm in for four."

Danielle was stunned. Her smile grew so large she grabbed her napkin to hide it. She wasn't sure if she should show him how happy she was about this. I told him about UCLA and how we tested the 1517 name out.

"1517?"

"We don't believe in indulgences."

He laughed, and just like that we had our first verbal commitment. I don't remember what we talked about for the rest of breakfast, mainly because I think I was so thrilled, but also because I was already worrying about whom we could possibly pitch next. Danielle and I walked out of that breakfast on fire. "We've got to knock on a lot of doors," she said to me as soon as Peter's front door closed. We were walking back to the office. "We have to send our pitch deck out to every single mentor in the Thiel Fellowship network. We have to ask them, do you know people with money? Because we need to talk to people with money!"

So we had to find strangers who believed in our mission. The very next call we set up was with Jaan Tallinn, one of the cofounders of Skype. Naturally enough, we took the call over Skype. He was in for $500k. We were on a roll. Then we hit up Nicolas Berggruen, the "Homeless Billionaire."[4] I met him once at a fundraiser for the Institute for Advanced Study. Nicolas was known to live out of hotels around the world. He didn't own a home. I emailed him asking if we could come to meet him. He replied that he would be in L.A. for a few days and we could try to catch him there.

So Danielle and I flew down and intercepted him where he was holding court at his usual table in the Polo Lounge at the Beverly Hills Hotel. The Milken Institute Conference was underway in Santa Monica and all the panjandrums of high finance were in town. The first hurdle was a small one. When I first met Nicolas, he only introduced himself by his first name. I had no idea how to pronounce his last name, Berggruen. When we walked up to the hostess's podium at the Polo Lounge, I had to stammer something. I went with, "We're here to see Nicolas Bregreerrurun."

The hostess cocked an eyebrow, smiled, and said, "Ah, yes, Nicolas, right this way."

She showed us to Nicolas's table. Handsome, puckish, and the center of attention, he was shaking hands and trading laughs with a few of the other one-percenters in town for the conference. Danielle and I approached him to shake hands and, before even trading any small talk, Nicolas dealt us a brushback fastball, high and tight. "Just to set expectations," he said, "I never invest in funds."

My God man! We were in the hole, and we hadn't even started. Coffee was served. We got down to business. I began our pitch by talking about the lack of progress in science and technology and the decline of institutions. Nicolas, who is German, took the conversation in a direction I did not anticipate.

"Yes, well, Europe is stagnating. And we know what happens when Germans try to be creative."

No matter the topic, references to Hitler pretty much destroy the momentum in any conversation. I thought this pitch was a straightforward loss. But now it was a dumpster fire. Then, suddenly, Danielle miraculously turned it around. "Alright, Nicolas, what are you interested in?"

"I'm investing in biotech, longevity research, and other deep tech."

"You know we discovered Laura Deming and backed her. Happy to make an introduction there. No one is further out in the frontier of life science than Laura. We can also introduce you to Austin Russell who is building the next generation perception system for driverless cars."

"Really." The clouds of Nicolas's doom-and-gloom were dispersing. "Interesting…" Our claim to having found the next generation of great innovators was gaining credibility. After we left the table, we made the intros to Laura and Austin. Nicolas spoke to both of them and then right away told us he would invest $500k into 1517.

We also had an early win from a group of investors and entrepreneurs from Guatemala, all of them affiliated with the Universidad Francisco Marroquín, a libertarian-leaning university in Guatemala City that had awarded Peter an honorary degree in 2009. They wanted to start Guatemala's very first venture capital fund. The success of the company Duolingo, which had been founded by a native of Guatemala City, sparked their imaginations. But they had hit an impasse. They spent months not knowing how to solve the chicken-and-egg problem for their country: without many startups in Guatemala, there wasn't a convincing reason to have a fund; but then without at least one fund, startups wouldn't have any access to capital, so no one would bother to start a company. The Guatemalan libertarians were stumped on this.

Then one of their crew, Helmuth Chávez, remembered that Danielle and I were throwing one of our conferences for the Thiel Fellowship community that summer. Helmuth and his daring and dashing colleague, Fernando Pontaza, flew up to San Francisco to check out the scene, talk to Danielle and me, and try to get a sense of whether they could mimic the fellowship ecosystem down in Guatemala.

We immersed Fernando in everything. We even drafted him as a judge in our micro-grant competition. He hadn't yet met with anyone in venture capital, but he'd met a lot of finance people during his career, and when it came to funds, he'd interviewed hundreds of private equity fund managers. He saw right away how different we were from that breed. Well, that—and we clicked. Over beers Fernando and I went on for forty-five minutes only speaking in movie quotes back and forth with each other. Danielle could only shake her head in disbelief at the strange rituals of male camaraderie.

Fernando returned to Guatemala and immediately told his team, "Look, these guys have a knack for finding young talent. We have to invest in their fund. Not only ask them for advice. We'll learn far more from working with them directly." Fernando showed his team the same one-pager detailing the success of the fellowship that we had shown Peter.

"Alright, let's make a commitment. What's the minimum?"

"One million."

"Let's do it."

And that's how Guatemala's very first venture capital fund came to be. They named it the Invariantes Fund. They nixed the idea of having a fund only dedicated to Guatemala. Instead, we inspired them to broaden their scope to invest in the United States and in other funds to balance out the investing they could do within Guatemala. That way they could slowly build up their ecosystem at home while making returns and learning best practices elsewhere.

Looking back on it, I asked Fernando what makes us so different from other VCs. "Everything," he said. "There is no one else like you out there. Since we're a hybrid fund that invests in both funds and companies, we've screened sixty funds a year over the past four years. And nobody does what you guys do. First, the working outside of college thing. That criterion. Nobody has that criterion. And you're shameless about it. You go out and say it point-blank to investors—boom! Second, the background of the team. A philosopher and a teacher—*Que onda*?! Highly unusual. Usually, someone has a background in finance or tech or they've founded a company in the past. But a teacher and a philosopher? *¡Dios Mío!* Third, the way you two conduct yourself. Your whole essence. Also not common in venture capital. Managers are usually corporate and professional. But now here's Danielle with her swimming-pool slip-on shoes and the leggings with cats on them."

Pretty soon after landing this first string of verbal commits, we started racking up the rejections. Not everyone found us intriguing. Sad to say, there are only so many Guatemalan libertarians and homeless billionaires. Some people couldn't get their heads around our investment thesis. "You're only investing in dropouts? How does that make any sense?" Others thought our backgrounds were a disadvantage. "How can you two, who aren't engineers or scientists, possibly investigate the feasibility of a technology?" Then there were those who thought that our track record with the Thiel Fellowship wasn't reliable. "How do I know you're not just lucky?" Somehow along the way, we were introduced to the financial team that manages the fortune of the family that invented Hot Pockets, the microwavable meat-stuffed turnovers no one eats before 1 a.m. There was something amusing to me about this team that ran the Hot Pockets fortune. These quantitative hedge fund guys kept asking Danielle and me if we could provide a mathematical risk model for the success rate of pre-seed startups. Risk model? There is no risk model. Either Jesus is in your heart, or he isn't. I couldn't convince them that the success of a startup at that stage can't be reduced to a die roll. They said no thanks.

But by the end of the summer in 2015, the winds shifted back in our favor. We had lots of commitments, but we couldn't yet close the fund and open for business until we had rounded up $10 million of the $15 million we were trying to raise. Then, through a mutual acquaintance, we got connected to Amy Huang, a general partner at a Hong Kong-based fund that helps companies go to market in Asia. She was new to venture capital investing, but even so, just hearing about us, she knew we were unlike other VCs. Above all, she had never heard of anyone going into venture from a non-profit. Who on earth with this background would think they could possibly raise a fund?

Amy came to meet Danielle and me in a co-working space in San Francisco where we rented an office. Her first impression was to notice my Rasputin beard. "Oh my god, this guy needs to shave!" Then she shook Danielle's hand and our whole vibe confirmed everything she had heard about us. "Yup, these are the least VC-like people I've ever met." She let us both know that right away. Amy has a blunt, devil-may-care sense of humor. She learned how to speak to Americans by watching *South Park* and listening to Eminem.

Amy sat down and heard our pitch. Danielle had cut out pictures and news stories about Thiel Fellows over the years and had taped them up on the wall. Amy had seen trophy walls before where people hang their prestigious degrees. But we had a collage of pictures. One of them was of the time Danielle and I bought a Thiel Fellow his first legal beer. The excitement we had telling her the story struck her as genuine and even a touch innocent. We weren't bragging about getting into some exclusive deal. Or about some big investment we made. Instead, she saw the biggest spark in our eyes when we were talking about getting the first beer with someone.

She went back to her office and talked to her business partner. He was skeptical. Danielle and I had emailed Amy our pitch deck. She told her partner it was the ugliest pitch deck she had ever seen. She said, either they refused to pay a professional to make their pitch deck slick, or they didn't even know these slides were ugly. Either way, that was a deal maker for her, not a deal breaker. She remembered her Oscar Wilde: only shallow people don't judge by appearances. Her partner dragged his feet.

As well as being a brash comedian, Amy has a taste for high fashion. She loves to wear luxurious designer shoes. The day we pitched her, she wore flats that had cute little cat faces on the tassels. Danielle, being a cat person, asked about them.

Amy told her they were $700 shoes. "Charlotte Olympia."

"I can't afford those."

"But I think one day you will buy the whole store."

Her business partner came around. Amy invested $2 million into 1517. We ended up raising $20 million in total. We were open for business, and it was time to start lighting the Paper Belt on fire.

· 10 ·

THE CRAM-DOWN

Darkness. An earthquake in a dream. No, it's not a dream. I can't tell exactly when I became conscious, but I'm awake, and now baffled…where am I? The room is so dark I can't make anything out. I can't remember where I fell asleep last night. Where the hell am I? Oh boy, it's a convulsion, turning earth into waves. The whole room seems to be rattling. I have no idea where I am, but the earth is shaking so it dawns on me that I must be in San Francisco. But I'm so confused. This isn't my apartment. A hangover too—it feels like a mad, metallic chaos, my thoughts, like three or four copper balls ricocheting on a pinball table inside my skull. Ding! Ding! Ding! The bed is now swaying so violently from side to side that it throws me to the floor.

But the ground is not shaking. Laying flat on the floor I see an alarm clock that looks like a bomb underneath the bed. This clanking, infernal device attached to the bed frame is shaking the entire bed, the headboard, and the side tables. It takes me a few clumsy, frantic button pushes, but eventually I turn the damn thing off. The stench of malodorous dirty laundry hits me…suddenly I remembered where I was. I was at a hacker house in Ann Arbor, Michigan. I raised the window shade. All was gray and snow-covered. It was winter, 2016.

I slept terribly because the hackers who lived here threw a party the night before. I had called it a night long before they did. But they partied deep into the early hours and at some point, they clogged the toilet of the only bathroom on the first floor of the house. That meant the closest working bathroom was in the bedroom they had lent me for the weekend. For the remainder of the night, hackers and the rest of their circus would walk through the room I was sleeping in to use the bathroom. At one point, I remembered two women coming out of the bathroom and they said in hushed tones to a guy walking in, "Don't flush. It'll wake him up!"

Danielle, of course, had it better. She slept in the attic, far from the madness where it was quieter. When I came downstairs that morning, she looked refreshed.

"Do you have any idea why my bed was shaking?" I asked some young dude I'd never met before. He was standing there in a doorway eating cereal, but then he burst into a laugh and dropped his spoon into his bowl.

"Tom didn't turn off his alarm clock!"

Tom, whose room I was sleeping in, apparently had such a hard time getting up in the morning that he installed a bed-shaking alarm clock to force himself out of his catatonic depths. This was par for the course at the Shift House, a hacker house located not far from the University of Michigan campus. The place had the feel of a frat house—a crumbling Tudor exterior, moldering mahogany walls, flaking paint, scuffed stairs, sticky floors, and that ever-present post-party mingled smell of stale beer and astringent cleaning fluid—nevertheless, the house was a magnet for engineering and design talent. It was no place for dilettantes. Danielle and I would come to Ann Arbor, and other places like it, to mix it up, talent spot, recruit, and offer whatever advice we could to the Shift House crew or anybody else they knew who was tinkering on a new idea.

After starting 1517, Danielle and I had turned totally out-bound for our recruiting, John Walker Lindh–style. We could no longer rely upon people filling out applications for the Thiel Fellowship. Instead of them finding us, we had to find them. Our strategy was to corral as many of the wayward comets as we could, any characters of weird and forceful originality long before they ever started a company. When we were taking meetings in our San Francisco offices or when we were on the road, we were not on the hunt for investments, but for the curious, the eccentric, the peculiar, the astonishing. Startup ideas, if anyone ever had one, would come in time. For many young makers and hackers—or anyone without a college degree, for that matter—it was enough for them to join our community, where they could meet like-minded outsiders and start friend-ships. And no wonder, too, since schools, parents, peers, and other small-town bullies had intimidated them into hiding their gifts. The most common reaction at our social events outside of any major city was always, "I can't believe there are other people here like me."

Every year, Danielle and I would travel and spend a few days or up to a week in a list of cities that could form the tour dates of a struggling mid-level rock band: Boston, Austin, Seattle, Toronto, La Jolla, Tulsa, Pittsburgh. Of course, we'd hit the big ones too—New York City, Miami, Chicago, and Los Angeles—as well as the hollowed-out, like Detroit and Cleveland. We'd also go to universities in the middle of nowhere: the University of Illinois at Urbana-Champaign, the University of Waterloo in Canada, the University of California at Merced. My phone is full of pictures of Danielle taking naps under a row of chairs at an airport gate or under the sponsor's table at a hackathon. It also has pictures of all the clock towers on just about every campus we ever visited. I didn't know where I was when I woke up in the Shift House partly because I had been in so many hotel and motel rooms. The inside of a La Quinta looks the same everywhere.

In time, we came to have a traveling salesman's knowledge of America. I can tell you where to find the best pancake in Los Angeles—the pumpkin pie pancake at the Griddle—or the best fruit smoothie in Michigan—the horribly named "What's in Your Cup?," in the town of Ypsilanti.

Our noses pressed up against the glass, breath fogging the window, we searched for the scientists' hangouts, where quantum physicists argued over beers. Or the campus cafes, where engineers plotted overthrowing Facebook, while fire-eyed poets and student songwriters expressed their doubts and frustrations on stage with a disturbing, if often incoherent power.

All through it, though, I remembered the research I had done when I interviewed with the CIA. I recalled what the disembodied voice explained to me on the phone about the clandestine service. He said the CIA had two roles for collecting and assessing intelligence: one that focused on looming trends and tracing the limits of what's known, the other tasked with building rapport and taking charge of recruitment. Whether unconsciously or not, this method formed the backbone of the 1517 working style.

What's going to happen in the future? Investors wish we were crystal balls, always asking us if we follow technological trends, but we say no, because if any technology has become a trend then it's already too late for us. We don't want to follow trends. We need to find the people who make them. The best way to predict the future, for us anyway, is to find the person who will create it. Admittedly, sometimes it feels like there's a sports analogy at work in our recruiting. Meeting an ace nineteen-year-old engineer in Tulsa bears a resemblance to scouting a linebacker who is playing in a Friday night football game way out in the sticks of West Texas. But the sports analogy breaks down because sports have well-defined rules and positions. The game by and large stays the same throughout the ages, and there are valid assumptions, many that can be quantified, in what to expect in the ideal linebacker. But innovation can take the most unexpected shapes and originate from the most unlikely of places. It is not one game. It is the game of all possible games. When we met Vitalik Buterin, we couldn't say we were scouting for blockchain inventors. We couldn't say that because there really weren't any besides Satoshi Nakamoto. And not even the FBI nor the CIA found him, despite the threat he presented to the Federal Reserve's dominance.

No, rather than sports, I've come to see intelligence as more fitting analogy. Like a couple of CIA case officers, but in this instance, spying on the edge of what's possible, Danielle and I talk to sources and recruit geniuses to help us build jigsaw puzzles that form a picture of a future that might be. The pieces are the extraordinary people we discover by traveling to distant places and by developing sources, any one of whom might one day influence the course of history. I take an irrational pride in the fact that the CIA didn't even see Ethereum coming, but we did. (Funny enough, the CIA has a venture capital fund called In-Q-Tel that has invested in a handful of our companies, but at a much later stage than we did. Paralyzed by bureaucratic, cover-your-ass thinking, they never invest as early in the life of a company as we do. Like other idiots along the Paper Belt, the CIA also requires that their employees have college degrees.)

Venture capital has its own information-gathering process. Above all, as the disembodied CIA voice told me on the phone during my interview, you can't search for intel about the future on Google or read about it on Twitter. There are some VCs that tap into online data sources which they believe can be used to make predictions about startup formation. As I understand it, they have algorithms that monitor LinkedIn and eavesdrop on various code repositories in order to track top engineers. If their algorithms detect several top engineers forming a new company, the firm will reach out to them. Whether that's effective or not, I can't say, but Danielle and I take the opposite approach. We believe in human intelligence. Any knowledge we learn about the future will come from people first—not books, not journals, not news stories, let alone through electronic signals or Internet tripwires. Individuals and teams invent things in small pockets. The garage startup is not a myth. But whatever they have invented has not yet rippled out into the wider world. Whether the team can make the jump from the garage to the market will be determined by their motivations, their commitment, their character—the critical things I don't believe any electronic signal can encode.

To that end, Danielle builds relationships and trust just about better than anyone I have ever met. Her easygoing charm and sound advice act as a gravity well for potential founders and for experts who can help us assess technical questions. Perhaps her greatest gift is her keen emotional intelligence, which gives her an uncanny judgment when it comes to assessing character and why people do things. That's of the utmost importance, because we believe that the future lies in the hands and the heart, as well as the head.

And while I've never been as good at building rapport as Danielle is, by 2016 I had developed a sense of the technological and scientific landscape and where anything we encountered fit within it. I am strong on the "so what?" and the "why" of what we find: I investigate what the consequences of an innovation might be and why it matters. A background of reading, talking to experts, and general curiosity informs my understanding of the context and helps me bring coherence to the puzzle pieces we come into contact with. How does it all fit together? Of course, that's not straightforward. I don't have the picture on the puzzle box cover to guide us to the solution, but I do have intuitions and hunches about what picture the pieces might be forming when taken together.

When the two of us use both of our strengths to evaluate a team, I have no doubt that the whole is greater than the sum of its parts. In fact, I have no idea how other VCs work alone. The interplay of our two strengths is the foundation of our process. Danielle and I spot wayward comets and they bring us to the edge of our understanding. What we learn there is not something anyone could ever read in a newspaper headline or detect in a repository of code. If anyone did, as I said, it'd already be too late.

What is intelligence? "φύσις κρύπτεσθαι φιλεῖ," the ancient Greek philosopher Heraclitus says, "Nature loves to hide her secrets." 1517's job is to find them before anyone else.

• • •

All of which is why I fell asleep in a bed in Ann Arbor, Michigan, on top of a device meant to awaken a narcoleptic college kid. We had agreed with the Shift House to take eight meetings that morning with their members in the house library, almost like professors hosting office hours. The library had hardly any books in it, but I noticed there was a dog-eared paperback by Kerouac chucked and forgotten in the corner. On the floor, right beside the table, was a discarded pair of Urban

Pipeline skinny jeans—size 32/32—the unbuckled belt still threaded through the belt loops. The pants sat there unclaimed through our meetings, as though someone had the bright idea of skinny dipping late in the night and had never come back to get dressed.

One by one people came in to tell us about what they were working on and what problems they had. One of them was a young man named Noah Shutty. Noah was a punky, nerdy guy with a lethargic rate of speech. He'd slowly speak half of a sentence, offer a big pause like he was taking a hit from a joint, and then finish the rest of the sentence in a deadpan. Maybe that came from staring deep into outer space for so long. Noah had teamed up with a post-doc physicist named Scott Stephenson to invent machine learning algorithms that could scan the skies for evidence of dark matter. Noah came to pitch us his idea for using those same algorithms for speech recognition. Since Google and Apple and Amazon were all working on speech recognition, using tremendous amounts of data to train their algorithms, it seemed an act of sheer folly that this slow-talking guy in Michigan could stand a chance against them. And yet, there was something captivating about him. His laid-back demeanor contrasted with the confidence behind his claims. He wasn't ready for an investment from us, but we wanted to encourage him and keep in touch. Danielle and I had pioneered giving $1,000 no-strings grants in situations like this back in the Thiel Fellowship. In my ideal world, I'd have ten $100 bills in a white envelope that I could take out of my inner coat pocket and slide across the desk. But in practice, for accounting reasons, we can't do that. So instead, we send $1,000 over PayPal or Venmo. With our grant, Noah could buy some of the supplies he needed, as well as some compute time on a cloud service to test some ideas out.

Over the years we've given out hundreds of these $1,000 grants, often in places like this with Noah. They work best when they're unexpected. One time in Detroit, a guy and his girlfriend cried when I told them I was going to send them $1,000 right then and there. They needed the money to buy parts to build a prototype and had no way to get started without it. Now, in truth, it's quite rare for these grant recipients to start companies that last. But I'm still surprised by the hit rate. There are something like twenty companies in our portfolio today that started as a $1,000 grant. That's incredible—to me, at any rate. Oftentimes the founders say they never would have started the company without it. And in many cases, they say it wasn't necessarily the money, but the fact that there were these two people from Silicon Valley, now here in Chattanooga, telling them they should try something they were afraid to test.

Months later, after some product development, Noah and Scott ended up starting their speech recognition company, Deepgram. 1517 is an investor. So is In-Q-Tel, the CIA fund. But we got there five years before them! Today the company is scaling in markets that Google and Apple and Amazon won't touch. They turn highly professional, jargon-filled speech into text. For example, Alexa and Siri can't recognize many of the specialized words and abbreviations used by doctors and lawyers (and apparently CIA officers). Deepgram's algorithms can hear them and transcribe them accurately, quickly, and cheaply.

So, by January of 2016, we were on our way to building our community of renegades and a portfolio of investments. We had refined our sources and methods. We were making $250,000 angel investments into startups led by dropouts or people who never went to college like it was something we'd always done. Naturally, the press still hated us. In a 2016 *New York Times* op-ed, science journalist and author Tom Clynes claimed that "radical innovation has yet to emerge" from anything related to the Thiel Fellowship, and that "the biggest hits have been the most pedestrian."[1] Antonio García Martínez, the author of the Silicon Valley memoir *Chaos Monkeys*, spewed forth his bile for us on social media. "For fans of ironic stupidity, Silicon Valley is a never-ending feast," he wrote on Facebook. He went on to explain, with great vulgarity, why our fund would fail by backing young dropouts. My favorite of all time has to be the challenge issued by Scott Galloway, a professor and bloviator in marketing from NYU's business school, who is also a popular podcaster. He and the journalist Kara Swisher take to the microphone twice a week on Vox Media to dish on happenings in the tech world. In 2017, Galloway told *Business Insider* that if he picked ten smart recent graduates from his alma mater, the University of California at Berkeley, they would outperform any ten dropouts we worked with on some dimension of success related to income or startup formation.[2] "Who would you bet on?" Galloway asks the camera. "There are always going to be the Jay-Zs of the world," Galloway continues, now addressing his audience. "There are going to be the Kobe Bryants, there are going to be the Mark Zuckerbergs, the people who drop out of college. You should assume you're not that person and go to college."

Fortunately, we were coming into contact with more and more young people who ignored Galloway. In January of 2016, a young man named Shahed Khan reached out to Danielle to ask for a meeting. We'd been keeping tabs on Shahed ever since he applied to the Thiel Fellowship when he was only fifteen years old. His idea was to start a Craigslist for chores. He didn't get a fellowship, but he'd email Danielle all the time. When we first met him, he was an earnest, buttoned-up teenager who wore a dress shirt with a school tie on. Now he was nineteen and a full-on hipster: dark skinny jeans, black bomber jacket, gelled hair. Shahed came to our office at 100 Broadway in San Francisco. Our office was a 150-square-foot closet with no windows. The HVAC was exposed on the ceiling. Shahed came in to tell us about a company he started only forty-five days ago with two of his friends. They called it Opentest.

Now, Danielle and I could handle the attacks from the media because we knew it didn't affect our business. No one actually cared what fake bets Scott Galloway wanted to make. But working with Opentest would reveal to us our strongest adversary, one that had the potential to crush 1517—namely, the old order of established venture capital funds on Sand Hill Road. As good as Danielle and I had become at pulling together that jigsaw puzzle of the future, we had a lot to learn as investors when it came to the lingering power of old gods. The plain fact was that while they couldn't care less about our mission, the old-line venture capital funds didn't like us encroaching on their territory.

In January 2016, Opentest had no users and was only a bare-bones product. Their idea was to build software for product managers so they could get feedback in the form of a video walk-through. Imagine surveys that collect videos of users while those users swipe through an app or browse a website. Shahed and his two co-founders, Joe Thomas and Vinay Hiremath, described the idea as "Mailchimp for software testing" in their first pitch deck, referencing the popular email marketing tool. We told them we'd be more inclined to invest once they ran a pilot test with a customer.

The Opentest team persisted. Their first customer was a website called BrainFM that relies on computers to generate meditation music. After a few more backs and forths with us over email explaining how BrainFM and a few other customers used their video survey tool, Danielle and I agreed to take a meeting with the team down in San Mateo where they lived and worked. "It was a powerful tool," Danielle remembers thinking. "But how many people are really going to use it?"

So we drove down to San Mateo from San Francisco to learn more. It turned out Joe, Vinay, and Shahed lived and worked together in the same cramped apartment. We told the guys we'd take them out to lunch. They quickly picked Chipotle. Once we sat down, the update they gave us on the product was impressive, but something else stood out for us as we crunched down on chips and guacamole. Shahed, Joe, and Vinay only ate half of their burritos. Each of them wrapped up the second half of the burrito in tin foil to bring it back to their apartment. To be sure, Chipotle tends to stuff way too much into their burritos. The burrito-folders behind the counter always have the hardest time fitting all of the ingredients into that flour tortilla. Half of the ingredients always spill out. Chipotle simply doesn't understand or respect the limits of maximum burrito capacity. But Danielle's spidey-sense immediately went off. Shahed, Joe, and Vinay are young men, she thought. They can totally house a whole messy Chipotle burrito. There's no way they're full.

"What are you doing?" she asked.

"We're saving this for dinner," they said.

The guys were days away from bankruptcy. They had to keep it lean, they told us. By the time we drove back to the city, Danielle and I had emailed them saying we were going to invest $200,000 into Opentest, the very first money into the company. Their grit and ability to execute won us over. And we'd always remember the half-burritos. We even wired them the money before all the paperwork was signed because they had bills to pay. We also sent the deal over to some other investors we had befriended. A firm called Elementum also put in a few hundred thousand. Opentest was on its way.

Then they caught fire. Over the next year, they had changed the product so that anyone could record a video of their computer screen while they worked. It became an essential tool for designers and engineers who could explain over video what changes they wanted to see instead of having to write it out in an email. They also added a cute bubble in the corner of the screen that displayed a person's face as they talked. It's the kind of product that's hard to explain, but that users just come to love. Their growth exploded. They changed their name from Opentest to Loom.

Soon after, they were becoming the darlings of Silicon Valley. When Loom hit the road to raise money for their seed round, they had no trouble getting meetings. Two firms came together to lead the round, General Catalyst and Point 9. Joe, Vinay, and Shahed asked to meet with us. They had to tell us some bad news. They were cramming us down.

The cram-down. A fundamental aspect of our investment strategy is to be the first money in. But then as we work with a company over the next few years, our philosophy is to follow on with more money in subsequent rounds of fundraising. Each round of venture financing has a name and a sequence. Angel or pre-seed starts it off. Then Seed, Series A, Series B, Series C, and so on until a company is acquired or goes public in an IPO. As part of our contract with a startup, when we write that first check, we ask for what are called "pro rata rights." This means the founders are contractually obligated to carve out some share of stock for us in those later rounds. Our fund's ability to deliver returns to our investors depends on these rights. Loom had invited us into a meeting to tell us that, despite promising us these rights, they could no longer honor the agreement. Not if they were going to work with General Catalyst and Point 9. These two funds insisted that the round had to look a certain way, leaving little to no room for our follow-on investment.

Now, even though we had a legal right by contract, we could never take the company to court to enforce it. That kind of antagonism would sour our reputation with startups we might work with in the future. They might decide not to accept our investment lest we sue them at a later stage. In addition to that fear, investors also don't want to undermine their own cash-strapped company with legal bills. So we have one of the strange dances in Silicon Valley, where companies agree to legal rights and then back out of them without penalty because they know their investors can't enforce them.

After our protest in that meeting with the Loom team, Joe managed to find some room in the round for us, another $200,000 investment. We were grateful for the opportunity to keep working with the company, and we recommended that Shahed become a Thiel Fellow, which happened in due course, but we still felt the sting of taking it on the chin.

Then, not long after that, Danielle and I were on one of our long road trips to the East Coast. There was a partner at General Catalyst based in New York City who liked to meet with us from time to time to talk shop. He was not the partner that led the Loom investment, but he worked alongside the guy who told Loom to cram us down. Peter Boyce II—aka "Bad Boy Boyce" on Twitter—is a Harvard alum who began a small side fund in 2012 for General Catalyst called Rough Draft Ventures. Rough Draft covers similar ground to us, as it invests tiny checks into student-run companies, but exclusively at prestigious Paper Belt schools such as Harvard, MIT, and Columbia. Since there was some overlap in our recruiting, Boyce liked to trade notes with us. When we arrived in New York City, Danielle and I agreed to meet with him at General Catalyst's offices on Broadway in SoHo.

Boyce often dressed like an Ivy League professor of English literature—rectangle glasses, fine worsted wool sports coats with cashmere V-neck sweaters, and a collared shirt underneath. He is supremely accomplished, polite, and elegant—but with a dash of Los Angeles's effusive insincerity. He'd always begin conversations with vacuous compliments. "I love what you guys are doing. Love it so much. Love it. Love. Love. Love it!" On this day, when we walked into General Catalyst's offices, Boyce showed us into a conference room to talk to his associate. He wanted her to pick our brain to steal our methods. As soon as any fund asks us about "community building" we hide what we do in a fog of abstractions. Not that they could copy us exactly, even if we told them, since Ivy Bots and Old Smoothy VCs aren't going to spend three days crashing at a hacker house in Ann Arbor. Nevertheless, sending us to his lackey so she could pump us for information was irritating. After twenty minutes, Boyce slid into the room. "You guys are fabulous. You're amazing."

"Well, anyway, we've got to talk about something," Danielle cut in.

The look on Boyce's face showed he knew exactly what issue we were about to raise.

"Your partner who co-led the Loom round," I said, "he went out of his way to push us out of our pro rata."

Boyce's L.A. facade crumbled. He clasped his hands into a praying mantis position on the table.

"Look," I said, "we want to continue to work with you guys. You're one of the best funds out there, but we're not going to send you companies if this is how we're treated."

Now the Ivy League professor disappeared. He wasn't going to take any blame for this. Boyce raised his two hands in the air like Richard Nixon, not in two Vs like Nixon, but with the index and middle fingers joined as pointers, and then he started moving his hands like a guy on a tarmac waving orange batons to guide an airplane to the gate. "Who makes the decisions?" he asked while doing this. "Who makes the decisions at the company?" Each time he said "who," the word was underscored by his two hands moving in the tarmac-guy motion pointing accusingly at us. The tone was of a schoolmarm instructing toddlers.

Danielle and I fell into that role, almost bowing our heads in shameful acknowledgment. "The CEO," we answered, like dutiful students.

"That's right!" Boyce exclaimed. "The CEO. The CEO makes the decisions. So your problem is with the CEO, not with my partner, not with General Catalyst."

Holy shit. Danielle suddenly had a vision of Boyce using this same demeanor to tell the Harvard Dean to change his B-plus paper into an A-minus. Who makes the decisions? The Dean makes the decisions.

We walked out furious and hopped into a taxi on Broadway. I'd never seen Danielle so livid. On her phone, she found a fifty-five-gallon drum of lubricant for sale on Amazon. She wanted to order it and send it to General Catalyst with a note that said, "Next time you fuck us, make sure you use this."

I grabbed her phone out of her hands before she could hit the buy-now button. By the time we got back to the Ace Hotel, I talked her down. "Let's get a drink." And we vented in the lobby bar.

Then, a year later, Loom crammed us down again. This time it was Kleiner Perkins. I can see old Tom Perkins smiling on his $150 million yacht. Loom continued to track hot. Joe wrote to tell us that Kleiner Perkins was leading their Series A. This time Kleiner would allow General Catalyst and Point 9 to claim their pro rata rights, but they weren't going to give Loom any room to give us ours. Also, Joe said they were squeezing in the actor Jared Leto because he wanted to invest. Apparently, his string of roles in terrifically bad movies, particularly as the Joker in the *Suicide Squad*, made him a valuable investor to have on the cap table.

If we were livid the first time, we were thermonuclear the second. We wrote an email to Joe:

Hey Joe—

We've been reflecting on the way you've structured this round and it appears to us that you've made a series of bad choices on honoring your relationships with us and other early investors.

We have been far from quiet money in your company. After rallying to get you all off the ground not only with our own capital but also with intros to others who ultimately funded you like Elementum, Andy Chou, and others who helped you out like Dylan Field—not to mention a Thiel Fellowship recommendation for Shahed—we find the act of not honoring the original agreement wanting in character. It is even worse that you have also found no way to remedy this action outside of cramming us down.

We have the contractual right to exercise our pro rata. It is not clear to us that you have communicated this to the partners you are working with at Kleiner, General Catalyst, and Point 9. It's also ironic to us that Point 9 just published a piece on Medium about not screwing your early investors.

If you are asking us to waive our pro rata and cram us down, we would like you to reply to this email thread asking for the waiver, explaining why you are cramming us down, and cc'ing the partners at these funds on that email.

Thanks,
Michael & Danielle

Joe never responded to the email. Instead, he said he'd talk to us at the Elementum Christmas party. So there we were, a couple of cocktails in, snagging hors d'oeuvres, chit-chatting over the Christmas music in the background, when Joe asked if we could talk. The three of us shuffled off to a couch in the corner of the room where it was quieter. Before he even started talking to us, tears were welling in Joe's eyes. And then he took a deep breath and told us how we're getting screwed again. He said they had to maintain what they saw as a fair share of equity for themselves and their other investors. He appeared to be sad about this. Even somewhat apologetic. But, like a boyfriend who is tired of his girlfriend, it felt more like he was sad because he had to have this conversation at all. The "it's not you, it's me" conversation. To this day, Danielle is still confused by the whole thing. Why would you choose to do this at a Christmas party?

In retrospect, now that we've worked with many successful companies, it's somewhat admirable that Joe wanted to appear apologetic because other founders we've since invested in have been blunt. They get interest from one of the legacy Sand Hill Road funds, cram us down, and say, "Well, this is how the game is played. Everybody knows it. No big deal."

And then—surprise, surprise—another year later, Loom crammed us down yet again. The company continued on its meteoric rise. This time around it was the Yankees: Sequoia Capital led Loom's Series B. It's known generally throughout Silicon Valley that Sequoia only hires partners who have a bottomless pathological need to win. When I was working for Peter Thiel, any time Michael Moritz's name was mentioned, I would notice Peter would get competitive, even slightly agitated. Moritz is one of the legendary long-time partners at Sequoia and served on the board of PayPal when Peter was CEO. One time when I was with Peter, Moritz's name came up and Peter launched into a *There Will Be Blood* Daniel Day-Lewis parody with Moritz yelling "I drink your milkshake!!" in Peter's telling.

Well, Sequoia drank our milkshake. We barely got to invest anything, and we didn't even bother to protest. We'd had enough crocodile tears. Today the company is cruising. As of its last valuation, Loom is worth $1.5 billion.

During one of our meetings with Loom in their offices, I hated feeling so powerless. I said to Joe, Vinay, and Shahed, "You know there's a famous moment in the Peloponnesian War."

Danielle and the guys looked at me like I was speaking gibberish, fluently. "The island of Melos wanted to stay neutral in the war between Athens and Sparta. But the Athenians wouldn't have it. If the Melians didn't side with Athens, they would be destroyed. The Melians protested that this was unjust. And then the Athenians said, 'We are not the first to have acted this way, for the strong do what they can, and the weak suffer what they must.'"

No one said anything. But the Loom guys nodded assent.

We left the meeting and were walking out onto Market Street in downtown San Francisco. "Ok Heraclitus," Danielle said. "That went shhhhhjjjjjjooooo over their heads." She flew her hand over her head as she said it.

"It's Thucydides."

"Whatever. It would have been better if you simply said, 'I'm disappointed. I wanted my pro rata.'"

She was right. But if we were going to beat Kleiner and Sequoia, not to mention overcome a hostile media and university system, we were going to have to have more cunning plan. "The strong do what they can, the weak suffer what they must." Well, not on my watch.

·11·

LIGHTS, CAMERA, ACTION

So we entered into a cold war against Sand Hill Road. Hostilities would always remain below a friendly, diplomatic surface. Our animosities were never to be found in the easily forgotten handshakes at conferences or in the mechanistic smiles at industry meet-ups. Email sign-offs would always end with an overly exuberant "thanks!"—that exclamation point beaming with passive-aggressive good cheer. And yet, for their part, behind the scenes, the top venture funds would continue to use their power and prestige to influence startups against us, dictating terms and trying to crown category winners.

For our part, well, we had one advantage they didn't know about. A young man named Austin Russell. The first thing anyone notices about Austin is a startling fusion. He is tall, six-foot-four, lanky, with sandy auburn hair and scruffy stubble. A native of Irvine, he looks and sounds like a Southern California surfer, especially when his belly laugh explodes out at the end of one of his war stories or explanations. But instead of laughing while telling you about eating it in a nasty wipeout or about carving it down a curling wave tube, Austin will laugh while telling you about the virtues of using the 1550-nanometer wavelength of light in the lidar system he invented. ("Lidar" is an acronym for sensors that use light to see and recognize objects in the world.) "Of course, you can't use the 905-nanometer wavelength to see anything at 200 meters without turning the power up to the point where it fries human eyes," he told me once, as if it was the funniest joke ever. "Your driverless car would give everyone on the sidewalk Lasik surgery!"

The first time Danielle and I met Austin was back in 2012 when he was seventeen. He came to a conference Danielle put together. When we met him, he'd already been tinkering around with lasers for years as a teenage lab rat at the Beckman Laser Institute at the University of California at Irvine, which was near his home. He had no formal connection to the university but fast talked his way into the lab, and he hated wasting his time in his high school classes. In his application to the Thiel Fellowship, Austin complained to us that his most recent high school homework assignment involved memorizing the names of people who played a role in the Salem Witch Trials. "This isn't what history should be about!" he grumbled. Meanwhile, he wrote to tell us that he had recently completed a proof-of-concept prototype that produced something he called "Spatially Dynamic Supercontinuum Coherent Radiation (SDSCR)." Then he told us what that meant:

> This project took years of advanced research, combined with a necessary solid technical background. Ultimately, I created a device that is essentially able to modulate light on a microscopic scale, to simulate and produce ANY frequency/wavelength in the visible and IR spectra and project it toward any location in 3D space. Simply put, with this device, we have full control over any desired property of light in your surrounding environment. This means that you are able to do everything from projecting

scalable and interactive three-dimensional holograms in midair, to efficiently transmitting power wirelessly over long distances, to detecting cancer far earlier than any other medical imaging system. Best of all, this revolutionary photonics-based platform is easily capable of being embedded into a handheld device. This is not just some "too-good-to-be-true" theoretical project either. I currently have a basic, but functional prototype.

Recall that Austin was seventeen when he wrote the phrases "years of advanced research" and "a necessary solid technical background" and then imagine him laughing about it as though he just shredded a 360 on a ten-foot wave surfing down in La Jolla. Like anyone reading this, we wondered if Austin's ideas were crazy, or crazy awesome. And truth be told, we couldn't tell at first.

But after some intense due diligence—we had one of our physicist friends dig into Austin's claims—we awarded Austin a Thiel Fellowship in the spring of 2013. His work was speculative, but not bananas, and that was good enough for us. Peter's $100,000 grant went a long way for Austin to continue his research and development on his technology. Across our first few quarterly meetings, he thought he'd develop its use for cameras in Hollywood. The core ideas powering his prototype could be repurposed for special effects so that green screens would become a thing of the past. But by then another trend had begun to build momentum and capture the public's imagination.

Google's self-driving car program began in 2009, and then the buzz, the mania, and the bold pronouncements crescendoed over the decade that followed. By 2014, Austin saw an enormous gap in all the hype. Despite companies claiming they were going to deliver full self-driving cars soon—even companies as big as Google and Tesla—the inadequacy of the current technology presented tremendous obstacles to their claims. The robots driving the cars were much worse than humans.

The problem came down to perception, the ability to learn, and cost. Autonomous vehicles need eyes to see and a brain to process the information and learn from experience. Throughout the 2010s, the overwhelming faith of the industry was in the brain, not the eyes. The orthodox view was that both the algorithms for object detection (the visual cortex) and the chips running the algorithms (the neurons) would become so fast that it didn't matter all that much what types of sensors a vehicle had. A simple video camera might do because, in the end, a system's increasingly powerful computation would compensate for the faint and noisy signal coming in from the world. For the most part, though they had big brains, many of the early experimental cars used weak lidar systems, radar, and cameras for eyes. These old lidar systems looked like a giant spinning Kentucky Fried Chicken bucket. But even with all the training in the world—and I saw fleets of these bucket-head cars endlessly circling the streets of San Francisco as though in some robotic purgatory—the algorithms couldn't learn to recognize the rare, but important edge cases: a plastic bag blowing in the wind, an open car door, a jaywalker looking the wrong way, a bike on a rack, a blind left turn. To add to these difficulties, the cost of the stronger fried chicken buckets was expensive, as high as $120,000 per unit.

Austin rejected the big data software-based approach and joined forces with another photonics ace, his mentor Jason Eichenholz of Open Photonics. Together they co-founded Luminar Technologies to build the hardware that could solve the problems their rivals didn't even acknowledge they had. Artificial intelligence and meticulous mapping were not enough. No amount of big data could make up for bad data. Instead,

Luminar would reinvent the whole perception stack from the ground up, starting with a lidar system more powerful and cheaper than any yet produced.

The company started in a nondescript warehouse in Irvine, California, with a bunch of physics geeks who liked to build things with lasers. When they weren't working on the first version of their lidar sensor, they built electric surfboards and go-carts for fun. (One surfboard caught fire out in the Pacific; thankfully no one was hurt.) In the meantime, Jason and Austin researched two thousand different ways to build a lidar system that could see. They found 1,999 ways that couldn't work. But then they discovered one that does.

It relies upon four key innovations. They are the laser, the receiver, the scanner, and the processor. A lidar system, in a truly astonishing act of magic and speed, fires trillions of photons out into the world. Those photons hit objects and then rebound back to the system, where its receiver catches the photons and registers them upon their return. The processor makes sense of that incoming information, timing each photon over the distance they travel. The scanner keeps the laser sweeping the horizon so as to detect even the slightest movement caught in the pico-second difference between two photons on their return home.

Most lidar systems in 2013 were producing green and black images of the world that looked like an old Atari video game with sparse green lines, dashes, and dots moving in a black void. The industry leader was a company called Velodyne. I gained a greater appreciation for the power of the computers that could translate those faint Atari pong blocks into a somewhat reliable representation of moving cars and people. That was impressive, but it wasn't enough to ensure that vehicles could be trusted on the road. The old systems were too nearsighted. They could only see a short distance, which limited their reaction times on the roads to one or two seconds tops, assuming they saw the object at all. A car ride full of last-second swerves and screeching stops would be nauseating at best and fatal at worst. If an autonomous vehicle was going to travel at 60 miles-per-hour down the road at night, it'd need more than seven seconds of reaction time. Austin understood from the beginning that his system would need to detect and recognize objects more than 200 meters out at night, even seeing elusive dark objects that reflect less than 10 percent of the light that strikes them.

To attain the necessary performance specs, Austin and Jason broke away from industry dogma. On the laser, most rivals used the 905-nanometer wavelength of light because it was closer to the visible light spectrum and could simulate what the human eye sees. But the 905-nanometer lasers were one of the main reasons the old systems were so nearsighted. Engineers had to limit their power, which then limited their range because increasing the power would endanger humans on the roads and sidewalks. Which is what Austin meant when he said that increasing the power would help those systems see better, but would give everyone Lasik surgery in the process. To avoid that problem, Austin and Jason developed a laser in the 1550-nanometer wavelength, which could be used at one million times the pulse energy of the 905 without hurting anyone's eyes.

That breakthrough, however, created other problems they had to solve. To use that kind of laser, they would need to invent a new receiver. The old silicon-based receivers were not sensitive enough to register the 1550 wavelength reliably. Austin and his team threw out the silicon and replaced it with an exotic high-performance alloy, indium gallium arsenide (or InGaAs, for short, pronounced "in gas.") InGaAs is insanely expensive. Austin held up a disk-like wafer of InGaAs for me once that was about a foot across in diameter. He said it cost $10,000.

Then Jason showed me the amount of InGaAs they were using on the receiver they'd invented. It was a tiny sliver, a millimeter at most, that sat precariously on the tip of Jason's index finger. Next, they embedded that tiny sliver into a microprocessor of their own custom design. Last of all, rather than using many lasers like their rivals—the Velodyne HDL-64, for example, the best performing fried chicken bucket, used sixty-four of them—Luminar built a new mechanism that raster scans the world into pixels, thousands of times per second with a single laser. The image output of Luminar's system is a spectacular view, a lifelike world painted in a prismatic array of colors, objects clear at 200–250 meters, with different colors representing the different distances of those objects out in the world.

Five years passed during which Austin, Jason, and the rest of the team refined the system. Not long after Danielle and I formed 1517, we invested $750,000 into Luminar. We were the first venture capital fund to put money into the company. We saw Luminar move its headquarters multiple times and grow from a few employees to four hundred. At one point they rented a mansion called the Pony Tracks Ranch in Portola Valley, a golden suburb tucked into the mountains on the edge of the Pacific near Silicon Valley. It was the perfect location for conducting research and testing their system. The ranch's former owner, Jacques M. Littlefield, had used his fortune and his 450-acre property to assemble perhaps the world's largest private collection of military equipment.[1] Littlefield owned a 73-ton British Conqueror tank, a 41-foot Soviet SCUD missile launcher, and an M48 Patton tank, in addition to numerous Sherman tanks, a Panzer, and mobile howitzers. After he died, Littlefield's family donated his collection to a military museum in 2014. But that left behind the perfect set of garages and workshop spaces for building out Luminar's lidar and testing it. During our visits, a ride in Luminar's souped-up car would often begin in the same garage bay that formerly housed a SCUD missile launcher.

Across the years, we'd drop in periodically to discuss strategy with Austin and assess the competition. By 2018, all of the big players predicted that the mass deployment of robotaxis was only years away. The mania was quite fantastic. After having acquired the entire robotics department at Carnegie Mellon University, Uber said it would have 100,000 driverless cars on the roads by 2020. Its competitor Lyft decreed the majority of its rides would be autonomous by 2021. In 2019, Elon Musk promised Tesla would be "operating robotaxis next year." To stay in the game, Detroit was so busy acquiring any startups they could that the price tag didn't matter. General Motors bought Cruise Automation for more than $1 billion in 2016, even though it was only a small team of software engineers with no hardware to speak of. Investors fought like rugby players in a scrum to get into hot deals. VCs were greedily passing around pitch decks related to anything driverless. Their eyes popped out of their sockets. Just about every pitch deck described the potential market size, not in the billions, but the trillions.

With all that money at stake, the competition in lidar and sensor systems went from a simmer to a psychotic overboil. Velodyne was still the industry leader, but new startups began to emerge, each attempting different lidar designs and architectures. A game of press release one-upmanship broke out, a childish charade of empty boasting, with each company claiming its system was more powerful, smaller, and cheaper than any before it. The valuations of these startups ballooned to extraordinary heights, despite many not even having a product, let alone revenue. One of the darlings of Silicon Valley, Quanergy Systems, raised $160 million by 2018, the last round of investment valuing the company at $1.5 billion.

Whenever we discussed the competitive landscape with Austin, we'd all shake our heads in disbelief. Some failures were public. Quanergy never met the deadlines it boasted it would, and it even shipped lidar units that didn't work as advertised.[2] Other failures and slights of hand were kept private. We'd get business intelligence from former employees or disgruntled investors who would reveal that some of the new companies were fudging data. It was not uncommon for some of the lidar startups to brag about having a 200-meter range with their system, yet what wasn't revealed was that the feat was accomplished indoors in a white lab room on an object with 100 percent reflectivity.

When it came to autonomy and anything related to it, pedigree and credentials, rather than substance, became objects of obsession with investors and the press. To be fair, this was partly because it was so difficult for outsiders to judge the relative merits of such complex technologies. But Danielle and I caught the prevailing mood one time during a meeting with an investor who represented a family office out of Ohio. He said he was passing on investing in 1517 because he had already invested in one of Luminar's competitors, Aeva Inc.

"What does Aeva have going for it?" I asked.

"Its founders used to work for Apple and graduated from Stanford."

That was it. That's all he offered, gloriously confident in his touching faith in these talismans of power. Much like a superstitious megalithic cult, circle-dancing around the stones of Stanford and Apple. But prestige and status are about the past, not the future. Austin has no college degree nor Ph.D. No matter. Luminar's superiority was evident among the people it mattered to the most—the customers. Small indicators would crop up in the strangest of places. For instance, in court discovery filings for the massive Uber v. Waymo lawsuit in 2017—Waymo had sued Uber for stealing trade secrets and for patent infringement—Anthony Levandowski was recorded telling his boss, Travis Kalanick, Uber's then-CEO, that Luminar's lidar "is 10x better than anything else, lots to learn from here. They've been building this in stealth for the last five years."[3]

Now it was true that the company was in stealth, meaning it didn't issue meaningless press releases with fraudulent data. But it wasn't so much that Luminar was in hiding as that the competition and the upper crust Sand Hill Road funds were distracted and deluded. To take one, Sequoia had backed a software company, Aurora, as its horse in the race. To this day, Aurora actually showcases using weak Velodyne systems on its website. Of course, Austin had talked to many of the top funds out there over the years, but they couldn't believe that Luminar was better than the other startups founded by people with sterling credentials. We advised Austin to steer clear of Kleiner, Sequoia, and the rest of Sand Hill.

Over the years we invested more and more money into Luminar, seeing it as a massive bet against credentials and Sand Hill Road. We invested $2 million out of 1517, the maximum we could, and then doubled, tripled, and quadrupled down into side funds dedicated solely to Luminar. In total, we invested $17 million into the company. As Sand Hill Road went its way and we and Luminar went ours, there was a tense, let 'em all come, chips down excitement building. Who would win?

We kept a guarded optimism. But even so, our whole fund and our mission were riding on it, perched on the knife's edge. If this investment didn't work out, our story was over. Still, there were glimmers of the future. One time in May 2019, our investor from Guatemala, Fernando Pontaza, came with us to visit Luminar's headquarters in Orlando, Florida where it had relocated and established a 50,000 square foot manufacturing facility.

Jason Eichenholz took us all out for a ride in a minivan outfitted with the company's newest lidar, something like the sixth generation after years of refinement. The competition was fixated on the range, which was certainly important, but there were other performance requirements that none of them were close to finding solutions for: interference, glare, point density, dynamic depth. What if the roads are full of other cars with lidar systems firing photons into the system on your car? Can your receiver tell the difference between your photons and theirs? Jason showed us that he and Austin solved the problem. What about blazing sunshine? They solved that, too. Then we pulled up perpendicular to a Bank of America, across the street from its entrance. Jason said "check this out." The front windows of the bank were tinted, completely opaque. But when Jason pointed the lidar system at the bank, suddenly we could see inside of it on the screen in the minivan. Jason hit some keys and then the computer showed us a bird's eye view of the inside of the bank. We saw people standing in line for the teller. We saw the loan officers at their desks. And then, much to my amazement, we could see a person opening the bathroom door in the back of the bank.

Danielle said her brain exploded: "There are lots of people who won't want this to work!"

Fernando said, "Holy shit—there is nothing like this out there."

Jason saw the looks on our faces. "Good thing we haven't taken any money from the government," he said. "They'd seize and classify this for the military immediately."

· 12 ·

A NEW NINETY-FIVE

Octtober 31, 2017, marked the five hundredth anniversary of Martin Luther's nailing of his ninety-five theses to a university's church door in Wittenberg, Germany.[1] (It was also the ninth anniversary of Satoshi Nakamoto's first email announcing the invention of Bitcoin.) Three days before the quincentennial we held an assembly in San Francisco to celebrate Luther's provocation. We brought together about five hundred people to honor those who shouldn't be doing what they're doing in the eyes of some authority. As keynote speakers, we invited my old co-conspirator, Balaji Srinivasan, Patrick Collison, a co-founder of the payments company Stripe, Roya Mahboob, a human rights activist, and Sadie Valeri, a classical painter. Our theme was that higher education had become America's national religion and that we were on a mission to disestablish the monopoly of this single church.

Luther's ninety-five theses were written as a "disputatio," which meant that he was announcing that he was open to debate his claims in public.[2] Likewise, we wanted to announce our willingness to discuss our claims about the problems in higher education. So I disappeared into a cabin in Wyoming for a week. When I emerged, I had a new ninety-five. We took a page from Luther's book and nailed—ok, taped—our own ninety-five propositions to the doors of universities across America on the night of October 31, 2017. Five hundred years after Luther on the dot.

We enlisted twenty members of our community to tape the theses I'd written to administration doors at their colleges. The theses were way larger than we had intended. Our commercial printer had misunderstood our request and printed them on tea-stained seven-foot-long scrolls. They were ridiculous. They looked like something from a Medieval Times dinner theater. But it turned out for the best. I have a picture of this enormous scroll covering the statue of John Harvard in Harvard Yard while two curious people try to make out what it is. Similar scenes played out at Yale, Baylor, Pitt, Notre Dame, the University of Illinois, and elsewhere. We encouraged the twenty students to take pictures and post them on social media with the tag, "I'm rallying against the classroom-to-cubicle pipeline with the New 95 today, what will you rally for? #new95."

Sadly, no universities wanted to debate us. But those pictures are some of the best keepers of any that I have. I'll list my first ten theses to give a sense of the message. The rest you can find on the Internet or on the dean's office door.

1. Life in the United States begins with a thirteen-year mandatory minimum sentence: K-12.
2. Anytime you see anxious parents sweating over their daughter's pre-school interview, remember that university admissions committees have established the system of rewards and punishments that even loom over juicy bottle time.
3. Higher education has become America's national religion, complete with heaven and hell, salvation and damnation. You're a winner or a sinner. It's Yale or jail.

4. A "well-rounded" student is often only a euphemism for a ruthless workaholic in a greyhound race for a useless mechanical lure.

5. What is a college application but a fight to the death for prestige?

6. "The worst kind of virtue never stops striving for virtue and so never achieves virtue."—Laozi

7. "Would you rather have a Princeton diploma without a Princeton education or a Princeton education without a Princeton diploma? If you pause to answer, you must think signaling is pretty important."—George Mason University economist Bryan Caplan

8. Why are there some 5,300 universities and colleges in the United States but only one point of view?

9. We have to have the freedom to be the only person who believes something.

10. There can be no safety without dangerous ideas.

· 13 ·

THE FRONTIER

Danielle is on the edge of tears. It's 2018 and we are standing in front of a kiosk at immigration and customs for entry into Shenzhen on mainland China. We arrived here on a subway from Hong Kong. Having deployed the $20 million we raised for our first fund, we've been traveling extensively to raise capital for our next. The second fund has been harder to raise than the first. We have commitments from all of our Fund I investors, but it's been a struggle to get new investors to believe in our dropout thesis. So while the trade wars had curtailed Chinese investment in the United States, it wasn't completely closed off. There was an investment fund in Shenzhen that wanted to meet with us. We said we'd be happy to talk. But now we're stuck at a kiosk trying to get a machine to record our fingerprints.

"Treat it like a game," I say to Danielle. "Experiment rolling your fingertips."

"That's not helping!" she snaps at me.

In addition to passports, visas, and other bureaucratic paperwork, you have to give the joyless Chinese authorities at the border your fingerprints, which a computer reads when you place your fingers on a glass surface. The sensor isn't very sensitive, however, so you have to move and press and roll your fingertips on the glass until a representation of all five fingers lights up green on the screen. Percentages under each finger image tell you how hot or cold your effort is. Danielle's have been cold.

For whatever reason—"I have faint fingerprints!"—Danielle is having a hard time of it. The computer can't pick up her prints and she's getting frustrated, then angry, then sad. To say the Chinese government takes entry into its country seriously is an understatement. Walking into this room involved walking underneath a nest of cameras, of all different kinds, all probably recording different aspects of our likenesses and facts about us, including our current body temperature (even pre-Covid in order to catch the feverish before they gain entry). Outside the building were the requisite armed soldiers, barbed wire, and watchtowers. Danielle is scared that if the computer won't read her fingerprints, then we're not going to get into Shenzhen to pitch investors. There is a feeling of urgency, given the hard time we've had convincing new investors to back us. But even greater than that is the presence of a threat, which hangs about the room because you suddenly remember the verb disappear can be used in the transitive sense. Step out of line—show any sympathy for Hong Kong's independence—and the Chinese immigration authorities can disappear you to some nightmarish place where anything could be done without anybody ever hearing of it. Five booksellers in Hong Kong had recently vanished because they sold books banned on the mainland.[1]

"Try flattening your hand," I say, uselessly. "Roll them around."

"I can't roll what I don't have!" Danielle's fingers do look smoother than any I've seen.

Fifty-eight, fifty-nine, sixty—eeeoooeeeooo!—a red sign

flashes "unsuccessful" on the screen, and then the computer resets. After what's probably the twentieth try at this, Danielle is totally demoralized.

We're stuck in this purgatory under the watchful eye of the Chinese government while a stream of people flows by us from Hong Kong into the mainland of China.

What the hell were we doing in China? The start of our fundraising had gone smoothly. We'd reached out to Peter and scheduled a meeting at his offices in the Presidio in San Francisco. Josh Piestrup, who had been let go from the hedge fund four years prior, asked us to retrieve *Baitless Hook* off the wall if it was still there. Walking past the Thiel Capital reception desk, I saw that it was. I'd get it on the way out. When we sat down to pitch Peter, I framed our effort as the best way to short the higher education bubble. He laughed.

"But is that pitch working with other investors?" he asked.

I said it was. And it was indeed—but only with our existing investors and a few new eccentrics. Danielle and I wanted to expand upon our mission, so we were attempting to raise more money. For our first fund, we raised $20 million. Now we were trying to raise $40 million. We wanted to find even more creative young people to back and support. But because the startups we invested in for our first fund were only three or four years old, our numbers weren't strong enough in the eyes of the typical venture capital investor. It takes time for startups to mature and then go public. Usually on the order of eight to ten years. So our rate of return was on the lower end but growing. Worse yet for us, the larger investors—the pension funds, the fund of funds, the sovereign wealth funds—none of them believed young people without degrees could innovate and lead companies. Most of them didn't even bother to take meetings with us.

Peter turned to Danielle. "Well, we know Michael hates discussing business. How much money do you need?" We sure thought we were on our way after that. We left Peter's office so excited that we forgot to snatch *Baitless Hook* off the wall for Josh.

Following that we had some early wins, but they weren't easy. Ari Emanuel, the famous Hollywood super-agent (on whom the character Ari Gold from HBO's *Entourage* is based), had heard about us from the author and investor George Gilder. George had invested in our first fund and wrote a chapter about us in his book *Life After Google*. Like his brother Rahm Emanuel, the former mayor of Chicago, Ari has a reputation for being blunt and brutal. He lived up to that reputation. Through his executive assistant, I was connected to him on a call.

"How much money do you want?" Ari asked. No hello, no chit-chat.

"$500,000."

"I'll talk to my investment manager." Click. He hung up.

Danielle and I didn't know what the next steps were. I didn't have Ari's phone number or email. There was no way to follow up. We only had his executive assistant's email. Three months passed during which we'd email Ari's assistant and she'd deflect us. "Ari's on a trip." "I haven't heard from Ari on that. Let me ask." Finally, we were at Peter's annual Christmas party and ran into a friend who had accepted an investment from Ari. He said he'd give us Ari's email but only on the condition that we absolutely never tell Ari how we got it. "Of course. We promise."

Danielle and I were discussing the best way to approach our email to Ari. How do you out-Ari Ari? So I took to the keyboard:

Ari,

You work with talent in entertainment, and we are the best scouts of young talent in technology. I think it could be a strong partnership. Plus, we'd make you money.

It's fuck or walk time—are you in or are you out?

Best,

Michael

Five minutes later, his investment manager replied saying Ari was in.

But soon the frustration of being rejected over and over again began to build. To add stress to that, we'd hired Nick Arnett and Zak Slayback to help us out, counting on the higher management fees to pay their salaries. They were strong additions to our team—plus neither of them had college degrees—but perhaps we had hired them too prematurely. Our budget was set for a $40 million fund. We had $25 million in commitments, but we couldn't seem to break that barrier to get to forty no matter whom we pitched. Danielle and I had to cut our own salaries in half so we could pay Nick and Zak. Nick was also moonlighting as a Lyft driver to pay his bills. We even took a pitch meeting with a university endowment—the enemy! This investment manager from Washington University in St. Louis got on the phone with us.

"Do you realize what you sent me in your pitch deck? On page two it says we're terrible at doing our jobs," he said.

"Yes, that's right," I told him. Our conversation quickly devolved into a twenty-minute argument about how universities are failing their students. On the side, I was texting Danielle, "You've got to jump in and save this conversation!" She did everything she could to change the subject and calm the guy down. It didn't work. No surprise, Washington University in St. Louis did not invest.

● ● ●

So we were in Hong Kong, trying to get into Shenzhen, rolling our fingerprints on glass for the surveillance state. It took us more than three hours to get into the city. It wasn't just Danielle's flat fingertips that held us back. I also brought the wrong bureaucratic paperwork from Hong Kong. I was carrying around a book on anarchist philosophy, too. "Did you really have to bring that to read today?" Danielle said. After sitting forever in the equivalent of a communist DMV to obtain a one-day visa, the system finally released us into the mainland. And then, as we exited the doors of officialdom, and walked out into the dim light of a drizzly morning, there stood China.

The differences between Hong Kong and Shenzhen were immediately striking. Everything in Shenzhen is brand spanking new. Hong Kong is wealthier, but older, more set in its ways, richer in its traditions. Nevertheless, beyond the differences, there was a family resemblance between the two as well, something faint and yet deeper, as grandparents might resemble their grandchildren. It was then that I realized we were walking through the most overlooked innovation of the century. It was an answer to Cardwell's Law.

The study of the rise and fall of nations is both understudied and mired in the apocalyptic.[2] Since Edward Gibbon wrote his 1776 masterpiece on the decline of Rome, hundreds of doom-vendors have followed with the same message: we are Rome, and the end is near. But while the fall of Rome is one case study, albeit an important one, there is a whole field of historical research with more instances that requires further investigation. There is currently no widely accepted general theory on the lifecycle of national innovation rates. The only thing scholars agree on is that there appears to be a biological pattern. We have a birth, an explosion of human ingenuity, a peak, a decline, and a death. Cardwell's Law encapsulates the phenomenon: no nation, city, or group remains creative for long. History shows that creative societies are rare, and their bursts of invention and discovery are almost always short-lived. Moreover, the distribution of creative genius is not even, neither across time, nor among nations, nor within nations. It tends to cluster. Its appearance is not random. Some countries are more innovative than others.[3] Why is all this so? Perhaps the biggest puzzle in the history of science and technology is the decline of China from its peak in 1400.[4] Just as the Renaissance began in Italy, China faded, despite having invented gunpowder, the printing press, and mighty ocean-going vessels for exploration. What are the factors that cause this degeneration?

Polybius, the ancient Greek historian, was perhaps the first to investigate the lifecycles of nations.[5] Writing in the second century BC, and building on the theoretical foundations of Plato and Aristotle, Polybius formulated a theory as to why Rome had risen so quickly and endured for so long. How had Rome extended its period of growth, where other empires and kingdoms failed? According to Polybius, it was because of the checks and balances in the mixed Roman constitution, which blended aspects of democracy with hierarchy. The dynamics of sclerosis and decline could be postponed, Polybius thought, if a state established competing institutions that could put a check on the slide into corruption and decadence, which only increased over time the more powerful and wealthy a nation became.

Polybius's ideas pretty much collected dust on the shelf until the 1780s, when James Madison blew the dust off the cover and incorporated them into the framing of the U.S. Constitution.[6] But while Madison was a genius, he saw checks and balances only as tools for preventing civil strife and for moderating factions. He did not see them as a way to protect and maintain the rate of innovation and progress. That was left for an economic historian named Joel Mokyr, who in the 1990s picked up the baton and investigated why China declined in 1400 while Europe rose to power. His answer is a set of stronger checks and balances than Polybius or Madison imagined.[7] In Renaissance Europe, no one controlled the entire continent. In China, the emperor did. When the emperor banned ocean exploration, it was banned everywhere. But Europe was fragmented into a maze of frontier enclaves, ethnic anomalies, duchies, kingdoms, and city-states. If innovation was banned in one place, an inventor could flee to a rival kingdom to develop it further, as Leonardo Da Vinci once moved from Italy to France, or as Benedict Spinoza moved from Spain to the Netherlands. The competition between all these European principalities meant reactionary societies lost out over time. No interest group within a single society could ever thwart progress on the continent as a whole. In China, the opposite was true. There was no getting around the state, and there was no competition. "If technological progress is ephemeral and rare, multiplying the number of societies in which the experiment is carried out and allowing some measure of competition among them improves the chances for continued progress," Mokyr writes in *The Lever of Riches*, his now-classic treatise on technological creativity and economic progress.[8] "As long as *some* societies remain creative," he concludes, "others will eventually be dragged along."

What most people don't understand about China today is that its rebirth and strength are due to Mokyr's insight. The biggest threat to U.S. dominance in science and technology isn't from China copying our intellectual property or from its grueling work ethic. No, the biggest threat is a truth we had once known but have chosen to forget—the dynamism of the American frontier. China is China today because it recreated something we lost.

In the late 1970s, the Chinese government had come to its senses after decades of immiserating its people (but, of course, they wouldn't frame it that way). First, Mao's Great Leap Forward had devastated the country—deaths from its resulting famine were in the tens of millions between 1958 and 1962.[9] The Cultural Revolution that followed ransacked and demolished the soul of what was left. Even more people were purged, displaced, or imprisoned. After Mao died in 1976 and the reformers took power, the mainland they ruled was in ruin. For anyone traveling out of China down the Pearl River Delta to Hong Kong, however, it was clear a different set of rules instituted by the British had produced a different outcome.

Hong Kong is a tiny spit of land. It's an archipelago of rocks, precipitous sea stacks, and barren islands sitting at the foot of a peninsula on the southeastern coast of China. The land has little to offer in the way of natural resources—80 percent of it is too mountainous and rocky to farm. There are no minerals to mine, no oil to drill. Just sand and rock. Nevertheless, in the span of just forty years or so, this tiny, hilly territory rose from being a small trading backwater to becoming an immense manufacturing and financial powerhouse, a futuristic city-state from whose harbors the wealth of nations ship.

The city is cleaved in two by a harbor full of junks with red-square sails, yachts, freighters, and ferries. On one side, the island side, sits Hong Kong city center; on the other, the peninsula Kowloon. On both sides, buildings cluster together, jam-packed. They rise in lush valleys, nooks, and on the angles of the green hillsides. It is one of the world's most expensive and densely populated cities. The median apartment—a 430-square-foot shoebox—costs nineteen times the median household income. In the darkness of night, the lights of the towering apartment blocks hang as though from the sky on Christmas light strings.

On our trip to pitch funds in Hong Kong, I quickly came to appreciate the grandeur and incalculable wealth of this unlikely place. Downtown Hong Kong is a labyrinth of footbridges and tunnels. The streets and alleyways bubble with frenetic ambition. We delivered one pitch at lunch amid sizzling woks, hot pots, tables covered with snails, tentacles, crustaceans, unknown sea creatures tangled in noodles, and wicker baskets full of steamed dumplings, after which we were then off to our next pitch meeting, dodging double-decker trams in the streets, weaving through pedestrians overflowing off the sidewalks, speed-walking through fifteen-story shopping malls chilled in a constant bath of cold air conditioning, until we at last arrived at a hedge fund perched on the twenty-seventh floor of a skyscraper with an oddly blurred, opaque view of the city. The sight held a mysterious beauty.

Where did this city come from? How did this garden of glass and concrete sprout from so barren a rock, such a tiny spit of land in such a short time? One might hope to track the traditional historical economic statistics, but none were collected for a long time. This is surprising, given the hallowed Chinese bureaucratic traditions—the elites of China have been competing in civil services exams for millennia. What's even more intriguing is that no one tallied anything because a shy, obstinate man didn't want them to.

John James Cowperthwaite was born in Scotland in 1915 but spent most of his life as the financial secretary in Hong Kong for the British government, laying the foundations for what became its economic miracle.[10] He is one of the 20th century's unsung heroes, on par with Norman Borlaug of the Green Revolution in agriculture. Having lifted tens of millions out of poverty, his ideas continue to ripple outward. And he is the only reason no official data on Hong Kong's economy was ever compiled from

1961 to 1971. Cowperthwaite batted away request after request. As he explained it to the economist Milton Friedman, he was convinced that "once the data was published there would be pressure to use them for government intervention in the economy."[11] Another time, once asked what the most important thing poor countries could do to develop their economy, Cowperthwaite quipped, "They should abolish the office of national statistics."[12] Sometimes, it seems, no data is better than big data.

Intervening in the economy was almost always a no-no under Cowperthwaite's watch. He called his economic philosophy "positive non-interventionism," which was essentially Adam Smith with a twist. The market would generate wealth—letting entrepreneurs and capital free to discover new goods and services—but public funds could be spent on housing and education, provided it was within the bounds of revenues collected on low taxes.[13] From the end of the Second World War to the mid-1970s, the government only required modest deficit spending twice. Every other year the government ran a surplus. It was the exact opposite of the Keynesian economic policies the United Kingdom pursued during the same time period, and it is the opposite of what the U.S. pursues now. The results were astonishing. When Cowperthwaite arrived in Hong Kong in 1945, the average income per resident was 30 percent less than that of the average in Britain, its colonial ruler. In 2018, it was Britain that was the poorer by a wide margin; income per capita was 40 percent greater in Hong Kong.

When Lee Kuan Yew came to power in Singapore in the 1960s, he took the Hong Kong–Cowperthwaite playbook and put it in play with some local adaptations and deviations.[14] Then Singapore took off. Now we have *Crazy Rich Asians*.

So when Deng Xiaoping and the other reformers came to power in China after Mao's death in 1976, they decided to try an experiment in economic development.[15] They'd been to Hong Kong and to Singapore and had seen those cities grow to dazzling heights out of bare rock in a single generation. If Cowperthwaite's ideas were that powerful, then they should work on the mainland, too. As Lee Kuan Yew told Deng over dinner in 1978, "We, Singapore Chinese, were the descendants of illiterate, landless peasants from Guangdong and Fujian in South China, whereas the scholars, Mandarins, and literati had stayed and left their progeny in China. There was nothing that Singapore had done which China could not do and do better."[16]

The Hong Kong and Singapore experiments settled it. The reformers decided to "appropriate capitalism for the good of socialism," as the National People's Congress put it in their legislation. Deng called it "socialism with Chinese characteristics." To test and understand how free-market policies worked, the reformers chose a village on the mainland to rezone under new rules—light on regulation, light on taxes. It would be a confined laboratory to protect the rest of China. They called it a "special economic zone," but they might as well have called it a Cowperthwaite zone. That village was Shenzhen.

• • •

Danielle and I are eating hot pot in Shenzhen with the two associates of a fund we pitched a few hours before. The table is covered with sliced beef, lettuce, mushrooms, lotus root, white carrots, and pepper sauce. This restaurant is inside a new mall that is part of a new plaza that is on the edge of a new outer ring of this new city. Newness is everywhere. The one thing we kept hearing from everyone we met in Shenzhen is that if you leave for as little as three months and come back, the city will look different, rapidly stretching upward and outward.

"What do young people do for fun on the weekends here?"
I ask one of the associates.

He pauses, holding his chopsticks in the air over his bowl,
then laughs. "What's a weekend?"

Shenzhen has grown rapidly in the Cowperthwaite style.
From its beginning, when it was designated a special economic
zone in 1980, the population has rocketed from just 30,000 people
to nearly 13 million today, as laborers, merchants, entrepreneurs,
and others have poured in. During one stretch, its economy grew
at the fantastic speed of 40 percent per year (remember that the
U.S. is lucky to eke out 3 percent). GDP per capita increased
from subsistence levels in 1980 to over $26,000 in 2016.

It is not uncommon to meet people working twelve-to-
fourteen-hour days in Shenzhen. They call it the "996"—wake
up at 9 a.m. and work until 9 p.m., six days a week. The associates we talked to said they all worked so hard because social
mobility was real in China. He said they all felt like they were
only one generation away from living in destitution, and they
weren't going back.

"The U.S. competitive edge over China may not be long,"
Kai-Fu Lee said in the *New York Times* around this time.[17] Lee
is chief executive of Sinovation Ventures, a Beijing VC fund. He
is also the author of a best-selling book, *AI Superpowers: China,
Silicon Valley, and the New World Order*.[18] Lee was merely the
first to express out loud what most were beginning to feel in
private. Michael Moritz from Sequoia also wrote an op-ed in
the *Financial Times* where he chastised American decadence.
"The work ethic in Chinese tech companies far outpaces their
U.S. rivals," he declared.[19] Another investor added, "To some
degree, it's like looking into the future."

Lee predicts China will take the lead in artificial intelligence research through the use of deep learning software

on an enormous scale. His theory is that data will become a kind of natural resource in the future, and China will have the most. If data is the new oil, then China is the "Saudi Arabia of data," he surmises.[20] Because China has fewer concerns about privacy, and because of the centralizing tendencies of its government, and its monopoly on platforms like WeChat, Chinese companies using deep learning will have more data sets to train their algorithms on. That will translate into greater accuracy, faster deployment, stronger predictions, and more. American companies will fall behind as they struggle to train algorithms at the same scale.

For all that, I say this is overblown. Western companies developing deep learning programs have tons of data to train on. There is no shortage. Take the entire Internet, for one. The only advantage China has in drawing inferences from data is in using its computers for social control. And in my book, that is no advantage.

No, the more impressive know-how China is perfecting is the ability to build experimental cities. With its program for special economic zones, it has prolonged the existence of a frontier. After the success of Shenzhen, it created six more zones. Taken together, this could be the most successful anti-poverty program in human history, as hundreds of millions of the poor have been lifted out of poverty in a mere twenty to thirty years. And this gets down to the problem that dawned on me as we traveled from Hong Kong to Shenzhen. The dynamism of the frontier is a truth America once knew but has now forgotten. California was so innovative a place in the 20th century, not because of the weather or because of some special policy, but because it was basically a fresh special economic zone where vested interests could not block experimentation. There was no political opposition to scientific and technological progress. In the early 1900s, for example, filmmakers left New York for Hollywood because the land was cheap, there were no labor unions, and they could evade Thomas Edison's aggressive patent enforcement. Silicon Valley could tell a similar story.[21]

But now the American frontier has closed. California has lived through Polybius's lifecycle of growth into sclerosis. And because the West has given up on innovating in governance, in experimenting with new rules in new cities, the end of history is looking less like liberal democracy and more like Chinese authoritarian dynamism.

Back in 2013 Larry Page, then CEO of Google, took to the stage at the annual Google I/O conference and offered a vision for a new social philosophy, a way to reopen the frontier. Page wondered aloud if old laws and rusty institutions were slowing down the rate of technological progress. His argument was that we were missing discoveries because we couldn't run small-scale experiments with wild technologies like flying cars and drones. "There are many, many exciting and important things you could do that you just can't do because they're illegal or they're not allowed by regulation," he said.[22]

His solution wasn't to propose a change to the laws of San Francisco or Mountain View. That was impossible. Instead, Page proposed something far more radical. He suggested building a new experimental city somewhere in America that would operate by a different set of rules and regulations from the rest of the United States. It would be a laboratory to run experiments. If only we could "set aside a small part of the world," he said, in which "a few people can try out different things and not everybody has to go."

Now, after social media has driven people mad, after big tech has censored conservative dissent, and after Theranos defrauded investors, the spirit of the age is calling for tighter regulation of tech, not less. Remembering this experimental city speech by Page, a technology correspondent for the *Financial Times* concluded, "It is hard to imagine any tech executive voicing such an idea today."[23]

Too bad. An America without a frontier will not remain innovative for long. Cardwell's Law ensures it. As far back as 1627 Francis Bacon published a utopian novel, *New Atlantis*, which envisioned an island city-state distinguished by its zeal for experiment and discovery. But Bacon's spirit has long been dead in the West. Opposition to scientific progress is too strong. The dogma of the Paper Belt has covered the entire North American continent with a stifling set of uniform rules. The new city of the future may well rise elsewhere. In Silicon Valley, the backlash against tech had driven the dreamers of new cities into anonymity. Meanwhile, in 2017 China announced it was breaking ground on a new city and special economic zone that will be three times the size of New York City. China has perfected the Cowperthwaite playbook—while most in the West don't even know who Cowperthwaite is.

It's not easy to get into China as an outsider. It is difficult to get out, even for capital. "We want to participate in your fund," Danielle and I were told, after a positive meeting with Shenzhen investors. "But we need to raise money in Hong Kong to do it, which is unlikely any time soon." China's policy of strong capital controls keeps investment behind the Great Fire Wall.

We took the high-speed rail back to Hong Kong. It took only fifteen minutes at a speed of nearly 200 kilometers per hour. The train had only been in operation for two weeks. Google maps didn't even know it existed when we searched for routes earlier that morning. But that's China. Building, faster, churning, new.

The irrefutable failure of communism led China to embrace

capitalism, though Xi Jinping seems to be having second thoughts. Hong Kong ceased to exist in 2020. The experiment of "One country, two systems" is over. At the same time, the irrefutable success of capitalism—as predicted by Polybius and Mokyr—has led the United States to decadence and failed institutions that become less reliable and trustworthy every year. Political resistance to progress is gaining ground. Like imperial China in 1400, and unlike Renaissance Italy, there will be nowhere for innovators and their ideas to flee to. From this perspective, it's hard to tell where innovation will flourish most, if at all.

• • •

Back in America, we left behind the colossal and unimaginable forces of politics and globalization, and focused on the task before us. Stubborn as ants, Danielle and I continued on our fundraising in frustration. That frustration broke through in one last meeting. For six months we had been courting a family office from Greenwich, Connecticut. Its investment manager, Claire, is a scorching hot former French model with bewitching eyes, a pouty mouth, and long giraffe legs. Always dressed in haute couture, she has a classy, European patrician bearing. We'd met with Claire three times, twice in New York City and once in Greenwich. It was time for her to make a decision. Danielle and I gave her a call.

"Claire, we need to know if you're going to invest."

"I'm sorry guys, we're going to have to pass. Your portfolio of companies is strong, but it's all unrealized gains at this point. That doesn't mean anything until it's real. It could all go to zero and where would you be then? Come back to us when you have an IPO."

That did it for me.

"Claire, here's what I'm going to do when we have an IPO.

I'm going to cut the story out of the *Wall Street Journal* and I'm going to send it to you. And then you're going to ask me for a meeting. And I'm going to take it. Then I'm going to tell you we don't need your money."

"My, my," she said. "You *are* bold."

Danielle's eyes were lit up like searchlights and she started making the knife across the throat gesture with her hand to tell me to knock it off. Claire did not invest. In the end, we closed our second fund out at $25 million, and we held a party to celebrate at the Mission Control hacker house in the Mission District in San Francisco. When we first started the fund, we never would have guessed that the end of the most innovative city in the world was only months away.

·14·

UNREAL CITY

Hardly anyone I know can resist the enchantment of the setting. San Francisco seen from the Golden Gate Bridge is the city seen in the shimmering promise of all that the future might hold. Coming down the highway from Sonoma, shooting out of the Robin Williams Tunnel in Sausalito, there is a glittering three-second moment, a snapshot of the most astonishing view of a city anywhere. A vaporous city in the sea-light, standing as the background to a fairy tale or an epic work of science fiction. The grand panorama of San Francisco's harbor is heart-wrenchingly beautiful. The Golden Gate Bridge stands so slim and serene above a fierce and cold current below. A thought crosses your mind. Just think of the tens of millions, from all over the world, who yearn to be in that city. Talent summoned from every nation, every continent. There it is, the Athens, the Florence, the Paris of the 21st century, the city of ambition, where the future would be built...and yet...by 2019 the party was over. Paper Belt dogma destroyed it. This once great city had survived earthquakes and fires, but it could not survive itself.

The philosopher Isaiah Berlin, paraphrasing the German poet Heinrich Heine, once observed that "philosophical concepts nurtured in the stillness of a professor's study could destroy a civilization."[1] San Francisco, the cradle of American ingenuity, would become a case in point. Admittedly, cities are nearly immortal; though they decline, they rarely die. Rome is still with us. It survived the fall of a civilization and a world war. San Francisco will still be with us. But creative clusters are fragile, fleeting things. Silicon Valley, what everyone thought was a vast and unrelenting machine of innovation, is dead. Since I witnessed it firsthand, I am here to write its obituary.

Magnificent in the distance, by the end of the decade San Francisco had become hideous up close. In the time I lived there, the city managed to achieve the seemingly impossible: It combined the expensive and the bland and the morally appalling into a new form of decadence. To the tourist's eye from a great distance, it might look magical: a city of the future, a city of gasps. Then, slowly, as you drove off the Golden Gate Bridge and into the Marina District, it would reveal itself as the city of lies. San Francisco's fatal flaw was always this illusion. The chasm between the promise and reality. A great city—generous, glittering, full of warmth and splendor, flush with wealth in a boom—but one also full of desolate boulevards. Each day the city seemed to take another step towards Hell. The streets had become a sad hospital for cracked misfits, indescribable squalor, wreckage, and exhaustion. Never has misery been so costly. Never has luxury been so tedious.

Up and down the city's disorienting hills, I began to notice more and more homeless men and women—junkies, winos, the dispossessed—passed out in the vestibules of empty storefronts on otherwise busy streets. Encampments of tents sprouted like mushrooms in every shadowy corner: under highway overpasses, down alleyways. Streets were increasingly peppered with used syringes. Strolling the sidewalks, you could smell the faint malodorous traces of human excrement and soiled clothing. Crowded thoroughfares such as Market Street, even in the light of midday, became a carnival of indecipherable outbursts and drug-induced thrashings about which the police would do nothing. The confused mumble, the incoherent finger-pointing tirade, the twitch, the cold daemonic stare, the drunken stumble and drool—these were the rhythms of a city on the edge of a schizophrenic explosion.

I would often walk from meeting to meeting to refresh after sitting at a table for an hour. On one nightmare of a stroll, I walked through the city's center of power, from City Hall through Civic Center Plaza to the Tenderloin, the city's most distressing neighborhood. At noon on a sunny Saturday, under the sculpture of Lady Justice on City Hall's facade, men were walking around like specters with soiled blankets draped over their heads. Others were keeled over in pain or intoxicated by numbness—I couldn't quite tell which extreme. I saw a cluster of people bringing a drug to a boil in an improvised tin foil bowl, while others stuck needles in their hands, in their thighs, and in the space between their toes. Women walked about shirtless, with loose and dangling breasts out in the open. I was saddened by the vacant stare of a man on a stairwell wiping himself with the pages of a magazine, as an elderly woman paused to plan a path around him. I then came upon a giant fenced-in tent encampment on Fulton Street, which I later learned the city was paying more than $61,000 per tent per year to maintain.[2] Like a clock that doesn't strike, Lady Justice was silent.

Over the decade, the city banned plastic straws, plastic bags, and McDonald's happy meals with toys. And yet, all the while, I more frequently came upon lawless scenes like I just described. San Francisco came to rank number one in the country in theft, burglary, vandalism, shoplifting, and anything else categorized under "property crime."[3] There were on average about sixty cars broken into per day. Shattered glass left on the street was the tell-tale sign of what happened overnight. Robbers could pillage cars and homes with the ease of Visigoth raiders, while the district attorney—a Rhodes Scholar—decided to unleash the floodgates, freeing repeat offenders who went on time and again to sow disorder, pain, devastation, and grief. Diseases arising from poor sanitation—typhoid, typhus, hepatitis A—were spreading at an increasing rate. Fentanyl was going for $20 a pill. The city department of public works deployed a battalion of feces cleaners every day—a "poop patrol"—to wash the malodorous filth from the sidewalks. Like apparitions out of no man's land in a chemical war, these platoons would appear on the streets in gas masks and fluorescent hazmat suits, with high-powered water hoses to wash away the city's excrement.

How did it come to this? The left wanted to blame unchecked capitalism. But San Francisco has been overwhelmingly Democratic since the early 1960s. The last Republican mayor won an election in 1956 and left office in 1964. It is undeniably a one-party city touting a civic philosophy now with its back to the wall. For decades, city Democrats paid lip service to helping the poor. But up close the facts were telling a different story. None of their policies in the last half-century did much to rescue the poor from poverty. They enacted just about any law they wanted, and the government was rolling in it. If the Bay Area were its own country, it would rank among the twenty largest economies in the world, producing $748 billion in goods and services in 2017—more than both Switzerland and Sweden.[4] With all that wealth creation, the state and city coffers swelled with tax revenues. California collected nearly $171.96 billion in taxes in 2020, up more than 50 percent from 2010 due to the success of tech companies and other mainstay industries.[5] In 2020, San

Francisco's budget skyrocketed up to $13.7 billion. That's more than double the $6.4 billion budget from a decade earlier.[6] The city spent $852 million on homelessness in 2020; with about eight thousand homeless people in the city, that works out to $106,500 per person.[7]

Nevertheless, politicians and media commentators would unanimously blame high-income employees at Google, Facebook, Uber, and other tech companies for the city's woes and expensive housing. The bitterness and resentment expressed in hatred for these employees, despite the taxes they paid, was really quite something. Here are some terms that appeared in op-eds and essays I collected over the years: "Tech bros," "Stanford douchebags with stock options," "technological privilege," "the equivalent of the Prussian Army invading Paris," "tech supremacists." The writer-activist Rebecca Solnit called it "the siege of San Francisco."[8] But how could it be their fault? Where does Solnit think the money to pay for the city's generous social programs comes from? If you want the honey, you can't kill the bees.

Meanwhile, our moralists in the media busily tsk-tsked Silicon Valley's greed and lust and hypocrisy and hubris, but they somehow missed the scoop of the decade right before their eyes: the death of a once-great city. Instead of covering that catastrophe, *Bloomberg*'s Emily Chang erroneously reported on drug-fueled sex parties that turned out not to have happened at all.[9] The *New York Times*'s Nellie Bowles ran story after story on fake trends that portrayed tech workers as childish and quirky. First, it was the "raw water" craze. Next, it was strained thumbs from too much texting.[10]

Though the media never reported it, the cause of San Francisco's blight is codified nostalgia and greed. The dynamics underpinning Cardwell's Law—the accumulation of bureaucratic gunk and sideshow cons—turned San Francisco's impressive gifts into disasters. Baby Boomer civil servants tried their best to act as urban taxidermists, stuffing and mounting a dead city so it would always resemble the past. Its bureaucracy was and is vampiric and vast. It is sustained by the life and energy drained from endless memoranda, applications in triplicate, committee comments, addenda, the minutes from the meeting, and the recorded votes. It is the height of Paper Belt stultification. They are there to ensure no one does anything fresh, new, or interesting.

Over the years the *San Francisco Chronicle* told us that there was indeed a city mayor, and maybe even a chief of police, but it was never clear who was actually in charge. Zoning committees and planning commissions obscured responsibility. And why not have it that way? What better way to thwart progress than by having faceless city functionaries administer labyrinthine regulations that benefit the rich over the poor, the old over the young, the here over those to come, the past over the future? It made it impossible to hold anyone accountable. Paper Belt progressivism claimed to protect the worst off from abuses of power and the advantages of insiders. Instead, it only strengthened them.

To take the most egregious example, San Francisco virtually banned new housing. It forbids multi-dimensional units, caps the number of small shoebox units to a few hundred, and has outlawed building anything taller than 40 feet across 80 percent of the city, which is why what few towering skyscrapers there are sit in a tiny grove near the base of the Bay Bridge. There was no end to the stupidity and triviality called for to preserve the character of a neighborhood and enrich its current inhabitants. Unsurprisingly, the upshot was the highest rent and housing prices in the country. Due to this politically constrained supply and stoked demand, the median price for a one-bedroom rental became the most expensive in the nation at $3700 per month. To buy a single-family home—a starter home—a family needed $1.5 million on average, and they'd better be a cash buyer. The cost to construct a single new apartment unit rose to over $700,000, nearly triple what it cost a decade earlier.

Rather than address the problem, however, the mayor, board of supervisors, planning commission, land use commission, and a myriad of has-been community groups constructed an obstacle course that even the most energetic minds could not fathom. The whole permit process is fraught with trap doors every step of the way, resulting in the highest-stakes game of Chutes and Ladders known to man. A shudder, a sense of fated financial ruin, would pass across the face of any developer as he is called yet again to a hearing before the planning commission. Just about anyone anywhere has the standing to protest and cause delays. If just one constituent worried over a cast shadow or the historical preservation of a laundromat, then—crack!—the trapdoor would open and our builder would fall back down all the way to square one in the process. Meanwhile, real estate developers have lost years and have spent millions for nada, zip.

Here are a few by no means extraordinary stories from the decade: It took one man forty-one years—he started the process in 1978—and over $2 million to get approval from the planning commission to build four duplexes in the Bernal Heights neighborhood.[11] One real-estate developer worked for five years and paid hundreds of thousands of dollars to show that a proposed housing development wouldn't cast shadows on a nearby playground or destroy the historic character of a laundromat.[12] In another sad story, it took two years for a woman to open an ice cream shop.[13]

Even for the government itself, it is nearly impossible to

build anything in San Francisco. Infrastructure projects balloon indefinitely. In 2001, the city proposed a new bus lane on Van Ness, one of the city's main arteries. The new lane's opening has been delayed until 2022 and Van Ness remains a mess of potholes, equipment, and orange detour signs. The project will cost $310 million, which comes to $100,000 per meter.[14] It wasn't always this way. The U.S. built a highway in Alaska in 1942. 1,700 miles of roadway were built over frozen tundra in only 234 days.[15] That cost $793 per meter in 2019 dollars. The Van Ness lane for a bus will have taken more than two decades to complete. How is this possible? The Golden Gate Bridge, still a marvel of engineering, was built in three-and-a-half years in the 1930s. To commemorate its completion, as an encore, the city built an artificial island, Treasure Island, in the middle of San Francisco Bay. That took under three years to finish. What happened to the skills and sensibilities that built the Golden Gate?

It is quite simply baffling. Housing restrictions made the situation worse and worse for decades. And yet, no one seemed to notice that the same debates played out time and again to no positive end. Instead, for commentary, reporters invariably trotted out someone who disguised greed with the piety of a San Franciscan born and raised. Ah, those picturesque locals! Those blissed-out hippies now full of sneer and grumble! Whatever sad story they tell, the plain fact was they shamelessly aimed to limit the housing supply, inflating the prices of their own properties. Meanwhile, the media printed their moralistic scolding of the gentrifiers, that is to say, anyone with an urge to build affordable housing. No one in the media or in city hall seemed to care about what went unseen: the people who never got to live in San Francisco because the apartments they would live in were never built, the bookstores never opened, the dance steps never tried, the poetry never recited because the rent's too damn high.

The progressive Left accused landlords of immorality and greed, even racism, but it was the inflexible limits on the housing supply that pushed marginalized groups even further to the margins. The stratospheric cost of housing forced poor families to the outer edges of the Bay Area, reinforcing segregation. A UC Berkeley study found that a 30 percent increase in the median rent led to a 28 percent decrease in the number of minority households in a neighborhood.[16] Whole neighborhoods from the city decamped to the hinterlands of Antioch and Vallejo. Stories of three-hour commutes from Stockton became common.

Painters, writers, mystics, and philosophers all fled the city. Today, the only poetry in North Beach can be found in a shabby museum to the Beats that looks like a rotting convenience store in a bus station. The San Francisco music scene disappeared. The Victorian townhouse the Grateful Dead lived in at 710 Ashbury Street during their formative years in the 1960s is now surrounded by properties that sell for $3 million and more.

The truth is, you can't build a successful startup from a garage, or start a band, if the garage costs three million bucks. The flow of new creations in the city was choked off because there were fewer and fewer cheap places for new things to start. The famous urbanist Jane Jacobs once remarked that new ideas come from old buildings, the types of places you can alter without permission because no one cares about them. Artists in an industrial loft, startups in a warehouse—the true creative class can't afford to rent expensive new studios or $3,700 per month one-bedrooms.

But perhaps the crowning achievement for Paper Belt progressive policy was to cut the power and literally send the Bay Area back to the dark ages. The monopoly utility, PG&E, began rolling blackouts in 2018 to prevent sparks in dry and windy weather. Many of the company's electric lines have components that go back to the 1950s; some even from the early 1920s. This rickety infrastructure has sparked 1,550 fires since 2014—all man-made.[17] The state's failure to build reliable sources of power—such as nuclear—and its negligence that left the power grid brittle and dangerous are Exhibits A and B in any argument about technological stagnation in California. To add to that, the ban on new housing in San Francisco forced the city to sprawl its way into the dry forests and probe farther into California's hot Central Valley. The 2018 Camp Fire, the deadliest in California's history, was caused by a broken hook on a tower. That hook had been bought for 22 cents in 1919.[18] *1919!* When it finally snapped, the resulting fire killed eighty-five people and torched 150,000 acres. A year later, near Sonoma and Napa, precious grape vineyards burned among 190,000 acres, and twenty-two people were killed. The smoke from these fires drifted over San Francisco and choked its residents for weeks. For the duration, San Francisco became one of the most polluted cities in the world. People now stock up on air filters and masks every October for a season of ash in the skies.

This city, the very Babylon of Capitalism, could spend a billion dollars and not even bat an eye to build an eighth wonder of the world, a colossus to human ingenuity, a tower reaching halfway to the stars, to honor the frenzied dynamism of Silicon Valley which has blessed its people for seventy years. Instead, there are orange polluted skies, pot-holed streets, and grubby, run-down, worn-out neighborhoods. The city's former values have all been turned on their head. Tolerance has become hate. Self-expression, nothing more than groupthink. Today, post-Covid, a profound melancholy fills in the air of the city, punctuated only by the shrieks of a junky dreaming of demons or the rat-tat-tat-bam of the occasional firework. (Or was that a gun?) Used needles, human excrement, For Sale signs everywhere— these are the relics of discredited values. Housing prices are finally coming down, but for the wrong reason. San Francisco established anarcho-tyranny. Everything was allowed, but nothing was permitted.

The first indicator for the fall for me was that Danielle and I noticed fewer and fewer young people coming to the Bay to start companies. Instead, they choose to stay in Austin, Boston, or Chicago. When we started 1517, maybe two out of every three investments were based in San Francisco or in Silicon Valley. By 2018, that was less than 50 percent. Now it is barely any. In 2018 Peter left. The old office in the Presidio closed its doors. Then Luminar relocated to Orlando. By the end of 2019, I decamped to Los Angeles.

The final blow was when Covid hit. It accelerated the city's nosedive. Tesla and Oracle left for Texas. The reservoir of talent drained out. Subcultures withered and died. The source and the fulcrum of Silicon Valley's magic have always been the people. Now they were gone. Some fled for rural California, but many left the state altogether. For the first time in the state's history, going back to 1850, its population shrank in 2020. Even for the big tech companies that still call the Bay home, many have seen their workforce flee, thanks to the flexibility of remote work. Stripe and other companies shifted most of their hiring to outside the Bay Area after 2020. By the end of 2021, 74 percent of Stripe's new hires were elsewhere.

I am calling it. Silicon Valley is dead. As the crow flies, the headquarters of Apple is five blocks down the road from the front door of the high school Steve Jobs attended as a teenager. Apple's donut-shaped headquarters is home to a company that today is worth nearly $3 trillion, arguably the most successful

American company in any industry of all time. It all started in a garage at 2066 Crist Drive, which Google Maps can tell you is an eight-minute drive away from CEO Tim Cook's office. A story like this will not happen again in this place. Silicon Valley—its ethos, its creative fires, its ideas—lives on only in the surviving four or five mega-corporations that have come to dominate the headlines and the stock market. All the rest of it—the garages, the coffee shop pitches, the change-the-world missionary zeal—is gone.

As a new decade opens, other American cities began to follow the San Francisco playbook. What city will Paper Belt dogma destroy next? Seattle? New York? Philadelphia? Chicago? All of them continue to commit to outcomes no one can understand through a set of processes all know to be corrupt. Nevertheless, year after year the Paper Belt elite, educated at America's finest institutions, run on and reach their arms out, their hopes always receding before them. No matter! Tomorrow more cities will pass even more restrictions, forbid even more housing developments, defund the police further... until one fine morning...

The night before I moved, I walked down to Crissy Field, through the Palace of Fine Arts, past the sculptures looking down into their boxes, past Peter's old house, where we started the fellowship that morning in 2010, and then on down to the beach, to say goodbye to the astonishing view. A celestial seaport had been silenced. I had a wistful moment staring at the flashing lights from the fishing boats passing beneath the Golden Gate Bridge in the dark of night, the air aromatic with eucalyptus and crisp with a brisk ocean breeze. It is sad to leave a place that you love. Sadder still if you suspect that it will never quite be the same again.

· 15 ·

BISHOP AND KNIGHT
VERSUS BISHOP ENDGAME

It's 8 a.m. on Tuesday, December 3, 2020, and Times Square is empty. I'm standing across the street from Nasdaq's headquarters on Forty-third Street in New York City, and it's so cold that I keep switching from hand to hand the warm coffee I just bought from Starbucks. Plumes of white steam, like geysers from a subterranean hot spring, rise out from grates on the sidewalk or out from the tops of orange tubes attached to manholes on the street. Covid has stilled the city's usual exhilarating rhythms at this hour. There are no commuters anywhere. No tourists. I seem to be the only person here. But the big bright electric signs are all still on, turning the atmosphere radium blue, flashing ads in every color known to man. The contrast gives the scene a touch of the eerie, as though in some post-apocalyptic movie where humanity has been wiped out, but the world carries on.

I'm here because Luminar is going public at 9:30 a.m. when the opening bell rings and markets open. Austin called me three days ago to invite me to join him and his team to ring the bell on their first day as a publicly traded company. It had been

Saturday of Thanksgiving weekend. He said, "Can you make it to San Jose by 4 p.m. tomorrow? We've chartered a jet to fly to New York from there." Then he let out one of his big surfer laughs. Huh, huh, ha ha ha!

I was in Venice Beach when he called. And it just so happened that I had a breakfast scheduled with Peter Thiel the next morning at his home in the Hollywood Hills. I checked the schedules. I could race to LAX immediately after breakfast with Peter, make a flight to SFO, and then catch a ride down to San Jose in time to make the jet. Danielle was in North Dakota deep in the sticks with her boyfriend visiting his family for the holiday. She couldn't find a way to get to New York in time. But I had to go. We had to celebrate this victory.

"Hell yes, I'm in!"

But when we got to New York, the realities of Covid made the plan more difficult. There were travel requirements that included quarantining at our hotel, The Soho Grand, and receiving a negative result on a Covid test, if we were lucky enough to find one, the day before the opening bell. I had managed to do all of that, but last night after dinner, Austin's chief of staff pulled me aside to say Nasdaq wasn't going to let me into the ceremony. They had to limit the number of people to ten, which meant I was out. It was only going to be Austin and a few executives from the company. So this morning I woke up, totally bummed out, and walked the forty blocks or so from Tribeca up to Times Square. I still wanted to see the moment Nasdaq announced Luminar's debut on their 120-foot sign outside of the building. Standing outside in Times Square, I blow on my hand to keep it warm. There's another hour to go. I pop the collar on my professorial brown corduroy blazer to shield my neck from the air. The last forty-eight hours have been a whirlwind. I take a look at the front doors of the building. With all the restrictions in place, Nasdaq might as well be an impenetrable fortress.

• • •

The day PayPal went public in February of 2002, one of the PayPal crew decided to set up a public chess challenge for Peter in the parking lot of the company's office. Ten chessboards were lined up for ten opponents at once. It was a geeky way to celebrate an IPO for sure, but Peter never backs down from a public challenge like this, particularly in chess.

A crowd formed outside to watch. Practically the entire company. There was a buzz in the air. Many people had already popped the champagne open earlier in the day after the bell rang to open the markets. Others were tipsy from celebratory keg stands. It was a $20 ante to get the chance to try to beat Peter in front of all the other PayPal employees. Ten brave souls—or suckers—stepped forward out from the crowd, many of the PayPal mafia among them. Everyone cheered.

Then the games began. The crowd crunched in for a closer view of the action. All ten of his opponents were sitting while Peter would walk down the row of players, making moves at each chessboard one by one, often after only a glance at the board, with scarcely even a moment's thought. Meanwhile, his opponents each had time to think through their next move, because Peter would have to orbit, working his way through the other nine players down the line before returning for his next turn. Despite this, it was not long before the first player was eliminated. Then another, and another. Extra time to think didn't matter against Peter.

Almost before anyone knew it, most of the players had been eliminated. But then an extraordinary thing happened. Peter was at David Sacks's chessboard. Sacks is one of Peter's oldest friends and has since gone on to become a wildly successful entrepreneur and investor himself. Peter took a snapshot assessment of the pieces, made his move at Sacks's chessboard, and then walked on to the next board. But then Sacks noticed something. "Wait!" he said. Suddenly the whole crowd was silent.

Peter stopped, turned on his heels to look back to the table, and frowned. Sacks had his hands up in the air in a stop-the-press moment. "I...yes. Yes!" He moved his piece tentatively. "Checkmate!" Peter stared at the board for a moment, still frowning, pondering Sacks's unwelcome assertion. "Checkmate! Checkmate!" Sacks was yelling, now more sure of himself, but still surprised. He grabbed both of the $20 bills on the chessboard—his and Peter's—one in each fist and then stood up in triumph, while the whole company cheered.

People said Peter looked a little amused at the situation, perhaps even a little happy for Sacks, but also stubborn and suspicious like he was pretty sure Sacks had just violated some fundamental law of the universe and he wasn't sure how.[1]

• • •

I was thinking about the Sacks chess story the morning I drove up the driveway to Peter's house in Los Angeles for breakfast. That was a hell of a way to celebrate an IPO. It also reminded me of this time Peter asked me about all the negative press that was being written about him.

I said, "You know, it's interesting. They never want to debate an issue with you. Instead, they always portray you as this chess mastermind, operating from the shadows, thinking six moves ahead."

Peter laughed. "But I am!"

• • •

As usual, Peter's chef sat me down at the dining room table. A few moments later, Peter came downstairs, poked his head into the kitchen door to say we were ready, and then he sat down at the head of the table. I was not surprised to see him in a ringer t-shirt and workout shorts.

"Where are you living now?" he asked.

"Venice Beach."

"Ah, little San Francisco."

"Funny. Yeah, a bit. But I'm moving to Colorado."

"Well, I've enjoyed reading your documentation of San Francisco's decline. Unlike me, you never got a message from the city. But they were kind enough to come to my front door to tell me to leave before it collapsed."

I can't help but laugh. Peter was referring to a protest that occurred once out on his front stoop in San Francisco. It was led by a few city hall bigwigs and popular activists. One protestor held a sign that said, "Peter Thiel is a vampire." Sonja Trauss, one of the organizers, held a sign that read, "Nazi Sympathies."[2] It was this level of idiocy that led Peter to leave San Francisco for the Hollywood Hills.

But we weren't going to discuss San Francisco, chess, or even Luminar's IPO. No, as usual, we were going to discuss God, Dostoevsky, communism, and the Antichrist. It was before 9 a.m. and I'd only had one cup of coffee. I needed that second cup fast.

"I'm thinking about teaching a class on the Antichrist," Peter began. Most people—especially the entire Paper Belt machinery—miss how devout Peter is. They all assume he is an unfeeling techno-Vulcan. And yet one of his main theories about the world is about how little people trust their own feelings. It is true, in public comments, he emphasizes how people should think for themselves. That sounds like the brain. But the theory of mimetic desire, which Peter espouses, isn't about thinking. It's about what we feel and why we feel it. We tend to want what other people want because we don't trust our own feelings.[3]

The first time I met Peter, when I interviewed for a job, we talked about the threat of a single world government. I had always understood the danger in terms of Cardwell's Law and stagnation. Progress has enemies. Within any country, political resistance to progress grows stronger over time as more interest groups form to protect the status quo. What was once a fervent, dynamic economy ossifies into a rusting collection of former winners wielding political power to protect their stagnant empires. At that point, the Orwellian paradoxes in a nation begin to pile up: scientists opposed to science, teachers against learning, academics silencing speech, publishers censoring knowledge. This is the road we are on today. But competition among different nations can at least weaken the influence of any factional interest group within a nation. Provided that there are many competing sovereignties, there will be enough political support to turn institutions toward increasing the rate of progress, instead of letting them get captured for political ends. Countries must face penalties for not innovating.[4] But were a single world government to emerge, then progress would grind to a halt. There would be no safety valve, nowhere to flee to, nowhere to innovate. The same dynamic that captures any one country would seize the entire world.

But today, ten years after our first conversation, Peter was wrestling with this problem from a theological direction and with a greater concern for existential risk. The most dangerous political development to avoid is a single world government. If such a thing were to emerge, it would, of course, begin peacefully and democratically through treaties and international communities. The attendees of the World Economic Forum in Davos tend to be nice and polite. But once a democratic world government came into being—as Polybius would predict—there is a small but non-negligible probability it would degenerate into a totalitarian OneState.[5] Since the main check on any totalitarian government in the past has been the existence of many other non-totalitarian governments, the transformation, in this case, would be irreversible. There would be no refuge for freedom. Dissent would be impossible.

Regulators often use the precautionary principle to justify extreme safeguards against innovations, because the consequences in a worst-case scenario, however unlikely, are too catastrophic. Best to take the worst-case scenario off the table, even if that limits the higher positive outcomes as well. Just think, for example, of the risk aversion many regulators hold against genetically modified food. But the same precautionary principle would demand even stronger regulations against a single world government. In the 20th century, totalitarian governments killed more than 100 million people.[6] A totalitarian OneState in the 21st century could kill even more.

Peter thought libertarians underestimated this threat. They tend to be too quick in ceding sovereignty to multi-national organizations and NGOs. They also miscalculate the dangers from foreign threats in the name of free trade. Economic union, as in Europe, often leads to political union. And there is a one-way ratchet in these agreements that libertarians seem blind to, particularly when it comes to expanding the size of a market.

On the other hand, those who call on the world to unite against other existential threats, like little Greta Thunberg, also seem blithely unaware of the dangers of totalitarian catastrophe. Runaway artificial intelligence, terrorism, an asteroid hit, climate change—take your pick. Unification against any of them could pose a greater threat to humanity than what these activists are calling on the world to unite against. (Assuming some of these threats are actually even existential: maybe they are hard problems, but not catastrophic problems.)

234 • PAPER BELT ON FIRE

Our discussion was wide-ranging, but instead of drawing on economics, Peter was drawing on passages from the Bible. It was a better source for examining the truly apocalyptic. "Christians can learn from libertarians that the state is not God. But there is a lot that libertarians can learn from Christianity," he said.

It is indeed an odd fact of the New Testament that the Antichrist seeks to unite the world into a single government. See, for instance, the three temptations of Christ in the wilderness.[7] Dostoevsky picked up on that and repurposed the episode in his famous chapter on the Grand Inquisitor in *The Brothers Karamazov*. The Grand Inquisitor berates Christ for not joining Satan to unite the world into a single benevolent dictatorship:

> ...you would have furnished all that man seeks on earth, that is: someone to bow down to, someone to take over his conscience, and a means for uniting everyone at last into a common, concordant, and incontestable anthill—for the need for universal union is the third and last torment of men.[8]

Peace and security are the political slogans of the Antichrist, not conquest and suffering. Destruction will come from the inside, cloaked in the appearance of the good. What is good and what only appears to be good—we can no longer tell the difference. Not with the same confidence. Our inability to distinguish the two is the hallmark of our age. The Antichrist as a name suggests an extreme polarity between good and evil, but the power of the idea is that the polarity is hidden behind differences we have trouble discerning. What is the highest good versus what appears to be good but is not—this is not the stark, epic battle between good and evil, but the subtle contest between appearance and reality, and the danger presented by those who would exploit our inability to distinguish between them.

But the Grand Inquisitor's anthill can be flattened. Peter pointed me to Paul's Second Letter to the Thessalonians, verses 6 and 7, where it is posited that we must look for a way to check the rise of a totalitarian world government. The mystery is that Thessalonians does not say explicitly what this "restrainer" of evil is—the "katechon" in Greek. But whatever it is, the katechon slows down the apocalypse, and so it was our task to identify it and support it until it was no longer needed. This was a lot to digest, but the surface was tantalizing. Ten years ago, I agreed to help teach a class with Peter on sovereignty and technological change. I told him I'd be happy to do it again if he needed my help. And with that, breakfast was finished, and Peter saw me out to the door. "Have fun in New York at Luminar's bell ringing."

● ● ●

Josh Piestrup picked me up at SFO. There was just enough time for us to grab lunch before I had to catch a car down to San Jose in time for the jet to New York. He also wanted to know if I had seen *Baitless Hook*. Was it brought down with the other art from the Thiel office in San Francisco to Los Angeles? We caught up over crab and beers at an outdoor shack on the shore of the Bay near the airport.

Josh had been let go from Peter's hedge fund a few years back, but that never meant he couldn't email Peter saying he had an idea. Peter is always receptive to great ideas. Down on his luck, after being fired, Josh would take some magazines, books, beers, and a beach chair down to Baker Beach near the Presidio. He was there so often he became good at peeing in the sand from his beach chair, with no one noticing in the noontime sun. But one day, an idea hit him so hard that he had to grab his empty beer bottles and beach chair and run home. What got him so excited was that he devised a hedge fund trading strategy that could combine two things that normally can't be brought together, positive expected return and long volatility. A positive expected return strategy performs well when there is no volatility. But if there's a crisis or a panic or a major downturn, then that strategy loses money. On the other hand, a strategy that makes money in a crisis is called being long volatility. During blue sky days, these strategies don't really perform so well. But if an investor could find a way to combine the two strategies, so a portfolio would do well in normal times, but then also perform extraordinarily well in a crisis, then that was the Holy Grail in hedge fund finance. Piestrup had known there was a way to do it with currencies under the right circumstances, but those conditions were rare. But on the beach that day, he figured out a way to do it with single-name equities through the use of options. "Options are options!" So he grabbed his beach chair and empty beer bottles and ran home. He just had to convince someone crazy enough to write a check. An old Thiel alum, Patrick Kenary came on board. Then they emailed Peter. "We have an idea." Where they had trouble explaining this complex trade to anyone else, Peter got it right away. In fact, he was going through the spreadsheets and pointing out numerical errors. "These numbers look too good to be true."

"They're actually better than that. This is without leverage."

He grokked it in fifteen seconds. "Yeah, I'm in."

So Josh and Patrick, both friends of mine, were back at it together, running a hedge fund. I'd often catch up with Josh like this over lunch to talk about macroeconomics and markets. He had a view of financial markets that I didn't see as a venture capitalist making investments in startups. But it was good for me to understand what was happening in the world of central banks, interest rates, and market sentiment. Eventually, like Luminar, some of our companies would make it to the public markets. In that case, it was good to get a refresher on the current financial landscape. Josh and Patrick were always great sources of information.

But as edifying as it was to talk shop, it was always fun to come back to some of our perennial topics of conversation. Like the fate of *Baitless Hook.*

"It was probably destroyed by the curator in charge of Peter's art collection."

"I don't know," Josh said, cracking crab shell. "I'm still tight with all the lawyers in Peter's office and there's a gentleman's agreement that I don't ask. When the whole art collection was moved to Southern California, it had to sit in storage for a bit. So insurance was needed. And appraisers came through. And that's the last it was seen by anybody. We're not sure what happened. I just know I'm not supposed to ask the lawyers about it at this point."

"It's like the end of *Raiders of the Lost Ark.* With the warehouse."

"Exactly. Top men are working on it. Top men."

My Lyft to San Jose had arrived at the crab shack. "Ok, I gotta split."

"Wait, I got something for your trip." Josh ran to his car and pulled out a sack full of iced wine bottles. I opened it up. It was full of five bottles of 2011 Jérôme Blin Les Caillasses Champagne.

"Damn man, you didn't have to do that."

"Share it with everyone on the flight!"

And with that, I was off to San Jose. I love the *Baitless Hook* caper because it illustrates Satoshi Nakamoto's analysis of the failure of institutions quite well. There is this timeless philosophical debate—what is art? Everyone agrees a portrait by Rembrandt is art, but what about the paintings that any five-year-old could do? Like paint spilled and splattered on a canvas? Or better yet, a canvas left blank? On one prominent theory, a work of art gains its status by the way works are accepted into the art world—the world of artists, critics, gallery owners, curators, and other experts. If this entire institution—"the art world"—recognizes something as art, then it's art.[9] Marcel Duchamp's *Fountain*—the infamous urinal on a plinth—is art on this theory because it was hailed as a masterpiece by the institutions of the art world. Likewise, in Josh's wildest dreams, if *Baitless Hook* were to be subsumed into Peter's art collection and then one day sold to another collector, then magically it would be transformed from a joke into a work of art.

But, as Nakamoto would say, institutions have to be trustworthy and reliable. Trusted third parties are security holes. The public often scratches its head at the buffoonery of post-modern art because it senses that the art world is neither trustworthy nor reliable. It can't be reliable at identifying masterpieces, because how on earth could they possibly recognize Chris Ofili's elephant dung Madonna as great art? The institution is also untrustworthy. Insiders tend to claim that works of art like the elephant dung Madonna are treasures because they stand to benefit by doing so.

When people see a work of art hanging on the wall of a prestigious art gallery, they rarely trust their own experience, the way they feel before it. Instead, they immediately read the little white label to the right of the painting, searching for status markers that will tell them what to feel. Their true response might be boredom, but this little card tells them they should be impressed. The same might be said of useless college degrees. They are like *Baitless Hook*, using their proximity to other prestigious things to pass themselves off as valuable. Like galleries, universities also have their own little expensive white label they attach to people. They call it a degree. Is it art? Or is it just a toilet?

I made it to the San Jose airfield with plenty of time. I had one carry-on bag and Josh's sack full of champagne. The pilot was checking people in. But it turned out there weren't any Luminar employees coming on the flight. I was surprised to see it was only Austin Russell's family—his brother, mom, and dad, all tall and sunny in the So Cal way. This was a lot of champagne just for the four of us! The pilot eyed the sack.

"We can't really let you on board with that," he told me. Then he saw how excited the family was. "But I tell you what, I'll turn the other way since it's such a special occasion. Just be careful and don't get crazy."

● ● ●

Once we had leveled off at cruising altitude and made our way over Nevada, I opened the first bottle of champagne. I figured it was a good time because the flight attendant was distracted talking to the pilots. Sadly, there was no warning on the back of the bottle saying "Do not open above 10,000 feet on a private jet." As soon as the cork popped, champagne sprayed all over the cabin. The bottle's interior pressure stayed the same, but as ours decreased in the cabin with greater altitude, it was as though the pressure inside the bottle had expanded. Boom! A powerful fruity and floral aroma filled the air. The carpet was wet. And the bottle kept fizzing. It wouldn't stop. How many bubbles could be in that thing? It was all over the seats and tray tables. Shit, get some napkins! Austin's mom, Shannon, ran to the back of the plane to get paper towels from the bathroom. I sopped up as much as I could with a sweatshirt from my bag. I patted the carpet dry. I looked up and saw the flight attendant was coming back. I got back in my seat.

"Is everything ok back there?"

"Yes, great, thanks!"

There was only enough champagne left in the bottle to fill a tiny bit in each of our glasses. I made a toast to Austin's parents, expressing my gratitude to them for raising such a great young man. I also said a few words to celebrate Luminar's accomplishments. But one sip of champagne was all that any of us got, so I said, ok, I'll open another bottle, but this time I'll do it carefully over the sink in the bathroom.

It didn't matter. I was facing the mirror, over the sink, when— boom!—again the champagne blew up and then sprayed, first all over the mirror and then all over the ceiling of the bathroom compartment. It looked like I had taken a shower. My button-down shirt was soaked. I used up all the paper towels in the dispenser to clean the mess up. When I got back to my seat, the flight attendant had returned. She saw my hair all wet and cocked an eyebrow in suspicion.

"Are you ok?"

"Yeah, fantastic!"

To quote the philosopher Taylor Swift, I had champagne problems. We all decided that was the last bottle we'd open. Meanwhile, Shannon and I were reminiscing about how far Luminar had come. She told me a story about this one time Austin decided he had to talk to a physics professor at Stanford. He was just a teenager and he insisted he had to go. Shannon drove him up to Palo Alto five hours from Irvine. She thought he had an appointment. He did not. But Austin kept knocking on the doors to different labs to find the professor. Eventually, Austin found him and then told the guy, this pre-eminent expert in photonics, that he had to check out the laser he just built. Shannon said the professor had this bemused, well isn't that sweet look on his face: how cute, a teenager playing with lasers. But then Austin told him about the performance levels he'd attained with a novel design. Suddenly the look on the guy's face shifted. Son, that's just not possible. And no sooner than he said that, Austin took the laser out of his backpack and turned it on. It was flashing all over the room like a lightsaber being wildly swung. "Ok, ok, put it away! Now, tell me how you built it." By the end of the conversation, the professor said to Austin that if he applied to Stanford, he could go directly into the graduate program in physics.

"That's Austin," Shannon said. "No one could ever stop him from getting to where he needed to go."

"That's so good, but, you know, I stopped Austin once," I said. Shannon didn't believe it. "Yeah, he showed up to the Thiel Capital offices one day back in 2012 or 2013. The receptionists didn't know what to do with this young man saying he wanted to show Peter Thiel the hologram machine he invented. So they went back to the trading floor to get me and then I took Austin into the front conference room. I heard him out. He explained his tech to me and how revolutionary it was going to be, and he said he knows Peter will love it and see the implications. And I told him, 'that's great, but you just can't show up and expect to meet with Peter.' We sat in that conference room for an hour. Austin kept trying to buy time with more explanations. I bet he was hoping Peter would walk by. Austin only gave up when I said we could schedule something in the months ahead. I don't even think he was a Thiel Fellow at that point."

"Yup, that's Austin," Shannon said.

• • •

So there I was, standing in the cold in Times Square across the street from Nasdaq. I saw five executives from the Luminar team walk in through the front door and approach the security desk. After some ID checks and temperature reads, the guard let them through.

I could learn a few things from Austin. I decided I'm getting in that place. I made a quick move for the door and then approached the security desk.

"Can I help you?" the guard asked.

"I'm with the Luminar executive team. Just fell behind."

He eyed me with suspicion. "Can I see your license?"

He took it and then scanned a list of names on a clipboard. "You're not on the list."

"Call upstairs," I risked.

And so he did, with a kind but condescending look. And then—I have no idea whom he talked to—but after some back and forth, his tone shifted, and he hung up the phone.

"Ok, you can come in." He took my temperature and buzzed me through the gates. Jackpot! I hustled up to the second floor where the Nasdaq television studio was. As in all studios, the stage area was terrifically bright and vivid, since it was surrounded by darkness and the overhead stage lights were all on. Austin and his team were standing on the stage, getting stage directions and the show flow from Nasdaq's TV producer. I sheepishly joined the group, trying to be as inconspicuous as possible. Eventually, Austin saw me and laughed.

"I snuck in here."

He shook his head and laughed some more. None of the other executives said anything. They all thought I was supposed to be there.

It was showtime. The host of the Nasdaq opening took to the white podium. Behind her, through the windows, was all of Times Square. In normal times, at the opening of the bell, maybe twenty or thirty people would cram behind that podium as the CEO of a company hit the button to open the market. But today, because of Covid, it was going to be Austin alone.

The host welcomed the Luminar team and then reeled off the company's accomplishments to the camera: fifty commercial partnerships, including with seven of the world's biggest auto-makers, production level contracts with Volvo, Daimler, and Intel's MobileEye unit, the only lidar company that has met all the stringent requirements for autonomy at highway speeds. Every company that gets listed on a public market gets a ticker symbol. She announced what Luminar's ticker would be, and it was perfect for Austin: LAZR.

Austin walked up to the podium. There were only eleven of us, but we gave all the hoots and claps we could. "Alright, well, thank you so much for having me here," Austin began. He went through a list of all the thank-yous he could fit into two minutes. And then he gave his final thoughts:

> When I founded the company eight years ago, autonomy was at a very nascent stage. We set out to solve a problem that many thought was impossible. We had this goal to make safe, scalable autonomy accessible to all. And it's funny—we were crazy enough to build our own lidar sensing system from the ground up. This is something we were laughed out of the room for plenty of times. "You want to do what?!" "You want to compete with some of the biggest tech companies and auto companies in the world!?" But I'm a firm believer that solving the most challenging problems of the 21st century requires a first principles, top-down approach to analyzing the problem, and a bottom-up clean slate approach to solving it. And that's exactly what we did.

And then and there Austin hit the button to open the mar-ket. A snowstorm of red confetti fell from the ceiling. Everyone went nuts. I was standing next to Jason Eichenholz and hugged him. Nasdaq pumped some corny, triumphant music over the speakers, which crescendoed right at the moment Austin hit the button to ring the opening bell. My phone was ringing like mad with calls from friends and family. Texts from 1517's investors were coming in faster than I could handle.

I texted Danielle in North Dakota. She was watching on TV. "We did it!"

"Hell yeah, we did!"

Then I got someone to take a picture of me at the podium on the studio stage. I texted it to Peter Thiel and added "Incredible morning! Thanks for believing in us first!"

"Congrats!" he texted back.

"Not too bad for a dropout philosophy professor and a former school principal! It wouldn't have been possible without your support. Really want to thank you for everything."

"It's been a wild decade," Peter wrote. "It felt that way already on that fall morning in 2010. We knew what we were doing." The chess master even added a smiley face. We knew what we were doing! Six moves ahead.

Putting together a ten-year plan is sheer madness to most. "Everyone has a plan," the heavyweight boxing champ Mike Tyson said once, "until they get punched in the face." But putting a ten-year plan in place and then pulling it off…it was exhilarating.

Success for Luminar would mean fewer lives lost on the roads. Success for 1517 meant we were on our way to building our endowment for the outsiders. It was the seed for a new higher education. We made our investors over $200 million. Austin has no credentials. No degrees. By the end of the day, he was the youngest self-made billionaire in the world. The companies backed by Sand Hill Road were dying, merging with others to stay alive, or switching to other markets. Sequoia and the others could eat it. Danielle was right. We did it.

The next day, I had one errand to run. The *Wall Street Journal* ran a story on Luminar on page 1 of the Business & Finance section. "Luminar Makes Young Founder a Billionaire."[10] It was even above the fold. Ace Frehley was blasting on my radio, "I'm back! Back in the New York groove!" I cut the story out and mailed it to Claire in Greenwich, the investor who passed on us because we hadn't had an IPO yet. I kept the note short on a yellow Post-It: "As promised. Michael Gibson."

· 16 ·

LAST NAME LAST

A trolley gathers speed and pushes on in front of me. Suspended above it, a massive red Swiss flag with its white cross hangs over the street. I find myself sitting on a bench along the leafy Bahnhofstrasse in Zurich, Switzerland, directly across the street from the head office of Julius Bär, an eminent Swiss bank of infallible calculation and infinite privacy. The street is flanked on the left and the right by the storefronts of luxury precision watch companies whose foundings pre-date the storming of the Bastille. It is a chic boulevard irrigated by imponderable wealth. Couples on bicycles drift by. A small crowd has queued to buy gelato at a stand, while friends swap gossip and laugh around cafe tables. It is the Day of Ascension in late May, a sunny national holiday for the Swiss at the start of the summer season. I bring my attention to the bank, taking a look at its side-street entrance. Then, to my left, a waist-high gray Lamborghini clears its throat, spits exhaust, and then turns the corner with a sputtering growl.

I am sitting outside Julius Bär because it houses some evidence I need to understand who my dad was. My dad had an account with the Swiss bank and told my mom that if anything should happen to him, she should contact them. He had given her a phone number. Two days after he died, she called the bank in Zurich—August 2, 1978. Confirming the phone call, the bank sent her an official letter the very next day on its stationary dated August 3, signed in ink by one of its employees. The bank attached a photostatic of a forwarding address for all correspondence, which my dad had written down in pen in his handwriting. "Mail to: Albert van Dam. London."

I'm in Zurich because I'd been thinking about my dad, loss, who I am, why I do what I do. Unlike the penniless philosopher-poet that tried the first time around, now I had the resources to search through the dust of what remained, to try to find out if there was anything behind what my dad told my mom three days before he died. He told her he feared for his life and that he was doing some work for an intelligence agency. I hired Kyle, a former FBI agent who specialized in counter-intelligence, to help me. We issued FOIA requests to the CIA, the NSA, and the FBI. They turned us down, saying they have a right to refuse information requests that touch upon sources and methods still in practice. But when I mentioned the Swiss Bank account to Kyle, he said, "Whoa, that's weird. Your dad worked as an engineer for NBC. His income was reported and taxed. You don't take reported and taxed income to Switzerland. Where was the source of this unreported income?" My mom is like a Delphic oracle. You have to ask her the right question to get the right answer. I asked her about the Swiss account, and she unearthed the letter from Julius Bär from out of her attic.

The bank's 1978 letter has a monogram at the top left of the page—JB&co—and now, as I sit across the street from the bank on this bench in Zurich, I notice something past the crowd in front of the gelato stand. I see the font for the lettering above

Julius Bär's side-street entrance: number 12 Peterstrauss. The font is the same as that on the letter.

• • •

A couple of days later, I met with my Swiss lawyer, Colette, in the small city of Lausanne on the shores of Lake Geneva. She is an expert in the law concerning unclaimed assets in Swiss banks. Her office is on the top floor of a Lausanne office building overlooking the lake.

"The people of Geneva call it Lake Geneva," she said when I marveled at the view out the window. "But we call it Lac Leman. Leman is as old as the Romans." Colette has short brown hair, with spunky spikes poking out here and there. Elegant but not too formal. She wore a white blouse, a khaki-colored suit, and gold bracelets and rings.

There were giant slanting skylight windows in her office letting light in through a pitched roof above us. These skylight windows were unlike any I have ever seen. Colette began turning a crank on the wall. First, the window glass receded and then a small balcony extended from a compartment out into the open air, like a plank extending with a thin railing around it. The sight of Lac Leman cradled by the mountains was gorgeous. There is a deceptive nonchalance to a Swiss town hanging by a thread on a mountainside.

We both sat down. Colette had spoken with Julius Bär's lawyers over the phone two days ago. They will not officially confirm or deny that my dad had an account without proof of legitimacy from me, inheritance documents, or a will. I have none of these. Nevertheless, off the record, they told Colette they had looked up the records for Frederick W. Smith, my dad. In their files, they found an application to open an account at the bank dating from 1974. But the peculiar thing is that this was the only information in the files. There was no evidence that the account, if there ever was one, was opened. However, he did say there was one more additional piece of information. With the 1974 application on file, there was a forwarding address attached. Again, to one Albert van Dam (the same name as in the letter sent to my mom in 1978), but this time the address was in Amsterdam, not London.

The banker finished by telling Colette he was at a loss. He does not know how to explain the letter I have in my possession from the bank to my mom.

"These efforts are often very difficult and often lead nowhere," Colette said to me by way of a preface. "All the documents are so old, and paper doesn't last like computers."

Colette and I had arranged to call Julius Bär again to set up an in-person meeting in their offices in Zurich on the Bahnhofstrasse. "Look, I'm not trying to find out if the account holds assets," I said. "What I want is the transaction history. My dad was up to something unusual, and I want to find out who he was."

"I am surprised that you have come this far," she said.

"Me too." We both let out a nervous laugh.

Then she launched into an explanation for why she found my case so mysterious. There were certain facts that didn't line up with the history of Swiss banking. She handed me a copy of her Ph.D. dissertation on the subject, "Les Avoirs Bancaires Non Reclames" ("Unclaimed Bank Assets"). Going back to before the Second World War, there were Jews who used trusted third parties in Zurich to hide their assets from German spies, who by German law could expropriate any Jewish property. These spies were constantly on the prowl to intercept and prevent Jewish assets from making their way into Swiss bank accounts. After the Holocaust, these trusted third parties had lost contact with the original depositors. Most likely, the depositors had died in concentration camps. Years passed. At some point, these former trusted third parties decided to take the money for themselves, because the accounts bore their names. They had legal authority over the deposits. Or, if it wasn't the supposed friends that did it, then the banks found a way to seize the assets. If some dishonorable bank employees noticed inactivity over long periods with Jewish names, they would start charging more in fees on an account until it was completely drained. (I immediately recalled Nick Szabo's and Satoshi Nakamoto's mantra: trusted third parties are security holes.)

All of this treachery came out into the open during the 1990s, when claims started being made against the Swiss banks by surviving Jewish relatives in places like New York. "These Swiss bankers, so perfect and unfeeling," Colette added. "When the requests from relatives first came in, these banks demanded to see death certificates for people killed in Auschwitz!"

"Terrible." Without a death certificate, the banks could claim someone's death was not certain.

"Historically Julius Bär, what?...it has no morality," she continued, "How to say this correctly in English? No candor. They were involved in South African trade during apartheid. Lots of scandals. In all of these cases, even though there was untoward behavior, the accounts and the documentation still existed. So when I look at your case, I see a few unusual things. First, it is very unusual that they would write a letter on official correspondence to your mother and give her a forwarding address. That should not have happened. Acknowledge the existence of an account to a distraught girlfriend on the phone? Impossible."

"It is very peculiar."

"So after your father died, maybe the bank account was closed and the documentation destroyed. We don't know how or by whom—but it is possible. Probably because an intelligence agency didn't want anyone to find out. But they would need someone inside the bank, an agent or a spy. I'm not surprised it's Julius Bär though. But by law a bank can only liquidate assets after no contact for fifty years. We are within that."

Colette dialed the number for our contact at Julius Bär. He picked up and she put us all on speakerphone.

"We can only give accurate information on accounts over the last ten years," he began. Colette put him on mute and told me he was saying this to cover his ass legally. The banker continued, "This is an alleged client relationship that goes back more than ten years. And such a relationship never became active. Even if you provide birth and inheritance documentation, I am quite sure we won't find more than this 1974 application."

I cut in. "But how do we have this 1978 letter with your employee names on it? Can you tell me if these men were employed by the bank?"

"That is so long ago," he offered as an excuse. He would not give theories as to how I have this 1978 letter or why the bank would send it, and why it would have a different forwarding address. Colette indicated to me she thought he was being honest and telling us all he knew as far as this goes. Then she jumped in. "Why would you keep an application on file that long? Is that normal?"

"It can occur that we keep the application. We only have to keep for ten years, but in some cases, we find things in case we wanted to keep track of relationships."

"But is it possible the account was opened and closed and then that you would have no documentation?" Collette followed.

"That would not happen," he admitted. "I think we would have more documentation in such a situation. But remember we are permitted to destroy any information after ten years if the account has no assets."

Colette asked him if he would be willing to meet me in person tomorrow.

"We have no interest in meeting to say the same thing we say now."

"Ok." I tried another angle. "What was required to open an account? Would you need to list assets in the application?"

"In the 1970s it was absolutely easier to open an account. You could bring cash from the U.S. and that is all."

"Can you tell me if there is any interesting, intriguing information on the application? Anything more than phone numbers and addresses?"

"I don't think so." Then he became sharp. "I shouldn't have even spoken with you about this." And he hung up.

Colette raised her eyebrows. "I think we have to conclude the account has been destroyed," she said. "I would not be surprised if the CIA or another intelligence agency had people on the inside of a bank like Julius Bär."

The banker did give me one lead. The forwarding address for Albert Van Dam on the application from 1974:

Albert van Dam
Maalderij 25
Bovenkerk
Amsterdam

It looks like I need to find Mr. Van Dam. He's probably dead. But maybe his family or the Dutch government has information. I thanked Colette as she walked me back to the elevator. "This is the farthest I have ever come," I mused.

"I am at your disposal if you find anything interesting." She smiled and nodded her head.

I entered the elevator and hit the button for the lobby. As soon as the elevator's door closed, I began to cry.

• • •

Back in the United States, I met with Kyle over a beer to discuss what I found. It was exactly like the dark wood and brass rails bar one would imagine us meeting in.

"Great work, man. Cheers." We clicked pint glasses.

"Colette is astute, and I think you got as much as possible through her. More than usual. I am just kind of blown away that you got what you did. You have to understand the CIA has a labyrinth of methods for moving money around the globe. Cash flowing through phony entities to illusions. In the 1970s it was the wild west. The idea of U.S. intel having a contact within Julius Bär is completely reasonable."

"That freaking letter they won't acknowledge is pretty bizarre."

"There are two things you have to keep in mind, as tantalizing as this little adventure has been. You have to consider that maybe this account was set up for personal reasons and had nothing to do with anything. Or, I hate to say it, the account could've been opened by your dad at the direction of a foreign intelligence service for a covert method of payment."

"Yeah, I've also thought about the foreign angle on my dad. That maybe he was some other country's asset. It can't be ruled out, of course. But I've done a ton of research on traitors and treason. I recently read *Circle of Treason* by Sandra Grimes and Jeanne Vertefeuille—just an incredible book by two women who had long careers at the CIA.[1] It should be a movie. They're the ones who caught Aldrich Ames. One of the things they get into is the psychological traits and motives of traitors in either the CIA or the FBI. All the motives for treason tend to be more about greed and narcissism or feeling like a victim. Thwarted careers, no recognition, debts, drugs. So far as I can tell from stories, my dad doesn't fit that profile at all. He worked at NBC from the early 1950s until his death. Never had money problems."

"Jesus, working with you is like working with another agent."

"Yeah, something like that I guess." I shrug and take a sip. "I'm pretty good at finding people."

"Investigating Van Dam—could be a very expensive endeavor. If you want me to take a stab at him, I think you need to set a firm budget, or else it will get out of control very quickly. Might cost up to $50k."

"Ok, we'll get to it."

• • •

Danielle and I are back to doing our thing. A friend of my colleague Zak Slayback introduced us to a twenty-one-year old guy who believes he's found a way to cure Type 2 diabetes. Working out of his parents' basement, he's developed a therapeutic using a new technique called RNA-interference. He's got all the traits we look for in founders. But there's one issue we keep getting stuck on. He legally changed his name to Tony Stark, in homage to the comic book character a.k.a. Iron Man.

"No one is going to take him seriously! How is he going to get grants from the government? They'll take one look at his name and throw his application out." I'm arguing with Danielle that we can't make an investment.

"It's only $50k," she says. "And we're the only people on the entire planet who can help him. We don't care what his name is. We only care if he can do what he says he can. This is what we do."

"Damn it. You're right. Ok, let's do this. But we have to talk to him."

So we call up Tony Stark.

"Look man, we want to support you and we're going to

invest," I tell him. "But we don't want this to hold you back. I think if you're applying for grants and stuff or raising money from other VCs, you might want to say you're Anthony Stark. People won't notice."

"I think that makes total sense," Iron Man says.

"I have to ask. Why did you decide to change your name?"

"I just always liked the idea of being a superhero. It gave me hope. Plus all my friends were already calling me Tony Stark in high school because I was building rockets and messing around with DNA in my parents' basement."

Danielle was right. A young man with no college degree. Thinks he has a cure for Type 2 diabetes. Goes by the name Tony Stark. We had to back this kid. Today, Tony has found that his novel therapeutic cures Type 2 diabetes in mice. To get ready for the FDA approval process, he's now experimenting on rats. Amazing to say, it looks like he's on his way.

What's in a name? A lot, I think. Not long after that, Danielle called me. "You're never going to guess!"

"What?"

"Our names are going to be on the moon!"

"What?"

"Yeah, Zeno is going to etch our names on their battery case, the one being sent to the moon. They wanted to honor us for believing in them when no one else would."

"Oh, shit" is always an understatement, but that's all I could say. Zeno is a company founded by three Vanderbilt students who realized the technology behind nuclear batteries hadn't improved in decades. They had some ideas for how to solve the radiation problem and wrote into our contact form. After they met with my colleague Nick, we invested. Three years later, they have contracts with the Air Force and another company that is making a probe for NASA to send to the moon.

I'm not one for oversimplified life lessons. Figuring out who I am came late to me. But all I can say is, search for the extraordinary: you might find yourself on the moon.

●   ●   ●

Both the *Iliad* and the *Odyssey* begin with the question of identity.[2] The *Iliad* begins by naming Achilles and his father. That puts Achilles center stage and roots him in the past. Whereas—to reverse the coin—the *Odyssey* begins with anonymity:

> That man, remember him, the tricky bastard
> who always found a way.

Odysseus isn't identified by name until a full twenty lines later. And then, unlike with Achilles, Odysseus's father isn't even mentioned. His past is obscure. Later, Odysseus calls himself "no one" to his adversary, the Cyclops. The drama of the poem can be conceived then as a story about a nameless man who returned to find his name. But it has two parts to it. Back home, we find the situation reversed. Odysseus's son Telemachus knows his father's name, but he does not know the man behind it. Because of his father's long absence, the fate of the city hangs in the balance and Telemachus's life is in danger. The suitors will destroy the kingdom and eventually kill Telemachus if life carries on as it has. The fortunes of all only begin to turn once Telemachus begins to care more for the father he never knew than for the property he thinks is his and that is being destroyed before his eyes. So he sets off on a fact-finding mission to discover the man behind the name he's known. We might say the poem is only completed when the man and the name are one.

CODA:
THE INVISIBLE COLLEGE

Problems on the Frontiers of Knowledge

At a conference at the Sorbonne in August of 1900, the great mathematician David Hilbert challenged his peers to attack twenty-three unsolved problems in the field. It was a bold move to open a new epoch, but owing to his commanding authority—he was the imposing mathematician's mathematician—his challenge motivated the greats of his era and set their research program over the next four decades. As of today, the consensus holds that eight of Hilbert's problems have been solved, with nine more solutions holding partial acceptance, leaving four problems left open. (Two of the original twenty-three problems have been deemed too vague to yield an answer.) In one of the more marvelous plot twists in the history of philosophy and mathematics, the otherworldly debate about whether numbers exist independently of the human mind led to the invention of the computer. Kurt Gödel's Incompleteness Theorem—demonstrated in 1931—addresses the second question in Hilbert's problem set and, with John von Neumann, Alonzo Church, and Alan Turing building on its dazzling insights, the Incompleteness Theorem opened the door to the invention of modern computing.

Although I do not possess a single atom of Hilbert's weighty German authority, I seem to have what our time considers a mad man's faith. I believe there is great merit in specifying, in an encyclopedic fashion, the fundamental problems that need to be solved. There can be no progress without a goal, and, by charting a course, Hilbert's problem set motivated the whole mathematics community to take action. In this coda, I lay out in summary what may be the top two or three unsolved challenges in various areas of science and technology. If these new problems are solved, many of the major crises of our time will disappear altogether. Some advances may make life much better and longer (as with a cure for cancer) or simply more thrilling (as with supersonic flights). But to keep the bounds somewhat reasonable, I've decided the solutions to these problems must also be within reach—say, within fifteen years at the outside. They shouldn't rest on fantastic assumptions. While I read widely in science fiction, I must therefore leave out far-fetched ideas like time travel, teleportation, and anti-gravity.

I find it surprising how few people work on important problems at a young age. Instead, our education system infantilizes teens and assumes they must wait and pay their wasteful dues. In lieu of any concrete goal, schools encourage vague ambitions like "leadership" and call aimlessness "self-exploration." They offer the general, abstract promise of preparing students for a shifting landscape, a rapidly changing world, a future that cannot be predicted. This is why schools emphasize that they do not teach people what to think, but how to think. However, as I hope I have shown, these notions are discredited. No wonder so many teens are cynical and apathetic, embarrassed by their advantages and so desperate to hide them. Their formative years are spent working on tasks of little consequence in great comfort towards a larger course of action that everyone pretends to be real but all suspect to be fake.

Even recent grads find themselves in a similar situation. Having joylessly strained to stand out by fitting in, they by and large aim to preserve the abstract promise of their education by pouring into abstract jobs at Wall Street banks, hedge funds in Connecticut, Big Tech in Palo Alto, and management consultancies sprinkled everywhere. Often their purpose is to gain valuable, high-status experience before finally resolving what to do with their lives. Commitment can wait, so they think, as they set forth on careers in invisible services—down the gaping maw they go, into banking, insuring, trading, optimizing, hedging, analyzing—all fluid jobs, hard to assess, difficult to explain to a child, yet commanding of respect and preposterous devotion. These jobs are preoccupied with analysis, but never creation—analysis of trends, analysis of policy, analysis of data, analysis of the opposing analysis. But imagine if, instead of 40–60 percent of every graduating class disgorging itself from the bowels of the Ivy League into analysis, they embarked on the great adventure of trying to solve these fiendishly difficult problems—what would that world look like? We will only know we have turned a cultural corner when Tiger moms glow radiant with pride the day their sons and daughters become plasma physicists or synthetic biologists instead of partners at the white-shoe law firm.

I submit that the best way to do future significant work is to begin working on significant problems now. No one is too young to do so. In this respect, child labor is good.

To accelerate progress, we need young people working at the frontiers of knowledge sooner than they have in the past. They also need greater freedom. What that means is institutions that trust them to take risks and demonstrate some edge control with their research. We must hold it as a fairly predictable law of creativity that the unknown must always pass through the strange before we can understand it.

Universities have served this research function in the past and will continue to do so. But they are plagued by four realities. The first is the slow speed of a formal, credential-based education. It takes four years to earn a bachelor's degree and then another seven or eight to earn a Ph.D. Second, universities have become hives of groupthink. Third, grant-giving is driven by prestige, credibility, and a cover-your-ass mentality. Fourth, the incentives of academic institutions reward shrewd political calculation, incrementalism, short-term horizons, and a status hierarchy in which demonstrating loyalty earns more reward than advancing knowledge.

Our institutions of learning simply don't trust younger people to do great work. They must spend all of their twenties gaining credibility through diplomas, recommendations, and grant approvals. Only then might they get the permission and funding to investigate something new. We must break this subservience to power.

1517 is an alternative to the university system that is capable of finding, funding, and supporting young people who could go on to produce Nobel Prize caliber work between the ages of twenty-four and thirty-six. To this end, we've started what we're calling the Invisible College, after the underground scientific community of the 17th century, which was a forerunner to the creation of the Royal Society and helped spark the Scientific Revolution.

The original Invisible College was an informal group of natural philosophers, centered around Robert Boyle, who exchanged ideas by letters and encouraged each other as they established the methods of discovery we all take for granted today. They had to keep the society secret because they feared the church, government, and other authorities of the period. The authorities of our own era seem ripe for subversion or end-arounds.

If I could mandate one thing for all universities, labs, startups, and research organizations, it would be that they all must list the top five unsolved problems in their respective field. *It is essential that we find solutions to the top unsolved problems in the following fields:* energy creation, transportation, health, education, computation, freshwater abundance, increasing crop yields for less, cleaning the air, and, lastly, the problem of human flourishing. There are other concerns besides these, undoubtedly, but I have started here given their importance.

In what follows, I mention established teams and projects that are already trying to make progress in each of these fields. Of course, we should root for them with zeal. But we cannot rest complacently, expecting progress while we await their return from an attempt upon some snowy, distant peak. The sad truth is that most of these teams will fail and never be heard from again. Stagnation is upon us. We should assume these problems are some of the most difficult and complex mankind has ever faced. Some of the teams mentioned here will be out of business by the time this book goes to print, thereby dating the book like a bad '80s pop song. I don't care. I admit I still listen to the Thompson Twins. It is worth knowing their approach, and if they fall short, why they did so. For we all die on the march, in our dated fashions, and we must pick up what others have left behind. I list the teams here as a point of reference.

A final word of caution to recall from H. L. Mencken, that great wit and savage curmudgeon: "For every complex problem there is an answer that is clear, simple, and wrong."

Energy Creation

Georgia O'Keeffe, painter of flower, bone, and light, was riveted by the intense Polish man across the room at the party.[1] He was unusual-looking, with magnetic green eyes. World-weary, but quite funny. Not knowing the man's wife was part of her conversational cluster, O'Keeffe raised her arm and pointed her imperious finger and exclaimed, "Who is that man?"

That man, if you asked his wife, was a study in contrasts and contradictions. She'd fallen in love with his self-confidence and optimism, even during the darkest hours in the Second World War. Though she was French and studied literature, she couldn't resist those damn charming rolling Slavic Rs whenever he spoke her native tongue. That man, she could have told O'Keeffe, was Stanislaw Ulam, one of the greatest mathematicians of the 20th century. Françoise loved that special look he got in his eyes whenever he was immersed in mathematical thought, which was often, even at parties like this, here in New Mexico. She'd come to see that her husband could live on two planes of consciousness simultaneously. The first, the world we live in—the world of bones, flowers, and deserts; the second, the Platonic realm of numbers and equations, to which few common mortals have access.

What O'Keeffe didn't know—what hardly anyone knew, since it was classified (and mostly still is)—was that Ulam had changed the nature of the universe. No small claim. For up until that point, beginning with the Big Bang, so far as we know, only the universe could give birth to a star. But one afternoon in 1951, staring out of his living room window, peering into the garden outside with that mathematical look in his eyes, Ulam figured out how it could be done on Earth. He devised a way to spark a star.

Françoise walked into their living room at lunchtime that day. She could tell he was not looking at the garden.

"I found a way to make it work," he said.

"What work?" Françoise asked.

"The Super," Ulam replied. "It is a totally different scheme, and it will change the course of history."

The Super referred to a bomb powered by a fusion reaction. Many had been convinced such a thing was impossible, including Ulam himself. The best of the best, John von Neumann, Enrico Fermi, and a team of women "computers," plus the world's first machine computer, ENIAC, had been running calculations for years to model whether it would be possible to ignite a fusion reaction, given the known designs and materials. Their results were cloudy at best. By June of 1950, after a series of calculations with his teammate Cornelius Everett, Ulam believed he had firmly shown it could not be done. Not with what they thought they knew.

But then, the window and the garden. After that day, everything was different. Edward Teller refined and built on Ulam's ideas, his biggest insight to use radiation as a form of compression to light the fusion match. Robert Oppenheimer famously—or perhaps infamously—called their solution "technically sweet." Not even two years later, on November 1, 1952, the U.S. military ignited the first sustained fusion reaction on Earth that produced excess energy. A piece of a star was let loose. It tore through the ocean and sky, almost all the way to the heavens, thirty miles high. The resulting explosion and blast wave on a tiny island in a South Pacific atoll was colossal and terrifying. Reckless, the product of some chamber of insanity. It literally shook the earth. Teller was able to measure the vibrations all the way from a lab in Berkeley, California. The island vanished.

But if it was a dark page of history, it was also the birth of an inexhaustible source of energy and a glimpse into the source of all things. Just about every atom in the universe besides hydrogen was forged by fusion in the crucible of a long-dead star. We are fusion stardust, the product of an ancient alchemy. As is our current energy. The only big difference between a thermonuclear explosion and our sun is that the sun is far away, and it is constantly exploding. The ultimate source of every energy we use—from oil to solar—is the fusion reaction at the center of our sun.

One summer I visited Los Alamos, New Mexico. The museum there has preserved Ulam's office. He was known to write equations and notes everywhere. If you open the drawer to his desk, written inside you find a puckish note, part warning, part expression of awe: "A mathematician does something on a piece of paper, and then lo & behold, a big explosion may occur."

A line can be drawn from that desk back to another desk drawer, but in Paris, 1896. The physicist Henri Becquerel kept a uranium compound wrapped in paper inside his dark drawer to test its properties. Much to his surprise, the compound emitted an unknown energy that could darken a photographic plate, even if the compound had not been struck by light or acted upon in any way. Becquerel had discovered radioactivity, and a year and a half later, Marie Curie named it—but neither knew they were dealing with nuclear energy. It took fifty-five years to go from that curious substance sitting in a dark drawer somewhere in Paris to igniting an uncontrolled piece of a star in the South Pacific—less than one average human lifetime. After that, progress ground to a near halt. More than seventy years after Ulam's discovery, power-generating controlled fusion still lies beyond our grasp.

No matter whether climate change is an impending cataclysm or a manageable problem to be reckoned with, the world needs to shift away from carbon dioxide–emitting sources of energy. Republicans and Democrats may continue to fight old battles, forever despising one another, but less pollution and abundant energy are a good thing for both alike, especially if it means not giving up our way of life and extending our prosperity. Air pollution alone reduces global life expectancy

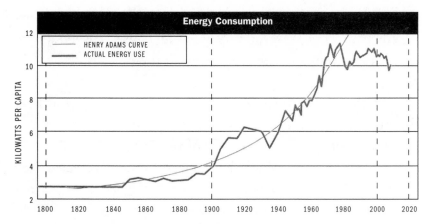

Credit: J. Storrs Hall, *Where Is My Flying Car*, Stripe Press 2021. The Henry Adams Curve represents a long-term trend in energy usage going back to the discovery of the steam engine, where up until 1971 or so we saw a steady increase of about 7 percent per year in the amount of energy we used. Thereafter the rate flattened.

by about 2.2 years on average.[2] But we can turn that around. There are at least seven potential sources of clean energy— fusion, nuclear, wind, solar, hydro, geothermal, and wave—but all of them involve outstanding problems requiring solutions. Natural gas is not so bad when it comes to carbon emissions, but I will leave that debate aside.

The importance of advances in energy creation is not only about the environment, however. Nor is it about making light, heat, air conditioning, farming, battery charging, and fresh water all dramatically cheaper—although it will certainly do those things. It's about abundance without end. By using more energy, we can do more as a civilization than is dreamt of in any of our philosophies. We can build a bridge to the planets, the moons, and, eventually, the stars. I will take each source one by one below. But a final crucial point: since 1971, consumption of energy in the United States has flatlined. Some see this as progress, hoping less energy use will hold back the threat of climate change. But it's not energy that's dangerous; it's dirty energy.

Fusion: The sun uses gravity to crush hydrogen atoms together in immense heat and pressure; those crushed atoms fuse into helium and release energy in the process. On earth, though, we can't use gravity. Instead, we have to use electricity, magnetism, and mechanical systems to squeeze and heat the atoms to 150 million degrees Celsius or more. (That's about ten times hotter than the center of the Sun.) But it's hard to confine this ferociously hot, dense plasma once it's created. The chief obstacle to generating fusion power resides in the plasma confinement systems, which to date have primarily used enormous magnets. Another mainstream approach, in an echo of the Ulam-Teller idea, uses lasers to compress and implode a pellet of atoms into a fusion reaction. With either method, the problem for physicists is that so far, fusion reactors using these systems consume more energy than they create.

Fusion energy is a dense, zero-carbon, clean source of power, involving no risk of meltdowns, no threat of it being used as a weapon, and, unlike most current renewables, is a viable replacement for always-on baseload power sources. It is no understatement to say that whoever achieves the first self-sustaining, energy-positive controlled fusion reaction will have dramatically changed human history.[3]

TEAMS TO WATCH: Commonwealth Fusion Systems, General Fusion, Zap Energy, First Light Fusion, Cortex Fusion, TAE Technologies, Tokamak Energy, Helion Energy, General Atomics, Princeton Fusion Systems, the ITER project in France.

Nuclear: Splitting atoms into a self-sustaining chain reaction generates tremendous amounts of energy from a relatively small amount of fuel. It emits no carbon dioxide and releases no dirty pollutants into the atmosphere. Like fusion, it would be a miracle but for three main problems: first, nuclear power produces a small amount of radioactive waste, which requires storage for a long period of time; second, in the past human error and natural disasters have caused reactor meltdowns, releasing radiation out into the world; and, third, nations or non-state actors can use the fuel to build nuclear weapons.

Nuclear energy, however, could yet save the world.[4] Today, nuclear is already safer, cleaner, and more reliable than all the other existing energy sources. The fear of nuclear power is far at odds with reality. Let us hope all the shouted slogans denouncing it grow silent. I point readers to *A Bright Future: How Some Countries Have Solved Climate Change and the Rest Can Follow* by Joshua Goldstein and Staffan Qvist for an eye-opening comparison among all of the alternative sources of energy. A few points are worth highlighting. Chernobyl, history's worst nuclear power accident, occurred in a despicable totalitarian state; the reactor had no containment shell (unlike any reactor in the West). And, much to my astonishment, no one in Japan has died from radiation as a result of the Fukushima meltdown. (Some people died from the hardship of evacuating, though.) The authors write: "So this, then, is the safety record of nuclear power over more than fifty years, encompassing more than 16,000 reactor-years: one serious fatal accident in the USSR with possibly, over time, up to 4,000 deaths; one Japanese 'disaster' that caused no deaths; and one American accident [Three Mile Island] that destroyed an expensive facility but otherwise just generated vast quantities of fearful hype. In the United States, nuclear power continues to produce about one-fifth of the nation's electric supply and has never killed anyone."

As safe as the old models already are, next-generation nuclear reactors aim to solve waste, safety, and proliferation issues. We can still make improvements on all three dimensions, and we can lower the costs. Given the considerable amounts of energy nuclear produces while only using small amounts of fuel, and with reactors taking up only a few acres of land, it's imperative that we continue to build them. Truly, there is no greener energy policy. For perverse stupidity look no further than states like New York and California, and countries like Germany, that claim to be leaders on climate issues, but that have arranged to shut down their last remaining reactors in the next year or so. The confused are always with us, alas.

TEAMS TO WATCH: Terrestrial Energy, TerraPower, NuScale, Oklo, Deep Isolation, Kairos Power, X-energy.

Wind and Solar: The two critical statistics used to understand our energy options are (1) the total amount of energy required to sustain the comforts of life as we know it, and (2) the ratio of inputs to outputs from any system—in short, whether the juice is worth the squeeze. Wind and solar are not promising sources of energy today because they require vast amounts of land to generate small amounts of power.[5] They cannot meet our needs, and we cannot decelerate gently. Well beyond the point of no turning back, our civilization cannot live by the counterclockwise philosophies of restraint and abstinence. To see the difference by comparison, the world's largest solar power station, the Noor Complex Power Station in Morocco, produces at best 582 megawatts, yet cost $2.5 billion to build and covers almost ten square miles. That's about the same power generation and cost as a single nuclear reactor deposited on just an acre of land. But there is yet an even bigger difference. What power solar farms do generate is inconsistent: solar doesn't operate at night or under cloudy skies. Windmills are motionless in a calm. There are seasonal issues as well. In the far north, such as in Scandinavia, the rare sunny days in the winter are too short to allow for much exposure.

The quality of energy output matters, of course. Coal is a potent energy source, for example, but it's so dirty that it kills no small number of people every year, in addition to filling the atmosphere with carbon dioxide. So solar and wind look relatively strong there. But the quality of input matters, too, and the components of solar panels are quite toxic. All in all, given how weak and inconsistent solar and wind currently are at generating power, they cannot be the only, let alone the main solution for our energy needs. Not unless we want to live like impoverished medieval peasants, huddled at the Equator, praying in a terrible heat to the inconsistent Gods of Light and Wind. Solving the power density problem seems improbable to me—note, it's not about the decreasing cost of panels, which seem to stay the same size—but I leave open the possibility that our ever-surprising human ingenuity may yet find a way. Grid-scale batteries or other energy storage systems aim to alleviate the intermittency problem, but more work needs to be done here as well and we are a long way off.

One far-out line of solar energy research is to move it from the earth to the heavens. There is a lot of space in space. And continuous sunshine. It is far-fetched at this point, but the physicist Freeman Dyson once imagined a sphere of light-absorbing material surrounding our entire solar system on its periphery. In science fiction these power systems have come to be known as "Dyson Spheres," and they represent a civilization's ability to harness all the energy of a star. A smaller Dyson Farm in orbit might be more feasible in the nearer term. But the high cost of launching materials into space and the challenge of sending power back to earth appear impossible to overcome.

Geothermal: Here we journey to the center of the earth. While it is not as hot as the center of the sun, the core of the earth still scorches, about 6,000 degrees Celsius, 4,000 miles below the surface. This intense heat from the earth's core represents an inexhaustible energy source that will last for billions of years. Today's geothermal power plants, which convert this heat into clean power, are located in areas where the earth's rising thermal energy naturally bubbles out from the core and escapes through the mantle to the surface: near volcanoes, hot springs, geysers, and the edges of tectonic plates.

Geothermal energy will remain limited to these unusual locations until engineers discover feasible ways of drilling down deeper into the earth from anywhere. Our current drills are not strong enough to descend low enough through nearly impenetrable rock. That will require a drilling breakthrough, probably involving non-rotary methods, which are still in their infancy. Beyond that, it will also require the invention of downhole electronics that are reliable at high temperatures and that are also resistant to pressure, shock, and vibration. The last hurdle would be to discover some cheap maneuverability at depth, allowing engineers to make arbitrary paths underground without it breaking the bank.

Despite these challenges, the potential is tantalizing. The Union of Concerned Scientists, an advocacy group, claims that "the amount of heat within 10,000 meters of Earth's surface contains 50,000 times more energy than all the oil and natural gas resources in the world."[6]

TEAMS TO WATCH: Quaise, Fervo, Sage Geosystems.

Hydro and wave: A handful of dams scattered across the American West are some of the most magnificent structures in the nation, with the Hoover Dam standing as the crowning triumph of early-20th-century engineering and stylish Art Deco design. There is a sturdy splendor to these sweeping blockades, as they pull power from flowing water, but their time has clearly passed. Almost all of the prime sites have been taken in the United States, and what few potential sites remain are untouchable due to environmental concerns.

That leaves the ocean. Unlocking power from the waves and tides is full of possibilities. The biggest challenge here, however, is devising a way to convert the energy from the wave to electricity efficiently. On top of that, the sea is a harsh mistress: ocean water is corrosive, and violent storms present frequent dangers. Developing a wave converter includes the same technical challenges as building a ship combined with an offshore platform. Nevertheless, a number of teams are working to overcome these hurdles.

TEAMS TO WATCH: CalWave, Corpower, Columbia Power, Oscialla Power, Marine Power Systems.

Transportation

The romance of the Jet Age cast its allure by combining speed, travel, and a better life into a single philosophy. Social mobility was not a metaphor, but a fact. By moving faster, progress happened faster. It was dazzling, aerodynamic, and, like Frank Sinatra sipping a dry martini, downright glamorous.

Yet our society's overall technical progress stalled at the same moment that our travel stopped getting faster. True, flights on today's 747s are much safer than they were in 1969, when the jumbo jet started flying passengers; they are quieter and more fuel-efficient, too. But they are no faster. Same for the newer Boeing 777s or the 787 Dreamliners. Consider that in 1958, the Boeing 707 could fly from New York to Paris in seven hours, traveling 500 to 600 miles per hour. With one exception, our speed limit has been Mach 0.85 ever since—for nearly sixty-five years. The rate of acceleration used to be a marvel. Just thirty years before the Jet Age, Charles Lindbergh had risked his hide in a sputtering prop plane to travel from New York to Paris in 33 hours and 30 minutes. Before that, it took four and a half days to cross the Atlantic on an ocean liner. Now, in 1958, Boeing was running an ad in magazines called "The coin, the watch, and the flower" to show that jet flight was so quiet you could hear your watch tick, so smooth you could spin a coin on a tray table, and so fast that the flowers you wore for your lover would still be fresh by the time you landed in Paris.

Today's symbol of travel is a drab, humorless, and disturbing affair. It is of a long line shuffling, suitcase to suitcase, winding its way back and forth as through the lower intestines of some bureaucratic beast, terminating in its plastic-glove pat-down. What would Sinatra say? Surely not "Come fly with me."

Supersonic jets: There is perhaps no more pathetic token of stagnation than the retirement of the Concorde in October of 2003, after twenty-seven years of service.[7] Though it was a commercial flop and only survived on subsidies from France and the United Kingdom, its now-ancient technology was still considered "advanced" at the time of its final flight. In fact, as far technology goes, it has been possible since the late 1950s to build an airliner capable of flying faster than the speed of sound. The original designs for the Concorde date from the early 1960s. But the economics of supersonic flight never proved tantalizing enough for the major airlines to bite. The planes carried few people, burned tons of fuel, and, due to a window-shattering sonic boom, only flew over oceans. Throughout the 1970s, the French and British governments begged and could not convince any commercial airlines to buy Concordes. In the end, the governments donated the fourteen supersonic crafts to their two national airlines and heavily subsidized their operations. (On the other hand, the U.S. government, over four decades, led by five presidents burning billions, has undertaken three research programs to build a supersonic passenger aircraft. All failed.)[8]

The four main problems standing in the way of supersonic travel are the nuisance of sonic booms, tremendous fuel consumption, extraordinary forces working upon the aircraft, and—for overcoming all that—a projected small financial return. Are there enough passengers per flight and flights per day to return the investment? It costs billions to design, build, test, and then clear the regulatory hurdles for launching any new airplane, sub- or supersonic. In yet another sign of stagnation, there are few players in the field who can even afford to try to innovate. In the 1980s, there were four manufacturers for commercial airliners in the world. Now we are down to two: Boeing and Airbus. Neither has made much effort to accelerate the speed of travel.

Even so, a few startups and NASA have taken up the challenge. All are developing more effective noise suppressors to quiet their aircraft's sonic boom, and they are banking on the discovery of cheaper and cleaner alternative jet fuels. It's a long shot, but the leader in the pack is Boom Supersonic, which aims to have a supersonic passenger aircraft operating by 2029. United Airlines announced in the summer of 2021 that it would purchase fifteen of Boom's airplanes. By the end of the decade, we may yet see a few of those long-thought extinct species, those goose-necked aircraft, with swept-back rakish wings, spearing their way across the Atlantic faster than the speed of sound. I hope they serve dirty martinis on board.

TEAMS TO WATCH: Boom Supersonic, Exosonic, Spike Aerospace, NASA's X-59 program.

Hypersonic jets & transatmospheric travel: Elon Musk's SpaceX has indicated that its reusable rockets might one day be used for travel around the earth. A rocket flight from Texas to Australia might take thirty minutes, with weightless views of outer space in between. Imagine that as a daily commute. Similarly, the idea of aircraft traveling at speeds in excess of Mach 3, using ramjets and scramjets, resurfaces from time to time. It is unlikely, however, that any of these modes of transport will become feasible within the next fifteen years.

Flying Cars: "The example of the bird does not prove that man can fly," Simon Newcomb infamously stated in 1901. (Newcomb—astronomer, mathematician, and authority of his era—very much looked like the stern, white-bearded Scottish Calvinist he sounded like.) He continued, "Imagine the proud possessor of an aeroplane darting through the air at a speed of several hundred feet per second. It is the speed alone that sustains him. How is he ever going to stop?"

Old Newcomb may sound like a crank to us, but he has a point about speed. Airplanes today descend and glide to a rolling stop on runways over a mile long. Take-off requires about the same distances. For anyone who has watched reruns of the *Jetsons* cartoons, and asked, "Dude, where's my flying car?," the answer is that no one has solved Newcomb's challenge: how to start and stop a flying aircraft on a dime. The main problems grounding flying cars are the extraordinary power requirements for takeoff, travel, and landing, the short duration of batteries and their heavy weight, the nuisance of noise thanks to multiple whirling blades, and ensuring safety in flight.

A handful of startups are attempting to address these challenges by building electric vehicles that take off and land vertically like helicopters, but then fly like planes (eVTOLs for short).

The FAA has yet to certify an electric plane, let alone a vertical take-off and landing vehicle for commercial use. Undaunted, some of these companies are promising to offer commuter taxi services by 2024 or so. All will require a pilot, and the companies have no plans to sell the vehicles, but instead aim to operate and maintain them as a fleet to ensure safety. Even so, we are still a long way off from George Jetson strapping into his bubble-pod flying car and then taking off for work from his Skypad apartment in Orbit City.

TEAMS TO WATCH: Joby Aviation, Kitty Hawk, Whisper Aero, Lilium, Archer, Vertical Aerospace.

Autonomous Vehicles: About 36,000 people died in vehicle crashes in the United States in 2019. For the world as a whole, it's about 1.3 million per year. In total, an estimated 60 million people were killed in motor vehicle accidents across the 20th century. Many of these fatalities are due to drunk-driving, which in the United States kills at a rate of twenty-eight people per day. If driving were a new technology, it would be banned for causing too many deaths.

This is not to say humans are always reckless drivers. Most of the time, they're actually pretty good. But sober robots promise to be even better, and they are never sick-at-sea. Driverless cars have long been a dream of science fiction since the earliest days of the genre. Arguably, the idea goes back to magic flying carpets and mystical moving thrones. The many scenarios depicting autonomous vehicles try to capture some of that magic by showing commuters preoccupied with their work or their friends instead of paying attention to the road, or perhaps more extravagantly, ads will tell stories of long-range caravans of autonomous vehicles, trains of driverless cars and buses swiftly moving at 150 miles per hour towards some fantastic destination in the night. But, whatever the fairy tale, at bottom autonomous vehicles are about safety. The ultimate dream is the uncrashable car.[9] Progress would mean fewer road fatalities and injuries, fewer accidents, and fewer fender-benders. The main problem facing the field, though, is that to date, no one has built a system that's as good or better than a human in all situations.

Today, there are two contending rivalries within the industry. In one corner are the incrementalists, who see automation evolving over the next decade step-by-step—as characterized in the jargon of the NHTSA—from Level 3 to Level 4 to Level 5 autonomy. Where we are today, Level 2, represents the "advanced driver assistance systems" that keep an eye out for human error. They can prevent cars from drifting across lanes, instantly brake when another car stops short, and park the car in tight spots. Incrementalists bring together cutting-edge components with top-tier legacy car companies: Volvo, Mercedes, Toyota, and so on. Their main advantage is in numbers and falling costs. They sell millions of cars every year to consumers. As their sensors collect data from every new Volvo or Toyota on the streets today, the sheer volume of the information will train each further generation to get better and better. In short, Level 3 must be mastered before Level 4, and so on. (Despite the reckless bravado of calling its system "FSD, full self-driving" this is Tesla's approach as well.)

Now, in the other corner of the ring, there are the brash tech diehards. They don't believe in evolution. They want a giant leap straight into Level 4 autonomy or death. What that means today is a full fleet of robotaxis that operate within ring-fenced, meticulously mapped locations under easy conditions. For example, Google's Waymo has been operating a small test fleet within a circumscribed zone in perpetually sunny and warm Phoenix, Arizona. (Level 5 would mean full autonomy anywhere anytime—imagine the same car working in a snowstorm at night on a winding road in the Colorado Rockies.) Waymo, GM's Cruise, Amazon's Zoox, and the venture-backed darling Aurora are all betting billions to prove they can make the big leap in this way to the driverless future. It's big tech versus the old auto-industry in a sudden-death showdown and, at this point, all bets are off. It should make for an exciting decade ahead. Either way, thankfully, the upshot will mean fewer deaths on the road. TEAMS TO WATCH: Luminar, Tesla, Aurora, Cruise, Waymo.

Traffic: It is difficult to fathom the time lost to traffic. My own private vision of hell is of being stuck in an endless traffic jam on a broiling hot day with no working air conditioner and talk radio turned on at a high volume. For many in Los Angeles, this is a daily commute. Elon Musk believes traffic is the "ultimate boss battle" and that drilling networks of tunnels under cities will relieve the pain of the problem. Perhaps he is right. Regardless, his unusual proposal shows how intractable the problem has become.

Health

The history of health and medicine has had its winning streaks. The most inspiring took place during the fifty years at the center of the last century, starting with the discovery of penicillin in 1928 and ending with the first test-tube baby in 1978. It is truly one of the most impressive eras of human achievement. The canon of supreme discoveries and inventions would at a minimum include antibiotics, steroids, the randomized controlled trial, smoking as a cause of lung cancer, the structure of DNA, ventilation, antipsychotic medications, the polio vaccine, open-heart surgery, the pill, new hips for the old, kidney transplants, heart transplants, understanding hypertension and the prevention of strokes, a treatment for childhood leukemia, the endoscope, the laparoscope, the Zeiss operating microscope, angioplasty, and the CAT scan. There are many others. In almost every case, the story involves a heroic struggle through years of suffering, a steep learning curve paid in death, early defeats, and the disapproval of colleagues. But even so, the advances came fast: all the great families of antibiotics appeared in a span of less than ten years. Fortunately for us, doctors and scientists persevered to find a cure, a treatment, a way to do the impossible. Sometimes they experimented on themselves first. Other times... well, the most peculiar story may well be that of John Gibbon, inventor of the pump that made open-heart surgery possible. Over four years in the late 1930s as a research fellow, he would catch stray cats off the streets of Boston and Philadelphia, enticing them with cans of tuna, then subjecting them to his Dr. Frankenstein experiments. He'd detach their hearts and pump their blood through his newfangled machine in an effort to oxygenate the blood outside the body. Then he'd reattach their hearts to see if the cats could survive. In the long run, his cat-snatching paid off, but it's hard to imagine a Harvard Medical School student roaming the streets of Boston like this today.

In any event, the benefits of this panoply of discoveries—plus better sanitation and clean water—translated into longer and healthier lives. Life expectancy at birth in the United States was about 47 years in 1900. By 1980, at the end of the golden era, that had jumped to 73.6 years. Though vastly fewer infants were dying—leading to a higher average life expectancy—it is also true that people were living much longer. In 1900, 4 percent of the U.S. population was older than 65; by 1980, that figure became 11.3 percent of a total population which was now nearly three times bigger.

But, just as in the other sectors of science, the rate of progress slowed down in the 1970s. The star was extinguished, but the light carried on, for a time. And so it was that at the beginning of that decade, expectations were running at all-time highs. And why not, given the success of the previous fifty years? Sidney Farber, the godfather of chemotherapy, told *Newsweek* that "the next ten years will be wonderful ones for cancer therapy. The time could come quite soon when the beast will be tamed." President Richard Nixon represented the apex of that optimism, launching a "War Against Cancer" in his 1971 State of the Union address. "The time has come," Nixon urged, "when the same kind of concerted effort that split the atom and took a man to the Moon should be turned towards conquering this dreaded disease."

The money flowed. Research expanded. Years passed. But the advances were not as easily won as they were before. The gifts from nature that had fallen into our lap by fortuitous accident, like antibiotics and cortisol, ran dry. One of the premier journals in science, *Nature*, published a gloomy paper in 1982, tolling the death knell of progress: "An End to the Search for New Drugs?" it asked. Cancer remained undefeated. Other diseases—Parkinson's, Alzheimer's—eluded our understanding. Ignorance of causes led to quackery. In dollars spent, the popularity of "alternative medicine" boomed. And despite the hype, early genetic engineering delivered only modest wins. The first wave of gene therapy, none. After the thalidomide tragedy in the 1960s—babies born without limbs due to a drug—the regulatory grip had tightened. As a result, by the 1980s the number of new drugs cleared each year declined, the cost of bringing a new drug to market skyrocketed, and innovation began to falter.

Many of the new drugs that did pass the hurdles were marginal improvements upon older medicines, rather than magic bullets for as-yet-untreatable diseases. Other drugs were more of a mixed blessing, less straightforward cures and more an anxious cloud of questions about efficacy and harmful side effects. It is true, the rate of progress from the late 1970s to the present was not zero. The last four decades saw its own achievements: stents, the discovery of the cause of peptic ulcers, a therapy for AIDS, clot-busting drugs, keyhole surgery, the MRI, sequencing the human genome, and…yes…Viagra. But as impressive as these discoveries are, it is hard for us today to appreciate how dangerous life was before penicillin, and therefore how miraculous, how momentous, how life-changing its discovery was. In fact, the first person administered penicillin, Albert Alexander, was on the verge of death because he had scratched his face on a rose bush. A rose bush! Such trivial cuts took people down all the time. Sadly, Alexander still died because the researchers couldn't make enough penicillin to see him through the doses needed to end his infection. But it was a true magic bullet: it killed the bacteria, and side-effects were minimal. Such miracles have run out.

Today, for the first time in a century, life expectancy in the U.S. has declined or stayed flat for five years straight. Due to Covid-19's toll, it now stands at 77.3 years, only three and a half years higher than it was in 1980.

There are an incalculable number of ways people can die. Any list quickly becomes a bewildering profusion, a chamber of horrors full of diseases and dysfunctions and traumas. Whenever I read medical memoirs, I'm struck by a heightened sense of my own fragility, particularly books by neurosurgeons like Henry Marsh or heart surgeons like Stephen Westaby. The narrow margin between life and death in their operating theaters is often thinner than an egg shell. Given all the ways things can go wrong, it's an absolute miracle we can walk and talk, and survive another day to do it again without cracking. It would take several volumes to list all the ways the body breaks down and all the ways researchers are investigating to treat it. But there are some hopeful lines of research and development that may reopen the frontier of health and medicine in the coming decade. I will cover a few, as well as some of the outstanding problems.

Immunotherapies: Jim Allison is a hog-stomping, beer-drinking, harmonica-playing, honky-tonk Texan who also happens to be one stubborn scientist.[10] When he came across another lab's results that didn't feel right, that didn't sit well with his understanding, he'd say, "We're gonna test this fucker to see if it's really right." His persistence through the 1980s and '90s paid off and led to a key breakthrough that deepened our understanding of how the immune system works. Allison was the first to discover the receptor on T cells that allows them to recognize and destroy diseased cells. He then uncovered how cancer cells disable this response from T cells, in effect hiding themselves from our body's own immune system. Tumors have the power to make themselves invisible by engaging another receptor on the T cell called CTLA-4, which puts the brakes on the immune response. It tells the T cell to stand down. Without that cloaking mechanism, our immune system would quickly identify and destroy cancer cells. It dawned on Allison that if he found a way to block the CTLA-4 checkpoint, much like breaking the end off a key in a lock, then our own immune system could cure cancer for us.

The challenge was to create the right antibody to act as the broken key in the lock. During Christmas in 1996, a postdoc in Allison's lab took off on vacation and asked Allison to check in on the mice they were testing a new antibody on. Before

Christmas, Allison measured and recorded that the tumors in the mice were growing. Then a funny thing happened. Swept up in the holiday, Allison forgot his promise to check on the mice. He said later that if the postdoc did that, he would've fired him. Christmas came and went, and then a few days later, Allison remembered the mice. When he came to the lab, he found that, for the mice that received the new antibody, the tumors were gone. Vanished. Their cancer had completely disappeared. The other mice that had received nothing were not so fortunate. They all had died.

That experiment marked the beginning of a new era in the treatment for some forms of cancer. It took fifteen years for Allison to bring the first cancer immunotherapy to market. Now a whole new field exists that investigates various ways of using the body's natural defenses to destroy tumor cells. Allison won the Nobel Prize in medicine in 2018.

There are still many unresolved problems. Checkpoint inhibitors only cure a subset of patients. Ipilimumab, the drug built from Allison's CTLA-4 work, reduced deaths from late-stage melanoma by 28–38 percent. We're still a long way from curing all cases. For other patients, taking the brakes off of the immune system can lead to toxic side effects. An overheated, unchecked immune system attacking our own tissues can lead to all sorts of negative complications.

The current wave of cancer immunotherapies shows stronger efficacy, more precision, and less toxicity. The newer class of checkpoint inhibitors, using different connections either on the cancer cell or on the T cell, can also stop the binding handshake that tells the T cells to stand down. (In the acronyms of the binding sites, these are classed as either PD-1 or PD-L1; welcome to the confusing alphabet soup of the field's jargon). The next wave beyond this will probably expand on what are called CAR-T therapies, another acronym worth remembering. It stands for chimeric antigen receptor T cell, which is immunology-speak for building the Wolverine or Captain America T cell. This therapy involves genetically engineering T cells to give them receptors specifically tailored to identify and destroy a patient's unique cancer cells. If the first generation of cancer immunotherapies unleashed the body's own army, then CAR-T therapies are about creating the mutant special forces. By sequencing the genome of the cancer cells, researchers can use that unique information to program mutant T cells to launch a pinpoint attack on the right target. There are CAR-T treatments available now that show strong success with blood cancers such as lymphoma, leukemia, and myeloma. They are not yet widely used for treating solid tumors. The challenge is to keep the engineered T cells activated for long enough to kill what's needed. They currently grow exhausted before fully eliminating solid tumors and they don't yet replicate themselves for reinforcements. Solving this problem could truly mean winning the war on cancer at last, more than fifty years after Nixon first announced it.

TEAMS TO WATCH: too many to list, as there are more than three thousand clinical trials in progress testing medicines that either unleash the immune system in a novel way or strengthen a soldier in the immune system army. But remember the alphabet soup.

Infectious Disease, BioError, BioTerror: In 1948, George C. Marshall, U.S. Secretary of State and architect of the Marshall Plan, made a bold prediction. He told the gathering of the Fourth International Congress on Tropical Medicine and Malaria that the world could expect the "imminent conquest of disease."[11] He was not laughed out of the room. Hardly anyone doubted that such an ambitious goal was possible. In fact, after witnessing the discovery of antibiotics—which, for the developed world, put an end to the millennia-long scourge of tuberculosis—most thought the end of infectious disease inevitable. Ten years later President Eisenhower called for the "unconditional surrender" of infectious microbes, while then-Senator John F. Kennedy predicted that those born in the 1960s would no longer have to fear pestilence.

Such optimism could claim one great triumph: the eradication of smallpox. Backed and supported by both the Soviet Union and the United States, even as the Cold War raged on, a team at the World Health Organization led a campaign to vaccinate the world, particularly in the most at-risk places in the developing world, despite war, dictatorship, famine, or natural disaster. It started in 1967, and just eight years later, the team was able to announce that a three-year-old Bangladeshi girl named Rahima Banu had been cured and was therefore the last case of the variola major in human history. Two years later, in 1977, the last case of variola minor would be cured in Somalia. Smallpox had been conquered.

But, as impressive as the victory was, the defeats had been mounting elsewhere. Malaria proved unstoppable. Marburg, Ebola, Lassa, Machupo: extremely deadly viruses no one had encountered before seemed to spring out from rats, bats, and monkeys to humans with uncomfortable regularity. Flu pandemics broke out in 1957, 1968, and 1977. And then there was HIV/AIDS, the cruel history-maker, which at first confounded and then haunted a generation.

Now we have Covid-19, and all of its variants. These outbreaks are not anomalies. If there is one prediction in this book I can make with near certainty, it's that we can expect the emergence and spread of new infectious diseases in the decades ahead.[12] Nature always has more surprises in store. Two factors make this certain: evolution and globalization. Viruses, bacteria, and parasites will continue to mutate and adapt, whether in man or animal. Meanwhile, Covid lockdowns notwithstanding, people travel more frequently and to more places every year. There are few regions that remain truly isolated from the rest of the world.

Gaëtan Dugas erroneously became one of the early scapegoats of the AIDS epidemic. Because four of the early AIDS cases in Los Angeles in 1981 named Dugas as a sexual partner, CDC investigators designated Dugas "Patient o," meaning he was the first node in the network they investigated.[13] The writer Randy Shilts, in his book *And the Band Played On*, misread that research and then renamed Dugas "Patient Zero," believing Dugas was the first person to transmit the disease to Americans. Thus, a malicious falsehood was born. What's more, researchers later said they intended to use "O" for "out of California" and not the number "o." Never has a typo defamed someone so badly.[14] At any rate, it is now known that HIV was transmitted to humans from primates, probably chimpanzees, somewhere in West Africa in the early 20th century. It is unknown how or when it mutated to become HIV, but the preponderance of evidence confirms the virus is descended from a virus that compromises the immune system of monkeys, chimpanzees, and other primates. There is simply no way Dugas was patient zero.

But if he was wrongly vilified, Dugas remains a symbol for the future of infectious disease. In a sense, he represents the dawn of an irreversibly tangled world, swift in its movement and dismissive of national borders. He was a Canadian flight attendant with sexual partners in just about every major North American city. Dugas told investigators he'd had sex with about 750 men from 1978 to 1982, from New York to Miami, Los Angeles, and San Francisco. But tracking its spread through people like Dugas was only partially helpful. It took nearly two years after the epidemic took off before researchers were able to identify

288 • PAPER BELT ON FIRE

the virus that caused the disease. The story should serve as a warning that speaks to the difficulty of detecting the emergence of something lethal and new, as well as to the futility of quarantining it. In this sense, the AIDS epidemic was not a one-off piece of bad luck, a once-in-a-lifetime natural catastrophe, but the beginning of a new era, a prelude to Covid-19, and a model for contagion in a modern world. We should be prepared for whatever will come next. And come it will.

Humans will always be humans. Social control—lockdowns, masks, and so on—may serve to limit exposure and slow the spread of infection, but it cannot save us. Early detection is important, and may serve to put out small fires, but above all we need to build the tools that either prevent infection or treat the disease after we have it. As Covid has made abundantly clear, we need cheap rapid tests, we need vaccines, and we need treatments. Social control alone can only make a calamity somewhat less bad than it otherwise might be. A virus or bug only has to escape once. To be effective, social control would have to run flawlessly every single time it came up against a new pathogen. Expecting that level of competence, adherence, and good luck over decades strains credulity.

There is another way. On January 10, 2020, scientists in China posted on the Internet the genetic sequence for a novel coronavirus, which they called the "Wuhan seafood market pneumonia virus." The next morning at home in Maryland, Barney Graham downloaded the information and set his team to work.[15] Graham, a director for vaccine research at the National Institute for Health, had been working on vaccines for coronaviruses for years. But most recently he had been working on vaccines for the Zika and the Nipah viruses with a Massachusetts-based company, Moderna. Moderna had invented a new way to program human cells to manufacture biological parts—the proteins unique to a virus—that our immune system needs to learn how to recognize in order to learn how to defend itself. By January 12, only two days after the Chinese scientists had posted the genetic information, Graham's team had designed a protein sequence to send to Moderna. Within two weeks Moderna was testing it in mice. Human safety trials began eight weeks later in March.

No vaccine had ever been created in less than four years. By the end of 2020—less than a year after Graham booted up his laptop—Pfizer, Moderna, and others had earned emergency use authorization approval from the FDA for vaccines against Covid-19. (Pfizer's vaccine was also based on Graham's spike protein research). This is an astonishing accomplishment that deserves its place in the annals of human achievement. Michael Lewis, arguably the best non-fiction writer in America, wrote a best-selling book, *The Premonition*, about the "heroic" team that came up with the best plan for social control and the government agencies that failed to implement it. Nowhere in his book does he mention Graham or his team or others who worked on vaccines. It boggles the mind how such a great writer turned in such a poor performance. It was only vaccines, treatments, and immunity—and not social control—that could save us.

But as miraculous as that story is, we need to be faster. New viruses, new bacteria, stronger multi-antibiotic resistant bacteria, new parasites—the entire phantasmagoria of human killers will continue to emerge anew. If not from nature, then from man, either as an accidental lab leak or as a genetically engineered act of bioterrorism. It is not out of the question that many of the most lethal viruses in the world can be made more contagious. Tuberculosis may return yet, stronger and more resilient. So we must head them all off at the pass. One of the biggest unsolved problems is how to create vaccines that prevent infection against all mutations of a flu virus or a coronavirus, rather than against one or a few variants. And while the FDA's three-stage process for drug approval is a gold standard, we need to allow for experimentation in testing safety and efficacy. The Phase 3 trials for Moderna and Pfizer's Covid-19 vaccines enlisted 30,000 people each and tracked them for months. Whether any of the participants encountered Covid-19 during that time was left to chance. There is an alternative process the FDA could have used that takes chance out of the equation and adds speed: the human challenge trial.

A human challenge trial is when test subjects are exposed to a virus after being vaccinated or being given a placebo. By subjecting the virus to the strongest possible test against a vaccine as fast as possible, scientists could gain more information more quickly about the efficacy of the treatment. Now, imagine this counterfactual: On May 9, 2020, Graham received an email from researchers at Vanderbilt who examined the effect of the Moderna vaccine on the eight Phase I participants. The results were beyond what Graham ever expected. After the Vanderbilt researchers sampled antibodies from the volunteers' blood and then tested them on infected cells in the lab, the Covid-19 virus stopped replicating. Outside of a high fever for a high-dose participant, there were no worrisome side effects. So how about this: what if the FDA decided to conduct human challenge trials at this time? It is hard to make certain estimates, but scientists could have obtained the information they needed on efficacy and safety in two to three months, rather than seven. How many lives could have been saved if the vaccines were available in August rather than December 2020? Hundreds of thousands. Maybe millions globally. Doctors, Nobel Prize-winning scientists, philosophers, and public intellectuals—all of unsurpassed eminence, 177 of them—signed an open letter to the NIH in

July of 2020 begging for human challenge trials and making the ethical argument.[16] They were ignored.

The future of nations may well hinge on their ability to adapt their institutions to the challenges of our time. The hardships of the Covid-19 epidemic put the world on edge. It's not going to get any easier, and what worked in the past is not adequate for the future. Just like our vaccines, the FDA must adapt to meet the lethal mutations ahead.

Diet, Nutrition, Obesity, Diabetes: Something else curious began in the 1970s, just as progress slowed down. The world began to get fatter.[17] By the 1990s, the CDC called it an epidemic. About one out of three Americans are obese. Two out of three are overweight. Eight percent qualify as extremely obese, as defined by the National Institute of Health. In fact, over the past four decades, on every continent, people are getting heavier. Even zoo animals, horses, pets, lab rats, and wild animals began to put on weight. It remains a mystery as to why.[18]

To make matters worse, no diet has ever proven to be better than the rest. Instead, fad diets backed by snake-oil pseudoscience abound. A raft of books touting new theories is published every year. One of the strongest signs of stagnation is an abundance of quackery. It betrays our ignorance. First, the fad was for no carbs, then it was for low-fat, then it was for only meat, then it was only for foods available during the Paleolithic era, when our lithe ancestors chased mammoth barefoot across the grass. There is a lot of money to be made off our gullibility and ignorance. Study after study—and meta-studies of those studies—find that on pretty much every diet, people lose a small amount of weight at first and then gain much of it back a year later. It didn't help, either, that the U.S. government, lobbied by special interests, promoted the wrong diet for over fifty years

in its now-infamous "food pyramid." Now, to be fair, researchers have found a few convincing strong correlations and causal
pathways that can prove helpful. Chief among them begins with
sugar. The more sugar in someone's diet, the more insulin in
their blood. Too much insulin, not at a torrential, but a persistent
rate on a year-to-year, decade-to-decade basis... well, there are
complex mechanisms at work here, but suffice to say insulin
can work to make us fatter. It increases the fat we store and
decreases the fat we burn. Eventually, our fat and muscle cells
gain resistance to insulin, then... catastrophe. So those trying
to lose weight would probably do well by eating fewer sugary
foods. A few experiments have also found a link between the
types of bacteria in our gut and how much energy a person
extracts from food.[19] The more energy we extract from the same
portion of food, the heavier we get.

It is shocking, however, how little we know about food,
motivation, and weight loss. Despite sugary foods being bad, in
general, and the cause of all sorts of bodily mischief, we all know
that one lucky bastard who lives on donuts and cakes and ices
and yet remains healthy and thin as a rail. On the other hand, we
also come across the preternaturally vigorous who run five half-
marathons a week, but who also seem to gain inches on the waist
every year. Cause and effect here are mysterious and uncertain.
And while it is a simple truth that eating less of everything will
cause someone to lose weight, life is never that simple. What
seems to work for some people doesn't work for someone else.
It appears that what constitutes a healthy diet depends not only
on what is being eaten, but *who* is eating it, their genetics, their
habits, their age, their hormone levels, and the composition of
the bacteria in their gut. To add to the problem, we have only
scratched the surface when it comes to understanding the psychology of diets and motivation.[20] Sugar can activate the same

reward centers in the brain as cocaine. Finding comfort in eating a tub of ice cream after getting dumped is not a joke. There is a pile of research finding a link between coping with anxiety and snacking.[21] Then there is our unconscious self-sabotage. People consistently miscalculate portion sizes, and they are poor at remembering what they ate earlier that day.[22]

We stand before an ocean of ignorance. The big questions—Why do we get fat? Why do we stay fat?—cannot be answered with confidence and clarity. The stakes are high. Obesity is strongly correlated with many illnesses, particularly Type 2 diabetes and heart disease, respectively numbers eight and one on the top ten chart for leading killers. There is currently no cure for Type 2 diabetes, and about one out of seven Americans have it. Diabetes increases the risk of heart attack, stroke, kidney failure, and the loss of limbs. The World Health Organization reports obesity rates have doubled around the world since 1980 and have accelerated in the last decade. Researchers have not pinned down whether obesity itself causes diabetes or whether there is some underlying cause that produces them both (along with an increased risk of heart disease). There are two leading candidates behind them all, much in the same way that smoking increases the likelihood of lung cancer, but we need more research. The first suspect would be sugar. The mechanisms whereby sugar works to make us fatter and ultimately diabetic are becoming better known. But there are confounding issues with sugar being the sole culprit in the obesity epidemic. For one, there are hunter-gatherer societies—the Hadza, the Mbuti, the Kuna—whose members consume as much or more sugar than Americans do, and yet they remain thin and healthy. Two—and much more troubling for the sweet tooth theory—sugar consumption has declined worldwide over the last two decades, by 15 to 23 percent, yet obesity rates and diabetes rates have continued to soar.[23] And so we are left with a second candidate, Contaminant X, which would be a toxic substance that we either breathe, drink, or eat, but have not yet identified.

In 1900, the average man in the United States weighed about 155 lbs., and only one percent of the population was obese.[24] Today, he weighs about 195 lbs., and a third of the country is obese. Until 1975, no country in the world had an obesity rate higher than 15 percent. Something changed around 1980. To quote one *Lancet* study, "There are no exemplar populations in which the obesity epidemic has been reversed by public health measures."[25] This is worse than stagnation. It is an absolute decline.

Longer, Healthier Lifespans: On June 23, 2006, Harriet died of a heart attack. A good-natured old lady, till her last day she loved munching on hibiscus flowers and napping by the pond. If she needed rest, it may have been because her long life had been quite the epic. When she was about five years old, she met Charles Darwin on an island of the Galápagos, where she was born, and he took her with him back to London. Years later Darwin would formulate his theory of evolution based on his visit to Harriet's home. But in the meantime, on the way to London, the captain of the HMS Beagle took a shine to Harriet—though he thought she was a he and called her Harry. She didn't seem to mind. After he retired from the British Royal Navy in 1841, Captain Wickham decided to bring Harriet to Australia, where she lived for the next 165 years, eventually under the care of Steve ("Crikey!!") Irwin, the famous "crocodile hunter." Harriet had lived through the American Civil War and two world wars. She napped when Einstein overthrew Newton. She witnessed the invention of the radio, the car, the skyscraper, the airplane, movies, and television, and she even saw a man play golf on the moon. This was all possible because Harriet was born with a special gift. Even though she aged, her risk of death from disease or organ failure never increased as she got older. It stayed low and constant till the end. Scientists call this good fortune "negligible senescence," which means Harriet could grow old without getting old. Harriet, you may have guessed, was a Galápagos tortoise. She lived to 175.

We are very different from Harriet. As we age, the risks of death, disease, and suffering increase exponentially. Aging is not only about retiring to Florida, counting our wrinkles and dyeing our gray hair. Aging is a broad set of biological changes that accelerate and accumulate over time.[26] Take any major disease—heart failure, cancer, dementia—and its root causes are ultimately age-related. By and large younger people simply do not die from these lethal afflictions, nor do they suffer from frailty, forgetfulness, or other sources of trouble. But as the years add up, the story gets darker. The older we get, the higher the chances that we suffer or die from a major illness. The odds of a healthy thirty-year-old dying in any year are somewhere just shy of one in one thousand. By the age of ninety it's about one in six.

But this need not be so. Nature provides her own proof that the rate of aging can be altered. All plants and animals age at different rates. Some animals, like Harriet, live much longer than humans. The bowhead whale is another example. The oldest recorded bowhead whale lived to somewhere around 211 years; another bowhead was recently found with a 19th-century harpoon still lodged into its body, an annoying childhood injury from the days of Moby Dick. Trees can live even longer. Sequoias can live for millennia. Meanwhile, other creatures, like mayflies, die in hours.

Why is this so?

There is no universal constant rate of aging, like a speed of light for biology or a gravitational constant for death. That variance among animals is the telltale sign that the building blocks of life—from the proteins to the cells to the organs—could all be tweaked in some way either to shorten or extend our lifespans. It is one of the great unsolved mysteries of our time to identify the causes underlying this process. An even bigger accomplishment would be to slow it down or reverse it. Anti-aging medicine is a young field. Hardly anyone took it seriously until the last decade. The Food and Drug Administration still refuses to classify aging as a disease. But the tide is starting to shift.

Aging isn't one change within us; it is many. Below are nine of the main categories of biological change that either cause aging or correlate strongly with it.[27] In some cases it's hard to tell if one of these hallmarks of aging is a root cause or the first effect of a deeper mechanism driving the change. Other times, these issues can serve as both cause and effect, with negative feedback loops accelerating decline over time. Progress in understanding the true underlying mechanisms in each category will illuminate the possible paths forward for slowing or reversing the biological clock. Suffice to say, there are many unsolved research problems in any of these categories of aging and a clear explanation of each would entail an entire book. I invite readers to dig in. The sources in the endnotes are good places to start learning. Nevertheless, in no particular order, the main categories of aging are:

1. accumulating damage and mutations to our DNA
2. telomeres shortening
3. defective proteins
4. epigenetic alterations
5. accumulating old cells that are not disposed of
6. mitochondria malfunction
7. chronic inflammation

8. depleted stem cells
9. a weakening immune system

Many approaches for addressing these issues have focused on garbage collection, in a sense. Out with the old and in with the new. For instance, proteins act as tiny bio-robots that gain their function by their form: how they fold when they are first made determines their function in our body. Therefore, proteins that are damaged or that haven't folded into their correct shape can wreak havoc if they spread and accumulate. Restricting our diet seems to help with this, as our body will in effect eat up these defective proteins for energy. (Some drugs, like metformin, that mimic the effects of dietary restriction also help with this.) In any event, we need a way to chop up these old and damaged proteins before they cause us trouble. Then there are aged cells that have ceased to divide but haven't destroyed themselves. These can accumulate in our tissues over time and accelerate aging. In the spirit of spring cleaning, some promising research programs have investigated ways of identifying and removing these misfolded proteins and senescent cells. But, as in all interventions, precision is difficult to achieve, and side-effects hard to contain.

By far the most promising line of anti-aging research aims to reprogram our cells to turn back their clocks. We've long known about the experimental potential of embryonic stem cells. But they were hard to come by and many people had moral qualms about their use. Then, in 2006, a Japanese scientist named Shinya Yamanaka discovered a breakthrough.[28] He and his team devised a way to transform a skin cell from a human body back into a stem cell. Now we no longer need embryos to create stem cells. By identifying four genes whose function is to govern and guide other genes—these are called transcription factors—Yamanaka found he could coax our cells back to the pluripotent state they were in when we were freshly conceived in our mother's womb. (Pluripotency means a stem cell has the potential to divide and turn into any kind of cell in the body.) The four genes Yamanaka identified are now known as "Yamanaka factors," and for their discovery he was awarded a Nobel Prize in 2012.

In the following decade, researchers have found that while Yamanaka could turn the clock back to zero for any cell, it is also possible to use Yamanaka factors to control the clock-winding with greater precision and restraint.[29] Instead of going all the way back to the very beginning, where cells lose their particular identity as a neuron, a muscle cell, a heart cell, or a skin cell, we can turn the clock back five years or ten years and so on without the cells losing their identity and corresponding functions. Cellular reprogramming in this controlled fashion can rejuvenate cells and now whole animals like mice by activating the Yamanaka factors for short periods of time at a spaced frequency. The total effect appears to be the reversal of aging. It is not yet known to what degree this will work on humans, or what the toxic side-effects might be.

Nevertheless, cellular reprogramming by Yamanaka factors could well be the hottest area of biology right now. A great deal of money is pouring into the research. For example, in early 2022 Jeff Bezos and Yuri Milner invested $3 billion in Los Altos Labs, a biotech anti-aging startup. The Los Altos Labs team is staffed with the leading lights of the field, including Shinya Yamanaka himself, as well as Jennifer Doudna, winner of the 2020 Nobel Prize for her co-discovery of the gene editing tool CRISPR-Cas9. While I am skeptical of colossal war chests being raised without any smaller milestones first being hit along the way—it shows a remarkable lack of edge control—I wish this all-star team the best.

Treating one disease at a time will only increase our lifespan by a small margin. Cure cancer, and we may only live an extra three years on average, because heart disease or another health issue will still kill us. Instead, we must address the deeper problem. Aging is the leading cause of death and suffering in the world. Though we cannot make time stand still, we may yet live like the tortoise and run like the hare.

Education

We are in the Dark Ages when it comes to teaching and learning—the bloodletting and leeches phase of our educational history. I make this harsh assessment based on how little progress there has been in the last fifty years. According to the U.S. Census Bureau, the U.S. government spent $752.3 billion on its public schools in 2019.[30] That's close to triple the spending per pupil since 1971, even adjusting for inflation. All the same, there are zero studies that find student outcomes are three times better than they were then. Not even close. Our schools fail to teach the basics: 23.1 percent of Californians over the age of fifteen are illiterate; more than half of all U.S. adults read below a sixth-grade level.[31]

We can broadly define learning as improving performance. There are many challenges in this field, but the six that stand out to me as the most important are the following: (1) figuring out how to spark curiosity and motivate students; (2) improving the rate at which students learn; (3) making sure students retain for years what they've learned; (4) teaching students how to transfer what they've learned in one domain to a new domain they've never encountered before; (5) cultivating creativity; and (6) doing all of these things at a decreasing cost and increasing scale. Progress in education would mean making advances on all these dimensions.

School is not education. A school is one method among

many for attempting to provide an education. Classrooms are not education. They too are merely a technique for teaching. And, I think, a rather poor one.

What, then, is the best way to learn?

All too often politicians, commentators, and the public focus on different issues. Many contentious arguments have broken out on what students should or shouldn't learn—the required curriculum—and on whether the government should run schools or not. I, for one, believe most of what public and private schools teach is worthless in preparing young people for the world. Consequently, I believe the government spends far too much money on schooling most students poorly. But that is neither here nor there when it comes to the fundamental questions of what methods and what techniques make for the best way to learn. That is an empirical question, independent of education's content or who pays for it, and the field is wide open for innovation.

It is sad to see how few advances in educational psychology are implemented in the classroom. In one exhaustive review, a group of psychologists and a neuroscientist examined a vast body of research on different learning techniques.[32] They focused on the ten most popular techniques and evaluated their relative performance. They also controlled for how well each technique works in different circumstances, across students of different abilities and ages, across different types of course materials, and for whether students were taking tests or writing essays.

The bad news is that the vast majority of students and teachers continue to rely heavily on terrible, ineffective learning techniques. In particular, the use of highlighting, underlining, rereading, and pouring over notes have little benefit. Despite many people reporting that they feel good doing these things, none of these techniques are good at helping students learn, nor at helping them remember what little they've learned after a time delay. One prominent book on the subject by two experts in learning and memory concludes, "Empirical research into how we learn and remember shows that much of what we take for gospel about how to learn turns out to be largely wasted effort."[33] Add on top of that the compulsion requiring a child to sit still in a chair in a row in a class for six hours a day, year after year. Boredom and subservience rule; students even must ask permission to use the bathroom. No wonder so many children hate school and cheer joyfully when a snowstorm cancels class.[34]

Part of the problem may be that no one has taught the teachers themselves. The researchers note that hardly any textbook in educational psychology offers a comprehensive overview of how effective different learning techniques are at boosting achievement. They conclude that it is highly unlikely that most teachers know what strategies work best and, worse yet, have no idea how to train students to use them.

The good news is that two cheap, relatively easy to use methods stand out as the most effective at boosting student performance: practice testing and distributed practice. Distributed practice is when students establish and stick to a consistent schedule of practice over time. (Its antithesis is cramming). Practice is not mere repetition, but a deliberate effort to improve performance in the Goldilocks zone where success is neither too easily gained, nor the challenge too hard. Self-testing as a technique should not be confused with high stakes standardized testing, but instead as a way of frequently probing the edge of knowledge in a field.

There have been thousands of education companies created in the last two decades, all of which offer courses of instruction, but I have not yet encountered a "test-making" company, beyond bare-bones sites like Quizlet. It would be useful to have a service that could quickly create one hundred practice tests on any subject of my choosing, whether on German Romanticism or quantum mechanics.

Consistent self-testing and distributed practice are the most effective learning techniques, but they are also the most painful, as both of these strategies require discipline, energy, and individual effort. Notice they do not require a classroom or a school. Maybe not even a teacher. As it is, however, the experience requires so much effort that some students report feeling as though they are not learning when in fact they are. (Strangely enough, the opposite is often true. There is a mistaken, pleasurable feeling of learning while using bad methods, creating an illusion of mastery, which convinces us we know more than we actually do.) Overcoming the anguish of the effort and the anxiety in the struggle to master a subject is not easy. Our minds and the reserves of our energy have severe and natural limits. Conscientiousness and fire are not easy traits to switch on at will. We need to understand coaching and motivation better—as with diets and working out—and how to stoke the flames of curiosity.

The bar is pretty low compared to where we are now, however. Today's typical classroom inspires dread and alienation. Just picture rows of desks lit by scalding overhead fluorescent lights, enclosed by cinder block walls with a few tiny windows, a stern teacher at the head of the class forcing students to memorize collections of dead facts for a test they don't care about. The horror!

Then there are the more intangible questions that require our attention. How can we encourage students to pursue the truth, independent of other people's approval? How do we teach civil disobedience, training our young to fight for what's right? Or how to practice delayed gratification for worthy long-term goals? Are these even possible to teach? No one has bothered to ask.

At any rate, we have the rudiments of a map for learning, but more work needs to be done. The techniques for learning must themselves be learned. How often students need to relearn the best techniques and how often they remember to use them when needed in the future is not yet known. Moreover, there may be newer methods driven by technology that we have not yet discovered or tested. Most education technology has failed, but I remain open to the possibility of progress.

As far as instruction goes, the most tantalizing topic in teaching and learning has become known as "Bloom's two sigma problem," after Benjamin Bloom, the education psychologist.[35] One-to-one tutoring far surpasses any other style of teaching when it comes to improving student performance. Bloom found tutored students performed two standard deviations better than those who are taught using conventional methods. That is an enormous statistical difference. Truly staggering. But the big unsolved problem is figuring out how to scale Bloom's findings. Imagine a tutor for every child. There are fifty million students in America's public schools. The costs of employing fifty million tutors for each of them would be astronomical, and we don't have enough teachers. It would require employing a sixth of the entire U.S. population. (Though, remember, we've been told repeatedly that the robots are taking all of our jobs.) To make matters worse, there is also a strong cultural resistance to the idea of tutoring as the primary mode of education. Many egalitarian intellectuals have denounced one-to-one tutoring as aristocratic and harmful to democracy.[36]

Nevertheless, Bloom's study offers hope. Alexander the

Great was tutored by Aristotle.[37] Now imagine an Aristotle for every child, helping her to develop her unique strengths, and to cultivate the self-discipline to improve upon those strengths. The future of education will look more like the past. But first we must break free from the Dark Age.

Computation

To any outsider it was an unlikely place, but the modern era of computers began on May 28, 1936, when the editors of the *Proceedings of the London Mathematical Society* received a paper with the rather cumbersome title, "On Computable Numbers, With an Application to the Entscheidungsproblem" by Alan M. Turing.

The Entscheidungsproblem, or "the decision problem," was one of the challenges put forth by the German mathematician David Hilbert in an esoteric field of research on the foundations of mathematics. Little did anyone know at the time that this obscure thirty-five-page paper from a twenty-three-year-old would build a road from logic and mathematics to cryptography, artificial intelligence, and an inquiry into the nature of the human mind.

Turing's 1936 paper on computable numbers hit that rare bull's eye, where philosophy and discovery overlap. The mathematician Alonzo Church at Princeton came to the same findings just months before Turing. But unlike Church, who used the standard abstractions of pure mathematics in his argument, Turing set forth thought experiments using machines, algorithms, ink, paper tape, and computation. (Before Turing, a "computer" referred not to a machine, but to a human being, more often than not a woman, who calculated by hand with paper and pencil.)

This unique blend of philosophical speculation, eccentricity, and logical rigor was Turing's signature throughout his astonishing career. Later on, after the end of the Second World War, after he'd cracked the German Engima cipher (while wearing pajamas and a gas mask to help with his allergies), Turing took it upon himself to defend thinking machines. He devised a test that was based on a popular parlor game. We would know machines could think, he claimed, when we couldn't tell if we were talking to a computer or a man, provided that a wall or a door prevented us from seeing which was which.

The Turing Test asks a deep question about what makes human intelligence, if at all, unique. What's odd is that so odd a man would seek to vindicate artificial intelligence by showing how it could imitate men in conversation. The truth is that computation is capable of so much more.

From our fingerprints to our hearts, we tend to believe that humans are very different from each other. Take a random set of talented people—Nietzsche, Dave Chappelle, Muhammad Ali, Ada Lovelace, Ghandi, Charles Dickens, you and your friends—and it is striking how different their geniuses are. Expand that set further to include all of mankind's differing abilities, interests, personalities, and talents. The task's scope boggles the mind.

But now think of computers, and this vast picture narrows quickly. From the bit to the interface, most people tend to see computers as all the same: a black box executing programs with the push of a button. Even the range of their physical shape seems extraordinarily small. Outside of humanoid robots in science fiction, most people struggle to imagine anything beyond desktops, laptops, phones, and tablets.

But while most people think that humans differ greatly and that computers are all pretty much the same, the truth is very different. In fact, the range of potential applications of computer intelligence is much larger than the range of human intelligence. Imitating mankind will prove to be a blind alley. Whereas much of the excitement surrounding computers today is tied to the search for the Holy Grail in the field—artificial general intelligence—I believe progress in computation will move in the opposite direction: towards greater and greater specialization and unique uses. "General" intelligence—programs that attempt to do thousands of tasks well—will prove to be less useful than specific programs that can do one thing extraordinarily well.

Computers and communications technology are the two outliers in the era of stagnation. Their rise, advance, and current dominance in our lives were so swift and so complete that the very idea of technology itself has shrunk to include only these two inventions. Gordon Moore's observation in 1965 that miniaturization and processing power increased at a predictably exponential rate became established as an inevitable iron law of progress. Half the area, twice as fast, every eighteen months or so. It happened like clockwork. Moore's Law was so clear and reliable that it convinced the world we were making more progress everywhere, not just in computers. The age of spiritual machines and hostile clever robots was upon us.

But sometime in the 2000s, Moore's Law hit a snag. The effort to keep pace with it became too costly. Most of the needs of the average consumer could be met with slightly better processors in laptops and phones. So Intel and the other chip makers gave up on going smaller and faster and turned their attention elsewhere. For the few remaining research programs continuing on the path laid down by Moore, they have recently begun to hit the limits of the universe. The bit, the smallest unit of information, is modeled by electrons passing through infinitesimally small gates that represent the 1s and 0s of our software systems. Those electrons cannot move faster than the speed of light, an important parameter for information processing on a silicon chip. Further, the laws of physics entail strange behaviors the smaller you get. When a single electron is interacting with gates only 5 nanometers long the universe gets funky: suddenly that electron becomes more a cloud of possibilities than a discrete element to course through a system. Precision is lost.

In response to these limits and market demand, chip makers and the inventors of other architectures have focused on specialization. The video game industry pioneered the use of computer chips dedicated to graphics processing: GPUs, graphics processing units. In an unanticipated twist, all the advances in what's advertised as artificial intelligence—machine learning and deep-learning algorithms—were made possible by the GPU. (Though perhaps it shouldn't come as a surprise that processors that mimic the visual cortex are also great for running algorithms to recognize objects and detect subtle statistical patterns.) It also happens that GPUs work well in solving Satoshi Nakamoto's math problems in the Bitcoin network. As a result, the price per share for Nvidia, the market leader in GPU chip-making, has skyrocketed nearly 1,000 percent over the last five years.

Meanwhile, other research programs are looking to use the funky laws of quantum mechanics to their advantage. Quantum computing replaces the silicon chip with its rules and logic for the strange properties of particles in quantum entanglement. In classical computing, the bit is modeled by two possible states: yes or no, 1 or 0, on or off. In quantum computing, the set of possibilities expands to four. A qubit—incredibly and mind-bogglingly—can process four states simultaneously: yes and yes,

yes and no, no and yes, and no and no. Connect enough of these qubits together—some researchers put it at 100 or so—and a quantum computer becomes vastly more powerful than a classical computer. Nevertheless, even quantum computers appear to be best at specialization. As of today, the most promising use cases involve problems requiring calculations that would take a classical computer years to perform: predicting the way proteins fold, modeling complex molecules for drug discovery or new materials, optimizing routes and traffic, making longer-term weather predictions, and cracking cryptographic codes.

Many unsolved problems remain in the field before we will see the benefits of quicker processing. At the top of the list is the challenge of keeping particles in that special entangled state. These quantum systems are currently unstable and decohere in milliseconds. Next would be to improve upon the error-corrections necessary to counter the mistakes made in such a fragile system. Lastly, it is difficult to string thousands of these unstable qubits into an information processing array. The teams working on these problems mainly differ by which quantum system they seek to manipulate: trapped ions, photons, electrons, or even whole atoms.

TEAMS TO WATCH: Rigetti, IBM, Honeywell, Google, IonQ, Xanadu, ColdQuanta, Atom Computing.

Alan Turing tried to show that machines could act like men, but the tragic irony of his life is that it ended with men expecting him to act like a reprogrammable machine. After his conviction for "gross indecency," the British government forced Turing to take estrogen to "cure" his homosexuality. Unable to bear this burden, he killed himself on June 7, 1954. Not every human thinks alike, but the little known secret is that not every machine does, either. Turing's biggest proof was its own limitation: computers can do more than imitate men.

Water, Soil, Air

The lakes, rivers, reservoirs, and aquifers of the American West are dying of thirst. For the first time in the region's history, dwindling reserves of water are threatening to shrink the size, the scale, and the power of its cities. Small towns in the most arid valleys may wither and die, left half-sunk in the sands, the barren relics of a lost civilization. Government agencies monitoring dry spells in western states say that more than half the land—64 percent—is currently undergoing an extreme drought or worse. From 2012 to 2016, California experienced one of its worst and longest droughts on record. The economic loss to farmers was ruinous, nearly $4 billion.[38] The U.S. Forest Service estimates 102 million forest trees died from lack of water, leaving a dried-out tinderbox to fuel the largest fires in California's history. At a 2015 press conference during the worst of it, California Governor Jerry Brown ushered in our new era of shriveled aspirations, parched soil, and gnarled trees: "The idea of your nice little green lawn getting watered every day— those days are past." After more than a century of expansion, the supreme optimism of the frontier spirit in the American West is over.

Around almost every lake in the western states, especially when seen from the sky, receding waters have left behind a white bathtub ring indicating the former high-water mark of abundance. One dramatic example is Lake Mead. Backstopped by the Hoover Dam, Lake Mead is the largest reservoir in the United States, serving 40 million people across seven states and northern Mexico. Los Angeles, San Diego, Phoenix, Tucson, and Las Vegas all depend on it. As of August 2021, it was filled to only 35 percent of its capacity, the lowest its water level has been since the Dust Bowl and the Great Depression.

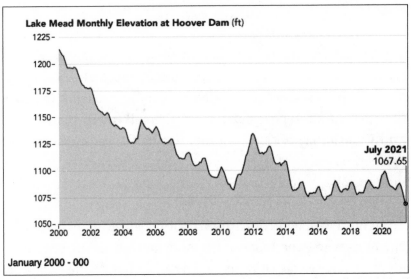

Source: NASA Earth Observatory, accessed at https://earthobservatory.nasa.gov/images/148758/lake-mead-drops-to-a-record-low.

But perhaps the bleakest of all is Salton City, a post-apocalyptic ghost town next to an evaporating, toxic lake, which becomes smaller, saltier, and more putrid every year under the broiling southern California sun. Salton Lake has contracted 45 square miles down from its size in 1999.[39] The former resort by the lake has become a place of desolation, an eerie menagerie of demolished homes, palm trees flattened to stumps, and one vacant yacht club.

We may shake our fists at the skies for the decline—bad luck or climate change—but there is not a scarcity of water. There is a scarcity of dynamism. Israel, a country founded in an arid desert, has channeled Moses and has struck water from a rock. Today, Israel's rainfall is half of what it was when the nation was founded in 1948. The population has grown tenfold. Its GDP has grown seventyfold. And yet, the country has become water-rich.[40] Former deserts have bloomed into lush farms so that Israel now exports fruits and vegetables. They accomplished this through wise governance and technological progress. Unlike in the United States, where water rights allow farmers to buy water at artificially depressed prices, in Israel farms and homes must pay the real price for the water they are using. The country has also consistently made it a priority to repair and renew its water system. Meanwhile, our superannuated water infrastructure leaks a staggering amount of water every day. Chicago loses a quarter of its water a day. One hard-to-repair leak cost New York City 35 million gallons of water every day for decades.[41] But more than any policy, Israel has innovated. They have improved productivity on their farms by inventing new, less wasteful forms of irrigation. They have seeded clouds to produce rain. They have bred plants that grow with less water. They have learned how to transform the sewage from their homes into clean water for their crops. And most impressive of all, they have discovered novel ways of turning seawater into fresh water.

Ignoring Israel's example, most people in the United States focus on small-scale innovations and altering personal behavior. Low-flush toilets, dual-flush toilets, shorter showers, and other water-efficient appliances may help us cultivate a frugal mindset, but their use saves only a minuscule amount of water compared to the gains to be made in farming and industry, where the overwhelming majority of water is used. In almost every nation around the world, agriculture accounts for 70 to 80 percent of all water use. In California, irrigation for farms accounts for 80 percent of water use. In Arizona, it's 87 percent. In New Mexico, close to 90 percent.[42] Asking someone to take shorter showers to save the planet is laughable. We need innovation where it matters most.

Most environmentalists would have us pursue conservation. But I am not interested only in efficiency gains or in saving fresh water. I am interested in creating even more. We should see our deserts bloom. A world without droughts is within our reach. We can achieve independence from the climate and immunity from adverse dry weather conditions. If the water dries up and our cities erode in the wind and sand, the fault will be ours and not the weather's.

Like sources of energy, sources of water must be consistent and reliable. Israel's desalination plants fit the bill and generate more than a quarter of the country's freshwater. But as it is, the plants remain expensive to build, and the desalination process is energy-intensive. Starting in the early 2000s, Israel built five new desalination plants along its Mediterranean coast. The last and most advanced in Soreq cost $400 million. At the same time, it took a decade to clear the legal thickets to break ground on a facility in Carlsbad, California, and the final bill for the project was $1 billion. There is a lot of room to improve.

TEAMS TO WATCH: IDE Technologies, Veolia, Hutchison Water.

Weather modification and rain-cloud seeding: The novelist Kurt Vonnegut's older brother Bernard was a co-inventor of the most widely used rain-cloud seeding process, which uses silver iodide as a condensation base for snowflakes and raindrops to form in clouds.[43] Silver iodide was recast by Kurt as "ice-nine" in his dystopian novel, *Cat's Cradle*. Ice-nine appears useful as a solid form of water, at first, but because it transforms any liquid water into solid ice-nine upon contact, the substance proves to be a doomsday catalyst for an apocalypse.

Fortunately Bernard's cloud seeding process is far safer to use, but there are many unsolved problems, including the dark shadow cast by Kurt's misplaced fears. One issue is that cloud seeding appears to increase the rain yield from a storm, but it requires clouds and fog to begin with. On a bright sunny day in a dry desert, the seeding is useless. The next problem is that it has proven difficult to measure how much the process increases the rain yield. Researchers in Wyoming have found the cloud seeding can increase the snowpack in a mountain range from 5 to 15 percent from winter storms. But skeptics say the evidence is sparse.[44] One startup boasts a meager 1 percent gain. The next and last challenge is the public's negative perception of meddling with nature. A Pew Research Center poll in 2021 found that seven out of ten Americans are worried about the unintended consequences of seeding clouds.[45] (Also worth noting: the same poll found more than half of Americans have never heard of the process.)

RAINMAKERS TO WATCH: North American Weather Consultants (NAWC), the Desert Research Institute, Weather Modification Incorporated (WMI), Ice Crystal Engineering.

Irrigation: The lawns in front of California homes may turn brown, but the farms and orchards are still lush. Because of California's dysfunctional system of water rights, farmers have no incentive to economize on water use or to find novel technologies to increase yield for less. They pay artificially depressed prices based on "rights" that allow owners to divert water from rivers and lakes for canals and irrigation. Some of these rights date back to the 19th century and have priority over all other claims. Unsurprisingly, then, most California farmers still irrigate their crops with a technique called flood irrigation, the same wasteful method that has been in use since the Pharaohs lorded over the Nile. The paragon for wanton water use is the almond farm, which requires one gallon of water to grow a single nut.[46] Despite water levels declining and the worst drought in generations, California's almond production doubled from 2003–15. Incentives matter.

In Israel, both the harsh conditions and real prices for water have pushed farmers to discover novel irrigation technologies. The most significant advance is precision drip irrigation, which delivers water drop by drop to the roots of crops or trees. Over the years, the technique has been refined by adding targeted nutrients and fertilizer. The upshot is that the widespread adoption of drip irrigation has reduced the amount of freshwater Israeli farmers use by 60 percent since the country's founding.[47] Flood irrigation has not been used there in decades. We could do worse than imitating Moses.

TEAMS TO WATCH: Netafim Irrigation, CropX, N-Drip.

Air: Watch any movie filmed in Los Angeles in the 1980s and the thick haze of smog in the air dates it. Today, the skies in American cities are clearer, but air pollution remains a cause of concern. Too many people are breathing in toxic particles that damage their lungs and enter their bloodstream. One estimate puts the global death toll from air pollution at about 7 million people per year.[48]

In addition to harmful fine particles, there are also the greenhouse gases—carbon dioxide, methane, and nitrous oxide. Without getting into debates about how sensitive temperatures are to increasing amounts of carbon dioxide, it is nevertheless true that we should discover ways to scrub the air and pull unwanted molecules out of it. The greater control we have over the weather and the atmosphere, the less vulnerable we are to any catastrophe, whether natural or man-made.

The world emits about 51 billion tons of carbon dioxide and its equivalents into the air every year. Most of the attention on this issue is cast on reducing emissions. And, as mentioned above, fusion and nuclear energy can help us get to zero faster. But then there is another strategy aside from curbing our emissions. We can pull greenhouse gases and other pollutants out of the sky and store them safely. This scientific field, carbon capture and storage, is relatively young, roughly only thirty years old. In a recent poll, nine out of ten Americans admitted they had never heard of it.[49]

Point of capture devices have been around for decades.[50] When emissions come out of a smokestack, they're highly concentrated. A point of capture system sits on the smokestack and traps the carbon dioxide before it's released into the atmosphere. The advantage here is that highly concentrated pollutants are easier to trap the closer they are to the source. But these devices are costly to run, and power plants and factories currently have no incentive to install them. The best current method uses amine chemicals, which are expensive, and the chemical scrubbing process that uses amine requires a lot of energy. Other methods use novel materials in membranes or cryogenic processes to separate gases by cooling them. These, too, are expensive and require further research and development.[51]

A direct air capture system, by contrast, pulls carbon dioxide out of the air long after it has spread far from its source. Trees, plants, and grass are very good at this, but reforestation is unlikely to scale to the size needed to meet the challenge of the issue. That leaves artificial techniques, which have their own difficulties. Because carbon dioxide is dispersed so widely in the air, the challenge is to find new materials that can trap and store such low concentrations. It can require a lot of energy as well. One of the best direct air capture systems at the cutting edge is operating near Zurich. Its developers say the facility will trap 900 tons of carbon dioxide from the sky per year.[52] Recall that the world dumps 51 billion tons of carbon dioxide and its equivalents into the atmosphere annually. That is quite a large gap. Another promising strategy uses kelp in the ocean to absorb carbon from the atmosphere, before sinking deep into the ocean for storage. But this, too, is unproven and early in its development.

TEAMS TO WATCH: Chart/SES Innovation, Running Tide, Climeworks AG, Ebb Carbon, Sustaera, Mission Zero.

Human Flourishing

James Stockdale's A-4 Skyhawk was on fire.[53] All the warning lights were flashing mad: fire alarms, hydraulic failure, electrical failure. Flak had hit his attack jet as he pulled it off a target. His plane was now hurtling just above the trees at 575 miles an hour. It was a beast out of control. There was nothing Stockdale could do. He had to punch out. Eject. Quick. Tick. Tick—boom!—eject.

His parachute opens. He is somewhere above North Vietnam, floating 200 feet over a small village. It's September 9, 1965. Stockdale figures he has maybe thirty seconds at the outside before his feet hit the ground. Rifle shots whir through the air. He whispers to himself in his descent, "Five years down there, at least." There is a lot of fighting left to this infernal war in which he'll now be a pawn. "I'm leaving the world of technology and entering the world of Epictetus."

Stockdale believed he would be a prisoner of war for five years. He sensed Epictetus would help him survive it. Who the hell was Epictetus?

Three years before this, before his plane was blown out of the sky, Stockdale received a book from his philosophy professor, Philip Rhinelander. He had stopped by Rhinelander's office one last time before leaving Stanford's campus to return to active duty. Stockdale had finagled his way into Rhinelander's tutelage when he should have been devoting his time to studying international relations. He was making a mid-career pitstop in grad school on the way to getting a desk in the Pentagon. Philosophy wasn't meant to be part of that, but Stockdale was hooked. He couldn't get enough. That day, Rhinelander handed him the collected teachings of a Roman slave, a Stoic named Epictetus. The collection had been put together nearly 1,900 years ago. Handing him the book, Rhinelander said, "You are a military man—take this booklet as a memento of our hours together. It provides a moral philosophy applicable to your profession." It was a bit foggy how this dead slave's ancient teachings were relevant to air combat and cutting-edge aeronautics. He was a fighter pilot in the Navy. What would a dead Stoic have to say about flying A-4s and supersonic F-8 Crusaders? He thought his teacher had no idea what his job required. This ancient rag was irrelevant.

Three years later, floating down like a mote of dust to his captors, Stockdale believed his professor was right.

The core of Stoic ethics is virtue, *arete* in the Greek, which connotes a blend of excellence, skill, strength, and valor—not a thing to be attained, like an Olympic gold medal or an Oscar, but a way of life, a way of doing things, a way of being. And if *arete* secures us anything at all, it is the fulfillment of our highest potential as humans—*eudaimonia*—sometimes translated as happiness in English, but its sense is less of a mood or a feeling and more akin to flourishing, like a majestic redwood fully grown in the sun.

The Stoics parted company from Aristotle and his students, not without controversy, by distilling the practice of virtue solely down to the exercise of the will and the purification of motive. For them, the success or failure of our actions is not our business. What matters is the inner citadel of one's soul, over which nobody else has control. So, what you or I might call the goods of life—wealth, health, family, lovers, friends—the Stoic is morally indifferent to, for what defines the sage is not that he possesses these good things or spends time with loved ones, but how he feels about their relationship to himself. No one is made good simply by having these good things; nor is a life filled with them necessarily a good one. Take what we cherish away, and without virtue, without *arete*, then our lives and our souls would crumble.

But that need not be the case. Instead, the Stoic implores you to consider: how deep may these so-called goods clutch into our hearts? Are they really necessary? We shouldn't believe, like crying children who have lost a toy, that losing the goods of life can hurt us. Quite the opposite. Often these very things can make our lives worse. We are twisted into the worst sorts of vice by hitching our innermost self to the fate of these external goods, jealously trying to protect them, greedily trying to possess more of them, debasing ourselves to hold on to them, to make permanent what can't last. It is all an endless torture. But the Stoic sage knows the way out. He can cultivate a moral, and therefore emotional detachment from these spurious goods, knowing that the sum of his worth factors no possessions in. Why feel grief for something over which you have no control?

Meanwhile, the other matters you and I might call bad—death, disease, catastrophe, poverty, imprisonment, undeserved notoriety, bodily harm, a broken heart—the Stoic sees them as neutral raw material or as the training ground for virtue. How do you conduct yourself undergoing these supposed bad things? How do you respond to them? How do you feel about them? That's the crux of it all. Not that anything in particular happened to you. In and of themselves, these events do not cause you to act badly. To the contrary: crisis, trauma, and deprivation could become strong material for virtuous action. The only thing that matters when our backs are to the wall is whether you let what is outside of your control rob you of your dignity. These events cannot touch the inner citadel of your soul. To the Stoic in extremis, there is always something unmanly about begging for your life in tears in the moments before your death.

"Philosophy does not promise to secure anything external for man," Epictetus tells us in *The Discourses*, the book Rhinelander had given to Stockdale. "To make the best of what is in our power, and take the rest as naturally happens."[54]

And what has the universe placed in our power? "The power to deal rightly with our impressions" or "impulses"—in short, the way we respond to events, objects, and people. All else remains beyond our control. Your grief, your joy, your sorrow, your passion—they're up to you. Therefore, the task of living well is to discipline our judgment about what is good. If you attend to this emotional response—examine it, train it, discipline the mind not to chase what merely appears to be good—then, Epictetus says, "you will not do a single thing against your will, you will have no enemy, and no one will harm you because no harm can affect you."

"Who, then, is the invincible man?" Epictetus concludes. "He whom nothing outside the sphere of choice can disconcert." We may not be able to control events, but our inviolable freedom is found in choosing how we respond to those events.

Stockdale's guess about being a prisoner for five years proved wrong. It ended up being closer to eight, with four years in solitary confinement wearing leg irons in an old French dungeon in Hanoi. He quickly learned there would be a lot of important things outside of the sphere of his choice.

As soon as his feet hit the ground that day in September, and he unfastened his parachute, he was overwhelmed by a mob of North Vietnamese militants. They pummeled him. Some had clubs. They shattered one of his legs and broke a bone in his back. He knew right away his leg would never properly heal. He wouldn't walk on it without crutches for a year.

Imprisoned, he was broken and humiliated. "You will help me," one captor told him. "You don't know it yet, but you will." But what about medical attention? His leg? His back? His wounds? "You have a medical problem, and you have a political problem," his captor said. "In this country we handle political problems first."[55] To coerce confessions, they would often bind him in tourniquet-tight ropes that cut the blood flow to his limbs. Then his interrogators would jackknife him forwards and down, his head towards his ankles, which were both secured in lugs attached to an iron bar. The blood would rush to his head. He would feel his upper body circulation slow to a near stop. Next, his arms were twisted upwards towards the ceiling. Then, pain. He would feel the most extreme pain. And then the panic of a world enclosing smaller... and then smaller... and then smaller to black. He tried his best to withhold information—all the captured pilots did—but eventually Stockdale would scream out true answers to the questions his interrogators would ask. It was inevitable. With their techniques (learned from their French colonial governors), the North Vietnamese could reduce a confident ace to a self-loathing mess in ten minutes. Even the most resilient could not last more than thirty minutes. This became known as "taking the ropes." He and his fellow American airmen would hold out for as long as humanly possible, eventually submit, give up whatever secrets they had, and confess guilt for things they never had done into tape recorders for propaganda. Afterwards they were thrown into a "cold soak," a month of isolation to ruminate upon their crimes.

Stockdale remembers spending his first New Year's as a prisoner shivering without a blanket, his legs in irons, hands in cuffs, lying in three days' worth of his own piss and shit. That was only three months in.

There were about fifty Americans imprisoned in the beginning. Week after week, month after month, more and more pilots and back-seaters were blown out of the sky by MiGs, missiles, and cannon fire. Many died in the air, but some ejected and floated down to prison. Over the years the total would accumulate to nearly five hundred. As a wing commander, Stockdale was the senior officer among them. He felt it was his duty to lead his fellow prisoners and maintain their cohesion as a group. They developed a secret community, a network mainly held together by tapping codes to each other through the prison walls. But these tapped codes didn't always stay secret. And sometimes the North Vietnamese would find notes or catch whispers and gestures. Every time they were caught, to the ropes they'd go.

Tortured and returned to their cells, the pilots slumped in shame. As strong as their wills were, there was always a breaking point. They would give their interrogators what they asked for, but they would cling to a tiny shred of defiance in making the torture team work for everything they took. Back among their friends, the pilots would weep, "I'm a traitor," utterly ashamed of the secrets they had cried out.

But their friends would respond, "There are no virgins in here; you should have heard what I told them." No one ever lashed out at someone for being weak. Everyone recognized his own fragility. But by relating each other's stories of defiance, always through wall taps, there emerged a band of brothers that was stronger together than any one alone.

Of Stoicism, Stockdale concluded: "It's a formula for maintaining self-respect and dignity in defiance of those who break your spirit for their own ends." He came to believe something Rhinelander had argued at Stanford, an outlook that had more of the flavor of Job than Epictetus: life is not fair; there is no double-entry moral bookkeeping in the universe, balancing out the good and the bad. Lots of bad things happen to good people for no reason. The only proper reckoning is the state of your inner self, the workings of your conscience, the purity of motive, your integrity. To the Stoic, and for Stockdale, the most grievous harm that can be done to anyone is not physical torture, but the harm a person can do to himself by shattering his own will—a suicide of conscience—destroying the good man within. What he most keenly remembered and felt was the remorse over breaking himself in confession and the shame of caving in too early.

After nearly eight years, the North Vietnamese released Stockdale, and he returned in 1973 to what he felt was the world of yakety-yak. Sadly, if anyone has heard of Stockdale today, more often than not it isn't because of his lectures on moral philosophy, but because of his terrible performance as Ross Perot's running mate in the debates during the 1992 presidential campaign. At one point on live TV, his hearing aid was turned off and so he didn't hear the moderator's question. Stockdale fumbled. A parody on *Saturday Night Live* made him look confused and dim. It was a total disaster. That became the lampoon skit, "Who am I? Why am I here?" and the crowds laughed at Stockdale's confusion.

Never a good politician, he instead wrote and spoke widely over the years about his prison experience, always grounding it in the context of Epictetus, Solzhenitsyn, and Dostoevsky—all of whom spent time enslaved or imprisoned. A syllabus for his philosophy course at the Naval War College runs from Socrates to Mill to Camus. His most lengthy essay on Stoicism carries the subtitle, "Testing Epictetus's Doctrines in a Laboratory of Human Behavior."

Stockdale died at his home in San Diego in 2005. He was eighty-one. If he were alive today, he would be shocked to discover just how big a commercial fad Stoicism had become.

• • •

"Stoicism is the new Zen," a columnist for the *Financial Times* proclaimed in 2016.[56] Over at the *New Yorker*, Elif Batuman doubled down: "Born nearly two thousand years before Darwin and Freud, Epictetus seems to have anticipated a way out of their prisons."[57]

As it was for the Romans, so it became for the American apex during the 2010s. Stoicism had secured its place as the ethos of choice for the continent-jumping, (self-proclaimed) industry-disrupting, CrossFit Millennial; self-help for the young TED Man, for sensitive people with the desire to do something great, but whose idea of greatness is a *TechCrunch* article and a keynote at South by Southwest for the janissaries of the Internet revolution.

The popular cult of Stoicism had managed to whittle the philosophy down from withstanding the iniquity of Roman tyrants to the task of managing disappointment and ten thousand unread emails. Inbox zero hero.

At the center of the mania for all things Stoic stands Ryan Holiday. In 2014 he published a book on how Stoicism can teach you "how to get unstuck, unfucked, and unleashed."[58] The marketing guru and strategy consultant called it *The Obstacle is the Way*, after a line by the Roman Emperor Marcus Aurelius. Holiday uses anecdotes about generals, inventors, industrial titans, and just about anyone else who's accomplished anything to offer object lessons in the effectiveness of Stoic principles. We are invited to join a Macy's balloon parade of Frederick the Great, Thomas Jefferson, Theodore Roosevelt, and George

Washington, all of whom Holiday says "explicitly studied and practiced Stoicism."

"There is no good or bad without us," Holiday writes, echoing his Stoic role models. "There is only perception."[59] In 2016, Holiday then followed up his bestselling *Obstacle* with *The Daily Stoic*, which offers "a daily devotional of Stoic insights and exercises," a regimen that has long been—we are assured—"the secret weapon of history's great figures from emperors to artists and activists."[60]

Next up in the parade is Tim Ferriss, the Stakhanov of Silicon Valley, who hosts a popular podcast with millions of listeners each week, in which he "deconstructs world class performance" through interviews with famous people. The author of the *Four Hour* book series says he has read Seneca's "The Moral Letters to Lucilius" more than one hundred times, and that it has been his constant companion for at least ten years. For Ferriss, "Stoicism is a no nonsense philosophical system." He is interested in results, not metaphysics. And, admittedly, it is true that certain Stoic practices have inspired modern therapies for depression that have found success, in particular cognitive-behavioral therapy. So this is no tail-chasing academic exercise. We're not writing esoteric definitions on invisible blackboards in non-existent chalk. "Think of it as the ideal operating system for thriving in high stress environments," Ferriss says.

Reading Holiday's *Obstacle* or listening to Ferriss's *Tao of Seneca*, I can't help but get swept away by their stoic gusto. But along the way I would suddenly awake from this carnival to realize how far we've come from the old Stoa. My favorite such moment is when Holiday uses General Ulysses S. Grant's attack on Vicksburg in 1863 to illustrate Epictetus's maxim to "persist and resist." Now hold yo' hosses right there partnah! When asked by a group of congressmen about his bellicose general,

Abraham Lincoln didn't ask what stoic philosopher the man had read. No, Lincoln asked what brand of whiskey the alcoholic loved to drink. The congressmen Lincoln was talking to didn't know the answer. "I urged them to ascertain and let me know," Lincoln recalled. "For if it made fighting generals like Grant, I should like to get some of it for distribution."

"Real strength lies in control or...the domestication of emotions," writes Holiday. Or in the case of Grant, in getting drunk and ordering other men into the inferno.

I am an admirer of both Holiday's and Ferris's work, but does this kind of Stoicism really serve us?

• • •

On the night of September 12, 2008, Karen Green came home to discover that her husband, David Foster Wallace, had hanged himself from the patio rafters. He is widely considered the greatest writer of his generation—a "once-in-a-century-talent," his editor said. Many critics rank his *Infinite Jest* as the greatest novel of the 1990s. He was forty-six.[61]

Like James Stockdale, Wallace is best known by the public for something other than his best work. In 2005 Wallace gave a commencement address at Kenyon College. It didn't take long for it to go viral and get packaged as a best-selling book.[62] From time to time the talk resurfaces: in May 2013, millions of people in a single night watched a video homage to the address before the Wallace estate shut it down.

The MacArthur Fellow spoke to the Kenyon graduating class that day about the importance of empathy. It was a simple message and Wallace knew it, but, as Wallace said, "banal platitudes can have life-or-death importance." Half of Wallace's appeal lies in his self-effacing, intellectually playful attitude. He tells us he is a student of the genre of commencement speeches, with their didactic little parables and "rhetorical bullshit." A satirical commencement speech about other commencement speeches—how devilishly funny! But then chip away his intellectual playfulness and we arrive at the ghost of Epictetus. At the thematic heart of his talk, Wallace serves us old wine in new bottles:

> "Learning how to think" really means learning how to exercise some control over how and what you think. It means being conscious and aware enough to choose what you pay attention to and to choose how you construct meaning from experience. Because if you cannot or will not exercise this kind of choice in life, you will be totally hosed.

Wallace says he's going to break free from the typical commencement clichés to tell us something that no one ever really talks about at graduation. He's going to tell us how to deal rightly with soul-crushing boredom and routine, how to overcome the day-in and day-out frustrations of long checkout lines at the grocery store and traffic jams packed with SUVs:

> If you've really learned how to think, how to pay attention, then you will know you have other options. It will actually be in your power to experience a crowded, hot, slow, consumer-hell-type situation as not only meaningful, but sacred, on fire with the same force that lit the stars—compassion, love, the subsurface unity of all things.

Wallace's 1,079 page novel *Infinite Jest* famously (or infamously) contains 388 endnotes. If he had one here, he'd have to *cf.* the Stoics—right down to the "unity of all things." "The only thing that's capital-T True," Wallace tells the graduating class, "is that you get to decide how you're going to try to see it." He offers a warning about the world they're about to enter. The routine real world is going to crowd in on you and grind you down in a repetitive rat race, and the simple truths are going to be forgotten, gradually slipping away from your awareness, not because they are useless, but because they're simple, just like the way a word loses its meaning when you repeat it over and over. And in place of those simple truths, he says, a nattering voice will dominate your life, lording it inside your skull-sized kingdom, unconsciously—that's the worst part of it!—convincing you to worship external goods like wealth, health, sex, fame, and power.

But there is a way out of this torture. Choosing how you respond to the world, Wallace concludes, "is real freedom."

In the hours before Wallace hanged himself, he organized and tidied the drafts of his last unfinished novel and left them in the house garage. The drafts, published posthumously as *The Pale King*, tell the story of a group of low-level IRS employees and how they cope with the boredom of their bureaucratic, soul-sucking jobs.

Wallace left a note with the drafts of the novel in the garage:

> Pay close attention to the most tedious thing you can find (Tax Returns, Televised Golf) and, in waves, a boredom like you've never known will wash over you and just about kill you. Ride these out, and it's like stepping from black and white into color. Like water after days in the desert. Instant bliss in every atom.

Wallace never made it out of the desert. This power he implored Kenyon's graduating seniors to exercise—to change how we feel about anything in the world, to create our own meaning in a flick of the mind alone, to find bliss even in reviewing IRS tax forms, to see even the pettiest frustration like Muzak in a crowded supermarket as not only meaningful but sacred—was in the end a fatal mirage.

Wallace had taken Nardil, an antidepressant, for almost twenty years. Feeling stable and also a bit fearful of the drug's long-term physical side effects, he tapered off it and onto other safer medications, but they didn't help. His depression came to rule him, and it wouldn't budge in the last year of his life. His doctors administered twelve electroconvulsive therapy sessions, sending electric shocks through his skull to trigger short seizures. It didn't help.

When the greatest writer of a generation commits suicide, we should read him in part as a canary in the coal mine. It may be that biological facts meant Wallace's depression was something outside of his control. Suicide is not always preventable. But judging by the popularity of his writing, and the critical acclaim for his ideas, he was attuned to the spirit of the age. In seeing how he was lost, we might catch our own resemblance in the mirror.

• • •

Prozac, Celexa, Tofranil, Wellbutrin, Lexapro, Paxil, Zoloft— something on the order of thirty million Americans have prescriptions for at least one antidepressant. About 2 million Americans admit they're addicted to painkillers. One in ten teenagers take medication for ADHD. Opioids kill more Americans per year than guns.

The CDC estimates about 93,000 people died from drug overdose in 2020, up more than 20,000 from the previous year. This is more than double the total from a decade earlier in 2010. The staggering, soaring rate of increase over the decade was driven by the spread and availability of fentanyl, which is fifty times more potent than heroin. About 57,000 deaths of the total for the last year were due to this grim synthetic opioid. That's equivalent to the total number of American deaths during the entire Vietnam War.

To add to that grim stat, over the last two decades, the American suicide rate has been steadily growing, despite greater spending and renewed efforts to help. More awareness campaigns, the expansion of suicide prevention programs, and increased mental health advocacy have all failed to reverse the trend, much to the confusion and frustration of researchers and healthcare providers. Maybe the loss would be worse without these efforts, but we can surely do better. The causes of suicide are not fully understood.[63] Psychiatry's encyclopedia of mental disorders, the *Diagnostic and Statistical Manual of Mental Disorders*, or *DSM* for short, features three hundred distinct diagnoses for various mental health issues.[64] The *DSM*'s diagnostic criteria still rely on pattern-matching observable behavioral symptoms, the same method used by psychiatrists two hundred years ago. Yet we still do not know what causes these disorders.

The number of books published on the topic of happiness jumped from fifty to over four thousand in less than a decade during the 2000s. People are looking for ways to cope, but an external disarray has anesthetized our inner lives. Americans confirm with greater and greater force T. S. Eliot's observation that "human kind/ Cannot bear very much reality." The mortality rate for white men in poor regions of America began to increase in the late 1990s and has consistently gone up since. Two economists, Anne Case and Angus Deaton, have tracked these "deaths of despair," whose causes include suicide, drug overdose, and alcoholism. They estimate some 600,000 Americans would still be alive if progress had gone on as expected in the 1990s.[65] This truly is devastation.

In the despair and the numbing, we can see the outlines of

the quest of our era, the quest for greater calm and security, the easing of pain, the resistance to change. Granted, for many mental health issues, we need faster scientific progress. The ocean of our ignorance is vast. All the same, it is also true that we have become a society dissatisfied with the way things are. But instead of risking change to an external world that angers or saddens or bores the hell out of us, we have chosen to focus on how we respond to it. We have chosen, instead, to Netflix and chill. Sometimes with pills.

We seem to be content with 5G streaming, but disturbed by our standards of living; happy with life in a virtual paradise, but surrounded by a physical purgatory; trigger-warned into a safe space with heart-emojis all around; child-proofed for $60,000 a year in tuition; segregated by income, zip code, and college degree. Ask your doctor if Diplomatis and Universemectin are right for you. Read our ad in *Good Housekeeping*. Did you get the e-vite from the planner of today's protest?

I have laid out the facts as I see them in all of the preceding pages. Progress in science, education, health, energy, transportation, agriculture, and so on has stalled. The consequences of this trend are much, much worse than feeling boredom in a long line at the grocery store or being stuck in traffic behind an asshole driving an SUV. All I ask is, what are we going to do about it?

"Question 46: Would you be happier with more control over what happens in your life or more control over your response to what happens?" Gregory Stock, Ph.D. *The Book of Questions*.

• • •

"Did I preach these things in prison?" James Stockdale writes. "Certainly not."

The truth was, despite the consolation it gave him, Stockdale never thought Stoicism would help his tortured cellmates. He never tapped Epictetus's maxims in code through the prison walls to his friends. "You soon realized that when you dared to spout high-minded philosophical suggestions through the wall, you always got a very reluctant response. No, I never tapped or mentioned Stoicism once."

Still, years later, people would want to know how they survived for so long. What kept the captured pilots going? Stockdale's answer was not Epictetus and the Stoics. It was the man next door. "Anybody who has been there knows that a neighbor in the cell block becomes the most precious thing on earth."

Three things kept Stockdale alive, and none of them were Stoic principles. Survival came down to cultivating a sense of belonging, purpose, and stewardship. Over a century ago, Emile Durkheim found that people are more likely to commit suicide when they are separated from their communities.[66] Durkheim noticed it was soul-destroying, not liberating, for people to be completely free from the bonds and expectations their relationships placed on them. The North Vietnamese prison wardens used this fact to their advantage.

Isolation obliterates. Separating each prisoner from his friends, the North Vietnamese could kick out the props supporting the pilots one by one. These men were welded into a family. They had been together in tight places. They had come to depend on each other. Exclusion eroded that sense of belonging. When you're in isolation for so long, there is a point at which the power of decision is lost. Alternatives creep into the mind and you become less certain of things. Your memories of language, poetry, and history slip away. Alone, anyone would grow so depressed after a year of solitary imprisonment that, according to Stockdale, they "would be willing to buy human contact at the price of collaboration with the enemy."

If they were going to survive, something had to be done.

Right and wrong were up for grabs. There was no cohesion in the group. Cardboard imperatives to obey the Code of Conduct were worse than nothing. Stockdale came up with a plan. He gave the group some rules: "we must all take torture before we do this and this and this." By "this" he meant a confession or submitting to what is false. And what was the threshold for that? "Not less than significant pain."

The group grew tighter because it felt like they were fighting back. Their lives started making sense. They had a sense of purpose.

Still, the men would come back from torture full of remorse—they should have held out longer before they submitted. They felt unworthy and full of shame. "I can never face my friends again." But tapping through the walls Stockdale and the others would tell the tortured that they themselves had all done that and worse.

This was the fighting and mending process: defiance against their captors, then shame, atonement, and catharsis through the band of brothers. The pilots found release in common knowledge. No matter what they were forced to say under torture, they shared the details through the wall. Their communion strengthened their resolve. It gave them the endurance they needed. To omit friends like these from an account of what truly matters—as the Stoics do—was for Aristotle to paint a thin portrait of life. In prison, Stockdale learned it was a life that couldn't be lived at all.

Against the Stoics, the Greek epic and tragic poets held that powerful emotions, including negative emotions like sorrow and fear, could be sources of wisdom. The poets knew that our emotions let us feel through what we care about, and that catharsis, whether individual or shared, is an important piece of our psychological well-being.

From Homer to Aeschylus to Sophocles, the poets portrayed lives made richer and deeper by external goods necessary to our flourishing. They also showed how we can be broken by that which lies beyond our control. In response, the Stoics recategorize these external goods as "preferred indifferents." That way one shouldn't feel so bad about losing them, even if that indifferent happens to be your child. But the tragic poets of Greece—and Plato wanted to banish them for this—invite us to live in the thundercloud, to grieve profoundly in the communion of the theater for the loss of what we love—not to shut our eyes to suffering, but to affirm life and the world as beautiful in spite of it.

I judge the character of a civilization in its relationship to pain. There are things outside our control that we feel deeply about. These things matter. Fight for them. A future worth having is only to be achieved by paying its price. Live in the thundercloud, even as a ship without a mast, barely better than drifting its way home, but still set in its reckoning on some monstrous and infinite sea. Above all, try to get home.

The rise of Stoicism™ is a sign of a civilization in decline. There is something decadent about a society trying to escape its own loss through a sour-grapes philosophy. Let us face reality. The answer isn't the self-induced trance of a yogi withstanding the flames or learning how to dream of the tropics while freezing in a snowstorm. Is how we feel on the inside the only important thing in life? Is it even a priority? Or can something be bad, no matter how we feel about it? Some of us dream of fire and poetry and marvel at the suggestion of mysteries and immensities beyond. We will keep reaching for them and, as Stockdale calls on us to do, come together with our friends, decide what we require of each other, and turn back the tide of decline.

This doesn't mean we shouldn't try to master our volatility when the chips are down, or that powerful reactions to false beliefs are healthy. Our emotions can be off, ill-fitting to a situation. But perhaps all we need is a good night's rest, less junk food, some time with friends, and good exercise. All of these help us gain emotional stability better than the sphincter-squeezing contortions of Stoic impulse control.

Learn to feel anger at the right things in the right moment at the right intensity. That is *arete*. Such virtue will take attention and discipline, but if you can't trust your emotion's guidance, you will totally get hosed.

for there is nothing either good or bad, but thinking makes it so.

So far, pure David Foster Wallace. Most people quote the line and leave it here. Perhaps, like Wallace, Shakespeare flirted with moral relativism. We can't really say, because the line is not Shakespeare's; it's Hamlet's. And he's shaking Rosencrantz and Guildenstern off his tail to avenge the death of his father, the king. Hamlet goes on:

O God, I could be bounded in a nutshell, and count myself a king of infinite space, were it not that I have bad dreams.

Alas, poor Wallace! What Hamlet knew well and Wallace didn't is that the free movement of the mind is only a misdirection—an infinite jest caught in an infinite nutshell.

We have bad dreams for a reason. Kings have been usurped. It is time to overthrow the usurpers.

ACKNOWLEDGMENTS

To undertake a book covering ten years at the edge of science and technology demands a mad courage. It would not have been possible without the love and support of my parents, Paula and John Corrado. Lots of love also to mi familia, my brothers and sister and all of their little ones.

I owe my biggest debt of gratitude to my partner in crime, Danielle Strachman, and our 1517 team: Zak Slayback, Nick Arnett, and Haylee Johnson. A big thanks to Peter Thiel for believing in us first. Il miglior fabbro: you are an American hero. To our investors who took the risk to back us—your names are carved in stone in my Hall of Fame.

Thanks also to all the founders we've worked with over the years. Austin Russell, for lighting up the skies. To the original gangster Thiel Fellows back in the old days, I salute you. We learned a lot.

I'd also like to thank my ambassador of quan, Ron Burg. Thank you, wise counselor!

Lastly, I'd like to thank all my friends, some mentioned in the book, others in the background. I love you all and you make me laugh. I thank Dr. Michelle Fleurat for teaching me the difference between a stroke and a heart attack, and for explaining my Dad's coroner's report to me. For reading early drafts of chapters and providing feedback, thanks also to Julia Thomson,

Charlene Ondak, Will Jack, Josh Piestrup, Derik Pridmore, and our 1517 community. For the "New 95," I have to tip my hat to the ever-funny Miss Ashley Grabill.

I would not have started this book were it not for the talent spotting of my agent, Toby Mundy. Thank you, my good man. And lastly, thanks to Roger Kimball, Andy Shea, and Amanda DeMatto at Encounter Books for seeing this through and for granting me creative freedom.

NOTES

PROLOGUE

1 Tyler Cowen, *The Great Stagnation: How America Ate All the Low Hanging Fruit of Modern History, Got Sick, and Will (Eventually) Feel Better* (New York: Dutton, 2011). Robert J. Gordon, *The Rise and Fall of American Growth: The U.S. Standard of Living Since the Civil War* (Princeton: Princeton University Press, 2016). For more recent overviews of the declining rate of scientific and technological progress, Peter Cauwels and Didier Sornette, "Are 'Flow of Ideas' and 'Research Productivity' in Secular Decline?" *Swiss Finance Institute Research*, (October 22, 2020) no. 20-90, available at SSRN: https://ssrn.com/abstract=3716939. The authors conclude: "Our main result is that scientific knowledge has been in clear secular decline since the early 1970s for the Flow of Ideas and since the early 1950s for the Research Productivity." For another account on the decline in the productivity of scientists over the same period, despite universities graduating more scientists, see Nicholas Bloom, Charles I. Jones, John Van Reenen, and Michael Webb, "Are Ideas Getting Harder to Find," *American Economic Review*, vol. 110, no. 4, April 2020, 1104–1144, available at https://web.stanford.edu/~chadj/IdeaPF.pdf. On stagnation in general, see Neal Stephenson, "Innovation Starvation," *World Policy Journal* (2011) no. 28 (3): 11–16; Mark Fisher, "The Slow Cancellation of the Future," in *Ghosts of My Life: Writings on Depression, Hauntology, and Lost Futures* (Washington: Zero Books, 2014) 2-29; and Patrick Collison and Michael Nielsen, "Science is

Getting Less Bang for its Buck," *The Atlantic*, November 16,
2018. For book length treatments of the topic from a cultural
perspective, see Franco "Bifo" Berardi, *After the Future*
(Oakland, CA: AK Press, 2011) and Ross Douthat, *The Decadent
Society: How We Became Victims of Our Own Success* (New York:
Avid Reader Press, 2020).

2 For one summary of the Varsity Blues scandal, see Jennifer
Levitz and Melissa Korn, "SAT Whiz Sentenced in Admissions
Scandal," *The Wall Street Journal*, April 9-10, 2022: "A federal
judge sentenced a test-taking whiz who admitted to fixing
college-entrance exams for wealthy teens to four months in
prison Friday, minutes after a jury down the hall returned
a guilty verdict against a former University of Southern
California water polo coach for his role in the sprawling
bribery and fraud scheme known as Varsity Blues...In
March 2019 federal agents took down an illegal enterprise
that helped teens from prominent families get into selective
colleges via bribes, falsified athletic credentials or bogus exam
scores. The investigation has led to 50 guilty pleas and three
convictions." The most remarkable unreported detail about
the Varsity Blues college admissions scandal is the silence
revealing what it says about learning. I can't find a single
reaction on record that says the scandal is no big deal because,
even if these unqualified applicants were admitted, surely the
difficult course work would root them out and surface their
inadequacies. Just about every commentator I've came across
takes it for granted that once these applicants got in, they
would be capable of graduating and then of earning a good
income in the labor market. By way of contrast, imagine if
someone used bribes and fake credentials to gain entrance into
the Navy Seals. That person's inadequacies would be detected
immediately.

3 A *Time* magazine cover story in March 2022 dubbed Vitalik
"the most influential person in crypto." Andrew R. Chow,
"The Prince of Crypto Has Concerns," *Time*, March 28, 2022,
54-61.

4 Scott Kuper, *Secrets of Sand Hill Road: Venture Capital and
How to Get It* (New York: Portfolio, 2019), 29-40. Sebastian

Mallaby, *The Power Law: Venture Capital and the Making of the New Future* (New York: Penguin Press, 2022), appendix. Tom Nicholas, *VC: An American History* (Cambridge, Massachusetts: 2019), 11-15. Dan Callahan and Michael Mouboussin, "Public to Private Equity in the United States: A Long-Term Look," *Counterpoint Global* (August 2020): 9-11.

5 David F. Swensen, *Pioneering Portfolio Management: An Unconventional Approach to Institutional Investment* (New York: Free Press, 2009), 235-242.

6 Max Chafkin, *The Contrarian: Peter Thiel and Silicon Valley's Pursuit of Power* (New York: Penguin Press, 2021), 169.

7 David Warsh, *Knowledge and the Wealth of Nations: A Story of Economic Discovery* (New York: W. W. Norton & Company, 2006), 147. Robert Solow, "Technical Change and the Aggregate Production Function," *The Review of Economics and Statistics* vol. 39, no. 3 (August 1957): 312-320. Paul Romer, "The Origins of Endogenous Growth," *Journal of Economic Perspectives* vol. 8, no. 1 (Winter 1994): 2-22.

CHAPTER 1: LAST NAME FIRST

1 Douglas London, *The Recruiter: Spying and the Lost Art of American Intelligence* (New York: Hachette, 2021), 69-71, 76-77.

2 Wilhelm Marbes, "Psychology of Treason," in *Inside CIA's Private World: Declassified Articles from the Agency's Internal Journal 1955-1992*, ed. H. Bradford Westerfield (New Haven: Yale University Press, 1995), 70-82.

3 Jonathan Lopez, *The Man Who Made Vermeers: Unvarnishing the Legend of Master Forger Han van Meegeren* (Boston: Mariner Books, 2009), 174 and 184. One estimate is about $30m in 1967 dollars.

CHAPTER 2: CARDWELL'S LAW

1 See, for instance, Lawrence Mishel, Elise Gould, and Josh Bivens, "Wage Stagnation in Nine Charts," *Economic Policy Institute Report* (January 6, 2015), https://www.epi.org/publication/charting-wage-stagnation/.

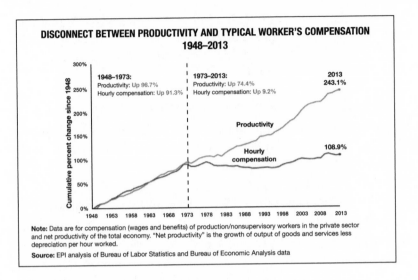

DISCONNECT BETWEEN PRODUCTIVITY AND TYPICAL WORKER'S COMPENSATION
1948–2013

1948–1973:
Productivity: Up 96.7%
Hourly compensation: Up 91.3%

1973–2013:
Productivity: Up 74.4%
Hourly compensation: Up 9.2%

2013
243.1%

Productivity

Hourly
compensation

108.9%

Note: Data are for compensation (wages and benefits) of production/nonsupervisory workers in the private sector and net productivity of the total economy. "Net productivity" is the growth of output of goods and services less depreciation per hour worked.
Source: EPI analysis of Bureau of Labor Statistics and Bureau of Economic Analysis data

In addition to Peter's main arguments, one can add one of the key measures economists use to track technological progress—total factor productivity, or TFP. Clear signs of stagnation are here as well:

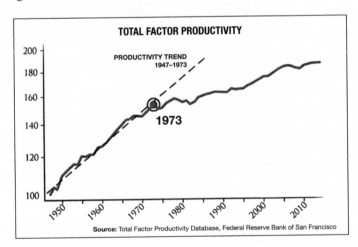

TOTAL FACTOR PRODUCTIVITY

PRODUCTIVITY TREND
1947–1973

1973

Source: Total Factor Productivity Database, Federal Reserve Bank of San Francisco

The solid line marks the U.S. decline in technological progress since 1973; dotted line shows where we would be if the rate of progress continued at the same rate prior to the early '70s. (Chart courtesy Marginal Revolution University).

Also, If America hadn't fallen off the rails in 1973, and had continued at previous rates of technological progress, the typical American household would be more than $30,000 richer today:

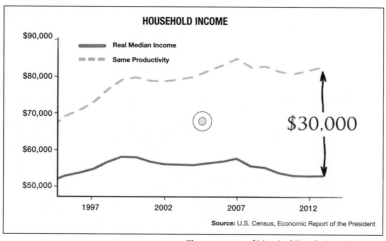

Chart courtesy of Marginal Revolution University.

2 Robert Wright, *Non-Zero: The Logic of Human Destiny* (New York: Vintage Books, 2000), 209-228.

3 Drawing on, Mancur Olson, *The Rise and Decline of Nations: Economic Growth, Stagflation, and Social Rigidities* (New Haven: Yale University Press, 1982), 17-35.

4 D.S.L. Cardwell, *Turning Points in Western Technology* (Canton, MA: Science History Publications/USA, 1972), 209-210. Also, Joel Mokyr, *The Lever of Riches: Technological Creativity and Economic Progress* (New York: University of Oxford Press, 1990), 207.

CHAPTER 3: THE ANTI-RHODES

5 Philip Ziegler, *Legacy: Cecil Rhodes, The Rhodes Trust, and Rhodes Scholarships* (New Haven: Yale University Press, 2008), x-xi and 13-19.

6 William Deresiewicz, "The Disadvantages of an Elite Education," *The American Scholar* (Summer 2008), https://theamericanscholar.org/the-disadvantages-of-an-elite-

education/. See also, William Deresiewicz, *Excellent Sheep: The Miseducation of the American Elite and the Way to a Meaningful Life* (New York: Free Press, 2014).

7 The locus classicus is Claudia Goldin and Lawrence Katz, *The Race Between Education and Technology* (Cambridge, MA: Harvard University Press, 2008). For wider social implications, Charles Murray *Coming Apart: The State of White America 1960-2010* (New York: Crown Forum, 2012).

8 Jeffrey T. Tilman, *Arthur Brown Jr.: Progressive Classicist* (New York: W. W. Norton & Company, 2006), 50-54.

9 David Kirkpatrick, *The Facebook Effect: The Inside Story of the Company That Is Connecting the World* (New York: Simon & Schuster, 2010), 66-85.

10 Kirkpatrick, *The Facebook Effect*, 87-89.

11 Catherine Rampell, "Out of Harvard, and into Finance," *The New York Times*, December 21, 2011, Economix Blog, https://economix.blogs.nytimes.com/2011/12/21/out-of-harvard-and-into-finance/.

12 Jacob Weisberg, "What's Wrong With Silicon Valley Libertarianism?" *Newsweek*, October 15, 2010, https://www.newsweek.com/whats-wrong-silicon-valley-libertarianism-73877.

CHAPTER 4: LEAVE THEM KIDS ALONE

1 Maria Montesorri, *The Montessori Method* (Scotts Valley, CA: CreateSpace Publishing, 2008).

CHAPTER 5: THE DESK

1 George Packer, *The Unwinding: An Inner History of the New America* (New York: Farrar, Straus, and Giroux, 2013), 213.

2 Jean Baudrillard, "Simulacra and Simulations," in *Selected Writings*, ed. Mark Poster (Stanford, CA: Stanford University Press, 2001), 175.

3 Peter Thiel, "The Straussian Moment," in *Politics and Apocalypse*, ed. Robert Hamerton-Kelly (East Lansing, MI: Michigan State University Press 2007), 189-218.

4 Rene Girard, *The Scapegoat* (Baltimore: Johns Hopkins University Press, 1986), 16.

5 Derek Parfit, *On What Matters: Volume One* (Oxford: Oxford University Press, 2011) preface xliv.

CHAPTER 6: INTELLIGENCE REDEFINED

1 As quoted in Gregory Ferenstein, "Thiel Fellows Program is 'Most Misdirected Piece of Philanthropy,' Says Larry Summers," *TechCrunch* October 10, 2013.

2 Benjamin F. Jones, "The Burden of Knowledge and the Death of the Renaissance Man: Is Innovation Getting Harder?" *The Review of Economic Studies*, vol. 76, issue 1, (January 2009), 283–317. Benjamin F. Jones, "Age and Great Invention," *Review of Economics and Statistics*, (2010), vol 92(1), 1-14. Benjamin F. Jones and Bruce Weinberg, "Age Dynamics in Scientific Creativity," *Proceedings of the National Academy of Sciences*, (November 2011), 108(47): 18855-19096. Benjamin F. Jones, E. J. Reedy, and Bruce A. Weinberg, "Age and Scientific Genius" (January 2014). NBER Working Paper No. w19866. For more recent research that documents and seeks to understand the short bursts of creativity of particular artists, movie directors, and scientists that occur over small periods of a person's life, see Lu Liu, Nima Dehmamy, Jillian Chown, C. Lee Giles, and Dashun Wang, "Understanding the Onset of Hot Streaks Across Artistic, Cultural, and Scientific Careers," *Nature Communications*, vol. 12, no. 5392, September 2021, 1-10. Available at https://www.nature.com/articles/s41467-021-25477-8. I find it strange that Wang et alia thoroughly document the existence of hot streaks, but then do not factor in the average age at which most hot streaks occur. It would be fascinating to see how that differs across different domains. Wang et alia find a pattern in most careers where the desire to explore new ideas and forms gives way to a blazing exploitation of those new discoveries. I can think of several research questions that follow: what is the minimum amount of exploration in a domain required before innovative exploitation? Do people ever go on hot streaks in multiple domains? Can people have two or more hot streaks in their life? And do hot streaks ever occur past the age of fifty and in what domains?

3 Benjamin F. Jones, "Age and Great Invention," 24.

4 Dean Keith Simonton, *The Genius Checklist: Nine Paradoxical Tips on How You Can Become a Creative Genius* (Cambridge, MA: MIT Press, 2018), 1-17.

5 Hubert L. Dreyfus and Stuart E. Dreyfus, *Mind Over Machine: The Power of Human Intuition and Expertise in the Era of the Computer* (New York: Free Press, 1986), 16-51. See also, Gary Klein, *Streetlights and Shadows: Searching for the Keys to Adaptive Decision Making* (Cambridge, MA: MIT Press, 2009).

6 Michael J. Mauboussin, *The Success Equation: Untangling Skill and Luck in Business, Sports, and Investing* (Boston: Harvard Business Review Press, 2012), 1-90.

7 Hugh Kenner, "Pound and Homer," in *Ezra Pound Among the Poets*, ed. George Bornstein (Chicago: University of Chicago Press, 1985), 1-12. See also, Jenny Strauss Clay, "Hide and Go Seek: Hermes in Homer," *Tracking Hermes Pursuing Mercury*, ed. John F. Miller and Jenny Strauss Clay (Oxford: Oxford University Press, 2019), 67-77.

8 For the most comprehensive overview of the psychological literature that I've come across, see Scott Barry Kaufman *Ungifted: The Truth About Talent, Practice, Creativity, and the Many Paths to Greatness* (New York: Basic Books, 2013). For more qualitative accounts that track contributing factors behind extraordinary achievement, see *Developing Talent in Young People*, ed. Benjamin Bloom (New York: Ballantine Books, 1985); David Epstein, *Range: Why Generalists Triumph in a Specialized World* (New York: Riverhead Books, 2019); Dean Keith Simonton, *Genius 101* (New York: Springer, 2009); and Ellen Winner, *Gifted Children: Myths and Realities* (New York: Basic Books, 1996).

9 Stephen Lyng, "Edgework and the Risk-Taking Experience," in *Edgework: The Sociology of Risk-Taking*, ed. Stephen Lyng (New York: Routledge, 2005), 3-16.

10 Scott Barry Kaufman, *Ungifted*, 264.

11 Here I must part ways with Mr. Thiel, the Jedi master, who will sometimes find it refreshingly contrarian when someone says they're in a company or a project for the money.

12 Scott Barry Kaufman, *Ungifted*, 279.

13 Scott Barry Kaufman, *Ungifted*, 269-279.

14 *Bhagavad Gita*, trans. Stephen Mitchell (New York: Harmony, 2000), 54.

15 T.S. Eliot, "The Dry Salvages," in *Four Quartets* (Boston: Mariner Books, 1943), 42.

16 Freeman Dyson, "Search for Artificial Stellar Sources of Infrared Radiation," *Science* vol. 131 (June 3, 1960) 1667-1668.

CHAPTER 7: THE CLOCK TOWER

1 Michael B. Farrell, "At MIT Event, Group Entices Students to Ditch School," *The Boston Globe*, October 10, 2013, https://www.bostonglobe.com/business/2013/10/09/mit-event-group-entices-students-ditch-school/4Rq3bpTLFHF5PcADma3YXI/story.html.

2 Yukari Iwatani Kane, "How I Spent My Summer: Hacking into iPhones with Friends," *The Wall Street Journal*, July 7, 2009, A1.

3 Gerhard Dohrn-van Rossum, *The History of the Hour: Clocks and Modern Temporal Orders* (Chicago: University of Chicago Press, 1996), 295-296.

4 David Landes, *Revolution in Time* (Cambridge, MA: Belknap Press, 2000), 85.

5 More celebrations in David Landes, *Revolution in Time*, 84-86. The 14th century poet-historian Jean Froissart in *L'horlage amoureuse*:

> The clock is, when you think about it,
>
> A very beautiful and remarkable instrument,
>
> And it's also pleasant and useful,
>
> Because night and day it tells us the hours
>
> By the subtlety of its mechanism
>
> Even when there is no sun.
>
> Hence all the more reason to prize one's machine,
>
> Because other instruments can't do this
>
> However artfully and precisely they may be made.

Hence do we hold him for valiant and wise

Who first invented this device

And with his knowledge undertook and made

A thing so noble and of such great price.

6 Bryan Caplan, *The Case Against Education: Why the Education System is a Waste of Time and Money* (Princeton: Princeton University Press, 2018), 97-102.

7 Anita Hamilton, "Not Too Cool for School: Tufts Offers Class on Hipsters," *Time*, August 21, 2014, https://time.com/3153922/tufts-hipster-culture-course/.

8 Bryan Caplan, *The Case Against Education*, 100.

9 Bryan Caplan, *The Case Against Education*, 3.

10 Louis Menand, *The Marketplace of Ideas: Reform and Resistance in the American University* (New York: W. W. Norton, 2010), 56.

11 Andrew Delbanco, *College: What It Was, Is, and Should Be* (Princeton: Princeton University Press, 2012), 29.

12 Martha Nussbaum, *Not For Profit: Why Democracy Needs the Humanities* (Princeton: Princeton University Press, 2010), 10.

13 Bryan Caplan, *The Case Against Education*, 50-59. See also, Samuel B. Day and Robert L. Goldstone, "The Import of Knowledge Export: Connecting Findings and Theories of Transfer of Learning," *Educational Psychologist* 47 (3) 2012, 1-24. For a good summary of the research on the negative evidence against transfer of learning, Fernand Gobet and Giovanni Sala, "Does Far Transfer Exist? Negative Evidence from Chess, Music, and Working Memory Training," *Current Directions in Psychological Science* vol. 26, issue 6, October 2017, 515-520.

14 Robert Haskell, *Transfer of Learning: Cognition, Instruction, and Reasoning* (San Diego: Academic Press, 2001), preface xiii. See also, Howard Gardner, *The Unschooled Mind: How Children Learn and How Schools Should Teach* (New York: Basic Books, 1991), 3. Gardner writes: "Researchers at Johns Hopkins, M.I.T., and other well-regarded universities have documented that students who receive honor grades in college-level physics

courses are frequently unable to solve basic problems and questions encountered in a form slightly different from that on which they have been formally instructed and tested."

15 Jason Brennan and Phillip Magness *Cracks in the Ivory Tower: The Moral Mess of Higher Education* (Oxford: Oxford University Press, 2019), 62-64.

16 Elizabeth Cascio and Douglas Staiger, "Knowledge, Tests, and Fadeout in Educational Interventions," NBER Working Paper no. 18038, https://www.nber.org/system/files/working_papers/w18038/w18038.pdf. Also, Brian Jacob, Lefgren Lars, and David Sims, "The Persistence of Teacher-Induced Learning," *Journal of Human Resources* (2010) no. 45(4), 915-43.

17 Richard Arum and Josipa Roksa, *Academically Adrift: Limited Learning on College Campuses*, (Chicago: University of Chicago Press, 2011). And their follow up, Richard Arum and Josipa Roksa, *Aspiring Adults Adrift: Tentative Transitions of College Graduates* (Chicago: University of Chicago Press, 2014).

18 Richard Arum and Josipa Roksa, *Academically Adrift*, 121.

19 Bryan Caplan estimates government spending on higher education alone to be $317 billion, not including loans and private spending. Bryan Caplan, *The Case Against Education*, 201.

20 Stacey Dale and Alan Krueger, "Estimating the Payoff to Attending a More Selective College: An Application of Selection on Observables and Unobservables," *Quarterly Journal of Economics* (2002) no. 117 (4), 1491-1527.

21 Gregg Easterbrook, "Who Needs Harvard?" *The Atlantic*, October 2004, https://www.theatlantic.com/magazine/archive/2004/10/who-needs-harvard/303521/.

CHAPTER 8: THE NAKAMOTO CONSENSUS

1 All of Satoshi's emails, forum posts, and his original whitepaper can be accessed at the Satoshi Nakamoto Institute's website, https://satoshi.nakamotoinstitute.org/.

2 Hugh Heclo, *On Thinking Institutionally* (Oxford: Oxford University Press, 2008), 48-50.

3 Yuval Levin, *A Time to Build: From Family and Community to Congress and the Campus, How Recommitting to Our Institutions Can Revive the American Dream* (New York: Basic Books, 2020), 18-19.

4 Nick Szabo, "A Measure of Sacrifice," (2005), self-published on the Internet. Available at, https://www.fon.hum.uva.nl/rob/Courses/InformationInSpeech/CDROM/Literature/LOTwinterschool2006/szabo.best.vwh.net/synch.html.

5 Nick Szabo, "Trusted Third Parties Are Security Holes," (2001) self-published, https://www.fon.hum.uva.nl/rob/Courses/InformationInSpeech/CDROM/Literature/LOTwinterschool2006/szabo.best.vwh.net/ttps.html.

6 For the first time it's named as the Byzantine Generals Problem, see Leslie Lamport, Robert Shostak, and Marshall Pease, "The Byzantine Generals Problem," *ACM Transactions on Programming Languages and Systems* (1982) no. 4 (3), 382–401.

7 Hsin-Yu Chen, Salvatore Vitale, and Francois Foucart, "The Relative Contribution to Heavy Metals Production from Binary Neutron Star Mergers and Neutron Star—Black Hole Mergers," *The Astrophysical Journal Letters*, (October 2021) vol. 920, no. 1, 1-6.

8 For an illuminating overview of gold and its role in the world economy, see Saifedean Ammous, *The Bitcoin Standard: The Decentralized Alternative to Central Banking* (Hoboken, NJ: Wiley, 2018), 17-40.

9 Saifedean Ammous, *The Bitcoin Standard*, 168-190.

10 Michael Gibson, "The Nakamoto Consensus" in *Panarchy: Political Theories of Non-Territorial States*, ed. Aviezer Tucker and Gian Piero de Bellis (New York: Routledge, 2016), 166-168.

11 For a proliferation of charts on various economic indicators that shifted and haven't been the same since 1971, visit the website, https://wtfhappenedin1971.com/. If I could, I would include just about every chart on this website in my appendix to substantiate the stagnation argument.

12 Raghuram G. Rajan *Fault Lines: How Hidden Fractures Still*

Threaten the World Economy (Princeton: Princeton University Press, 2010), 21-45.

13 For edifying histories of the failure of the Federal Reserve, see Milton Friedman and Anna Jacobson Schwartz, *The Great Contraction: 1929-1933* (Princeton: Princeton University Press, 2008). And, Robert Samuelson, *The Great Inflation and Its Aftermath: The Past and Future of Affluence* (New York: Random House, 2010).

14 Robert Kanigel, *The Man Who Knew Infinity: A Life of the Genius Ramanujan* (New York: Washington Square Press, 1991).

15 Robert Kanigel, *The Man Who Knew Infinity*, 312.

CHAPTER 9: 1517

1 Scott Kuper, *Secrets of Sand Hill Road*, 30.

2 Tom Perkins, *Valley Boy: The Education of Tom Perkins* (New York: Gotham Books, 2008).

3 Adrienne Green, "What's It Like to Be a Woman in Venture Capital?" *The Atlantic*, September 26, 2016.

4 Robert Frank, "The Homeless Billionaire," *The Wall Street Journal*, May 19, 2008.

CHAPTER 10: THE CRAM-DOWN

1 Tom Clynes, "Peter Thiel's Dropout Army," *The New York Times*, June 4, 2016.

2 Interview with Scott Galloway, *Business Insider*, November 14, 2017.

CHAPTER 11: LIGHTS, CAMERA, ACTION

1 Bruce Newman, "Tanks for The Memories: Historic Collection of Military Might Auctioned For More Than $10 Million." *Mercury News*, July 13, 2014.

2 Joshua Brustein and Mark Bergen, "How a Billion-Dollar Autonomous Vehicle Startup Lost Its Way," *Bloomberg*, August 13, 2018.

3 *Uber vs. Waymo*, Court Discovery Filings, August 15, 2017.

CHAPTER 12: A NEW NINETY-FIVE

1 For understanding Luther's role in the Reformation, Diarmaid MacCulloch, *The Reformation: A History* (New York: Penguin, 2005) and Heiko A. Oberman, *Luther: Man Between God and the Devil* (New Haven: Yale University Press, 1989). For understanding the role of the printing press in fomenting the Reformation, William J. Bernstein, *Masters of the Word: How Media Shaped History From the Alphabet to the Internet* (New York: Grove Press, 2013), 139-179.

2 Diarmaid MacCulloch, *The Reformation*, 123.

CHAPTER 13: THE FRONTIER

1 Alex W. Palmer, "The Case of Hong Kong's Missing Booksellers," *The New York Times*, April 3, 2018.

2 A good, sober place to start: Daron Acemoglu and James A. Robinson *Why Nations Fail: The Origins of Power, Prosperity, and Poverty* (New York: Currency, 2012); Ray Dalio, *The Changing World Order: Why Nations Succeed and Fail* (New York: Avid Reader Press, 2021); Niall Ferguson, *Civilization: The West and the Rest* (New York: Penguin Books, 2011); Paul Kennedy, *The Rise and Fall of the Great Powers: Economic Change and Military Conflict 1500-2000* (New York: Vintage Books, 1989); Mancur Olson, *The Rise and Decline of Nations*; Carroll Quigley, *The Evolution of Civilizations: An Introduction to Historical Analysis* (Indianapolis: Liberty Fund, 1979). While all of these books seek to explain the necessary factors that give rise to economic growth, they do not investigate scientific and technological creativity, the rate of innovation, and creative clusters.

3 A good beginning to the study of the factors that make some countries quicker than others in their rate of progress, Mark Zachary Taylor, *The Politics of Innovation: Why Some Countries Are Better Than Others at Science and Technology* (Oxford: Oxford University Press, 2016).

4 Joel Mokyr, *The Lever of Riches*, 209-238.

5 Polybius, *The Histories* trans. Robin Waterfield (Oxford: Oxford University Press, 2010), 371-385. Also, Frank W. Walbank, *Polybius, Rome and the Hellenistic World: Essays and Reflections* (Cambridge, UK: Cambridge University Press, 2002), 193-211.

6 Colleen A. Sheehan, *The Mind of James Madison: The Legacy of Classical Republicanism* (Cambridge, UK: Cambridge University Press, 2015), 54-55 and 87-88.

7 Joel Mokyr, *The Lever of Riches*, 233. For a thorough examination of how the fall of Rome's empire allowed for the political fragmentation of Europe and, therefore, cleared the way for the rise of the modern world, Walter Scheidel, *Escape from Rome: The Failure of Empire and the Road to Prosperity* (Princeton: Princeton University Press, 2019).

8 Joel Mokyr, *The Lever of Riches*, 302.

9 Stephan Courtois, Nicolas Werth, Jean-Louis Panne, Andrzej Paczkowski, Karel Bartosek, and Jean-Louis Margolin, *The Black Book of Communism: Crimes, Terror, Repression* (Cambridge, MA: Harvard University Press, 1999), 463-546.

10 Neil Monnery *Architect of Prosperity: Sir John Cowperthwaite and the Making of Hong Kong* (London: London Publishing Partnership, 2017).

11 Neil Monnery, *Architect of Prosperity*, 261.

12 Neil Monnery, *A Tale of Two Economies: Hong Kong, Cuba, and the Two Men Who Shaped Them* (London: Gulielmus Occamus & Co, 2019), 106.

13 Neil Monnery, *A Tale of Two Economies*, 148-169.

14 Lee Kuan Yew, *From Third World to First: The Singapore Story 1965-2000* (New York: Harper Collins, 2000), 544.

15 Ronald Coase and Ning Wang, *How China Became Capitalist* (New York: Palgrave McMillan, 2012), 1-68.

16 V. Suryanarayan, "Lee Kuan Yew and China's Transformation," *The New Indian Express*, July 31, 2021.

17 Li Yuan, "Crazy Work Hours and Lots of Cameras: Silicon Valley Goes to China," *The New York Times*, November 5, 2018.

18 Kai-Fu Lee, *AI Superpowers: China, Silicon Valley, and the New World Order* (New York: Houghton Mifflin, 2018).

19 Michael Moritz, "Silicon Valley Would Be Wise to Follow China's Lead," *The Financial Times*, January 17, 2018.

20 Kai-Fu Lee, *AI Superpowers*, 55.

21 Tom Wolfe, "Two Young Men Who Went West," in *Hooking Up* (New York: Farrar Straus Giroux, 2000), 17-65.

22 Nathan Ingraham, "Larry Page Wants to 'Set Aside a Part of the World' for Unregulated Experimentation," *The Verge*, May 15, 2013.

23 Tim Bradshaw, "Robo-taxis or High-Tech Tunnels? The Race for Traffic Utopia," *The Financial Times*, November 22, 2018.

CHAPTER 14: UNREAL CITY

1 Isaiah Berlin quoted in the preface of *The Power of Ideas*, ed. Henry Hardy (Princeton: Princeton University Press, 2013), xxv.

2 Trisha Thadani, "S.F. Pays $61,000 a Year For One Tent in a Site to Shelter the Homeless. Why?" *The San Francisco Chronicle* March 4, 2011.

3 Megan Cassidy and Sarah Ravani, "San Francisco Ranks No. 1 in Property Crime," *The San Francisco Chronicle*, October 2, 2018.

4 George Avalos, "Immense Growth Makes Bay Area World's 19th Largest Economy, If It Were a Nation," *The Mercury News*, July 10, 2018.

5 Accessed at: https://www.statista.com/statistics/248932/us-state-government-tax-revenue-by-state/

6 The Mayor of San Francisco, London Breed, "San Francisco's Budget: How It Works and What You Need to Know," self-published essay, https://londonbreed.medium.com/san-franciscos-budget-how-it-works-and-what-you-need-to-know-cf45df1f8ec#:~:text=The%20annual%20budget%20for%20FY,second%20year%20of%20the%20budget.

7 Lee Ohanian, "Only In San Francisco: $61,000 Tents And $350,000 Public Toilets," *Hoover Institution*, March 9, 2021.

8 Rebecca Solnit and Susan Schwartzenberg, *Hollow City: The Siege of San Francisco and the Crisis of American Urbanism* (New York: Verso, 2018).

9 Chris Matyszczyk, "Elon Musk: So-Called Valley Sex Party Was Just Nerds on a Couch," *CNET* January 12, 2018.

10 Nellie Bowles, "Unfiltered Fervor: The Rush to Get Off the Water Grid," *The New York Times*, December 29, 2017; "Me and My Numb Thumb: A Tale of Texts and Tendons," *The New York Times*, May 18, 2018.

11 Adam Brinklow, "Bernal Heights Housing Project Approved After 41 Years," *SF Curbed*, December 16, 2019.

12 Julian Mark, "SF Mission's 'Historic' Laundromat Development Delayed Again Over Shadow Study," *Mission Local*, September 28, 2018.

13 Scott James, "Before Ice Cream Shop Can Open, City's Slow Churn," *The New York Times*, February 3, 2012.

14 Joe Kukura, "Scathing New Report Details Why Van Ness Construction Went Years Past Deadline, Way Over Budget," *The SFist*, June 28, 2021.

15 Kenneth S. Coates and William R. Morrison, *The Alaska Highway in World War II: The U.S. Army of Occupation in Canada's Northwest* (Norman: University of Oklahoma Press, 1992).

16 UC Berkeley Public Affairs, "Rising Housing Costs Are Re-segregating the Bay Area, Study Shows," *Berkeley News*, September 19, 2018.

17 Russell Gold, Katherine Blunt, and Rebecca Smith "PG&E Sparked at Least 1500 California Fires. Now the Utility Faces Collapse," *The Wall Street Journal*, January 13, 2019. See also, Lizzie Johnson, *Paradise: One Town's Struggle to Survive an American Wildfire* (New York: Crown, 2021).

18 Lizzie Johnson, *Paradise*, 332.

CHAPTER 15: BISHOP AND KNIGHT VERSUS BISHOP ENDGAME

1 Thanks for this anecdote to PayPal alum James Hogan, one of the ten who lost against Peter that day.

2 As can be seen in the photograph accompanying Anna Wiener, "Why Protesters Gathered Outside Peter Thiel's Mansion This Weekend," *The New Yorker*, March 14, 2017.

3 René Girard, *Deceit, Desire, and the Novel: Self and Other in Literary Structure* (Baltimore: Johns Hopkins University Press, 1976). For a recent exposition of Girard's theory for a popular audience, see Luke Burgis, *Wanting: The Power of Mimetic Desire in Everyday Life* (New York: St. Martin's Press, 2021).

4 Mark Zachary Taylor, *The Politics of Innovation*, 215-242.

5 I take the name OneState from Yevgeny Zamyatin's dystopian masterpiece, *We*, trans. Clarence Brown (New York: Penguin Books, 2021). On the catastrophic risk of a totalitarian world government, see also Bryan Caplan, "The Totalitarian Threat," in *Global Catastrophic Risks* ed. Nick Bostrom and Milan M. Ćirković (Oxford: Oxford University Press, 2008), 504-519.

6 Stephan Courtois, et alii, *The Black Book of Communism*; Caplan, "The Totalitarian Threat," 504.

7 See, for instance, the temptations of Christ in the wilderness. King James Bible, Luke 4 5–8:

> "And the devil, taking him up into a high mountain, shewed unto him all the kingdoms of the world in a moment of time. And the devil said unto him, All this power will I give thee, and the glory of them: for that is delivered unto me; and to whomsoever I will give it. If thou therefore wilt worship me, all shall be thine. And Jesus answered and said unto him, Get thee behind me, Satan: for it is written, Thou shalt worship the Lord thy God, and him only shalt thou serve."

As well as Matthew 4 8–10:

> "Again, the devil taketh him up into an exceeding high mountain, and sheweth him all the kingdoms of the world, and the glory of them; and saith unto him, All these things will I give thee, if thou wilt fall down and worship me. Then saith Jesus unto him, Get thee hence, Satan: for it is written, Thou shalt worship the Lord thy God, and him only shalt thou serve."

I am no theologian. I can only speculate that it would appear as though Satan has some prior influence or power over the nations of the world that would become most potent when unified. There is a latent, fallen spiritual force within the organizing principle of a kingdom. It is puzzling, to say the least, that Satan could grant all of the kingdoms to Jesus. That already implies a strong skepticism of political power. They are his to move. Then, quite bluntly, to seek to unify all the kingdoms of the world—presumably in some non-voluntary way—is in some sense to serve Satan. That's his plan, after all. And the worship of God is against this.

8 Fyodor Dostoevsky, *The Brothers Karamazov* trans. Richard Pevear and Larissa Volokhonsky (New York: Picador, 2021), 274.

9 See, for instance, Arthur Danto, *The Transfiguration of the Commonplace: A Philosophy of Art* (Cambridge, MA: Harvard University Press, 1983).

10 Matt Grossman, "Luminar Makes Young Founder a Billionaire," *The Wall Street Journal*, December 3, 2020.

CHAPTER 16: LAST NAME LAST

1 Sandra Grimes and Jeanne Vertefeuille, *Circle of Treason: A CIA Account of Traitor Aldrich Ames and the Men He Betrayed* (Annapolis: Naval Institute Press, 2012).

2 Seth Benardete, *The Bow and the Lyre: A Platonic Reading of the Odyssey* (Lanham: Rowman & Littlefield, 1997), 1-5, 11-16.

CODA: THE INVISIBLE COLLEGE

Energy Creation

GENERAL READING

Robert Bryce, *A Question of Power: Electricity and the Wealth of Nations* (New York: Public Affairs, 2020).

Joshua S. Goldstein and Staffan A. Qvist, *A Bright Future: How Some Countries Have Solved Climate Change and the Rest Can Follow* (New York: Public Affairs, 2019).

Vaclav Smil, *Energy and Civilization: A History* (Cambridge, MA: MIT, 2017).

• • •

1 As recounted in the postscript written by Françoise Ulam in
   Stanislaw Ulam, *Adventures of a Mathematician* (Berkeley, CA:
   Univ of California Press, 1991) 305-315. For additional details
   on Ulam and Teller, see Kenneth W. Ford, *Building the H
   Bomb: A Personal History* (Hackensack, NJ: World Scientific,
   2015).

2 Ken Lee and Michael Greenstone, "Air Quality of Life Index,"
   AQLI Annual Update, University of Chicago, September 202.

3 Daniel Clery, *A Piece of the Sun: The Quest for Fusion Energy*
   (New York: Overlook Duckworth, 2013). See also, Arthur
   Turrell, *The Star Builders: Nuclear Fusion and the Race to Power
   the Planet* (New York: Scribner, 2021) and Tom Clynes, "Five
   Big Ideas for Making Fusion Power a Reality," *IEEE Spectrum*,
   January 28, 2020.

4 In addition to Joshua S. Goldstein and Staffan A. Qvist,
   A Bright Future, for a thorough overview and history see,
   Stewart Brand, *Whole Earth Discipline: Why Dense Cities,
   Nuclear Power, Transgenic Crops, Restored Wildlands, and
   Geoengineering Are Necessary* (New York: Penguin, 2010);
   Gwyneth Cravens, *Power to Save the World: The Truth About
   Nuclear Energy* (New York: Vintage, 2007); and Michael
   Shellenberger, *Apocalypse Never: Why Environmental Alarmism
   Hurts Us All* (Harper, 2020).

5 For a good accounting of how much energy we need, and how
   inefficient wind and solar are, see Robert Bryce, *Power Hungry:
   The Myths of "Green" Energy and the Real Fuels of the Future*
   (New York: Public Affairs, 2010) 83-130; for a more balanced,
   but still pessimistic view, Bill Gates, *How to Avoid a Climate
   Disaster: The Solutions We Have and the Breakthroughs We Need*
   (New York, Knopf 2021) 56-58 and 66-97. For an optimistic
   overview, see Varun Sivaram, *Taming the Sun: Innovations to
   Harness Solar Energy and Power the Planet* (Cambridge, MA:
   MIT Press, 2018).

6 Eli Dourado, "The New Productivity Revolution," *City Journal*,
   Spring 2021.

Transportation

GENERAL READING

J Storrs Hall, *Where is My Flying Car?* (San Francisco: Stripe Press, 2022).

Vanessa R. Schwartz, *Jet Age Aesthetic: The Glamour of Media in Motion* (New Haven: Yale, 2020).

• • •

7 For a history and analysis of the Concorde's struggles, see Jonathan Glancey, *Concorde: The Rise and Fall of the Supersonic Airliner* (London: Atlantic Books, 2015).

8 Erik M. Conway, *High-Speed Dreams: NASA and the Technopolitics of Supersonic Transportation* (Baltimore: Johns Hopkins University Press, 2005).

9 For speculation on how ubiquitous autonomous vehicles will change society and industry, see Lawrence Burns, *Autonomy: The Quest to Build the Driverless Car - And How It Will Reshape Our World* (New York: William Collins, 2018); Anthony Raymond, *How Autonomous Vehicles Will Change the World (Amazon, 2020)*; and Anthony M. Townsend, *Ghost Road: Beyond the Driverless Car* (New York: Norton, 2020).

Health

GENERAL READING

Daniel M. Davis, *The Secret Body: How the New Science of the Human Body is Changing the Way We Live* (Princeton, NJ: Princeton Univ. Press, 2021).

Steven Johnson, *Extra Life: A Short History of Living Longer* (Riverhead Books, 2021).

James Le Fanu, *The Rise and Fall of Modern Medicine* (New York: Basic Books, 2012).

Roy Porter, *The Greatest Benefit to Mankind: A Medical History of Humanity* (New York: Norton, 1998).

William Rosen, *Miracle Cure: The Creation of Antibiotics and the Birth of Modern Medicine* (New York: Penguin, 2017).

Jacob Stegenga, *Medical Nihilism* (Oxford: OUP, 2018).

David Wootton, *Bad Medicine: Doctors Doing Harm Since Hippocrates* (Oxford: OUP, 2006).

• • •

10 For a wonderful profile of Allison, see *Jim Allison: Breakthrough*, a 2019 documentary film directed by Bill Haney; for a history of the field and how the immune system and cancer interact, see Charles Graeber, *The Breakthrough: Immunotherapy and the Race to Cure Cancer* (New York: Twelve, 2018), and Matt Richtel, *An Elegant Defense: The Extraordinary New Science of the Immune System* (William Morrow, 2019).

11 Laurie Garret, *The Coming Plague: Newly Emerging Diseases in a World Out of Balance* (New York: Picador, 1994) 30-32.

12 Betsy McCaughey, *The Next Pandemic* (New York: Encounter Books, 2020).

13 David France, *How to Survive a Plague: The Story of How Activists and Scientists Tamed AIDS* (New York: Vintage, 2016), 86-87.

14 Brian D. Johnson, "How a Typo Created a Scapegoat for the AIDS Epidemic," *Maclean's*, April 17, 2019.

15 For background on Graham and his team's work, see "Luck, Foresight, and Science: How an Unheralded Team Developed a Covid-19 Vaccine in Record Time" by David Heath and Gus Garcia-Roberts, January 26, 2021, *USA Today*; and, "Shot in the Arm: Groundbreaking Covid-19 Research by Alumnus Barney Graham Began at Vanderbilt Decades Ago" by Michael Blanding, March 17, 2021, *Vanderbilt University Research News*. For a history of the development of mRNA vaccines, see Elie Dolgin, "The Tangled History of mRNA Vaccines," *Nature* vol. 597, September 16, 2021.

16 "US: Human Challenge Trials for Covid-19" an open letter, archived at https://www.1daysooner.org/us-open-letter

17 "Trends in adult body-mass index in 200 countries from 1975 to 2014: a pooled analysis of 1698 population-based measurement studies with 19.2 million participants," *Lancet* 387 (2018), 1377-96.

18 To get a handle the different sides of the debate and the open issues, I have relied on Zoe Harcombe, *The Obesity Epidemic: What Caused It? How Can We Stop It?*, (Newark, OH: Columbus Publishing, 2010); Tim Spector, *The Diet Myth: The Real Science Behind What We Eat* (London: Weidenfeld & Nicolson, 2015); Gary Taubes, *Why We Get Fat and What to Do About It* (New York: Anchor Books, 2010); Gary Taubes, *The Case Against Sugar* (New York: Anchor Books, 2017); and Stephen Guyenet, *The Hungry Brain: Outsmarting the Instincts That Make Us Overeat* (New York: Flatiron Books, 2017).

19 Ley, R.E., Turnbaugh, P.J., Klein, S. and Gordon, J. I., "Microbial Ecology: Human Gut Microbes Associated with Obesity" *Nature* 444 (2006), pp. 1022-3.

20 Hall, K. "How Strongly Does Appetite Counter Weight Loss? Quantification of the Feedback Control of Human Energy Intake" *Obesity* 2016 Nov, pp. 2289-2295.

21 For a good literature review, see Potenza, M. "Stress and Eating Behavior" *Minerva Endocrinologica*, 2013 Sep; 38(3): pp. 255–267.

22 Archer, E. "Validity of US Nutritional surveillance: National Health and Nutrition Examination Survey Caloric Energy Intake Data, 1971-2010" *PLOS One*, October 9, 2013.

23 See Stephen Guyenet, "References for My Debate with Gary Taubes" March 19, 2019, archived at: http://www.stephanguyenet.com/references-for-my-debate-with-gary-taubes-on-the-joe-rogan-experience/

24 Scott Carson "US Male Obesity from 1800-2000: A Long Term Perspective" *CESifo Working Paper*, No. 4366, 2013, Center for Economic Studies and IFO Institute, Munich.

25 Boyd Swinburn et alii "The Global Obesity Pandemic: Shaped by Global Drivers and Local Environments" *The Lancet*, August 17, 2011, 804-814.

26 Andrew Steele, *Ageless: The New Science of Getting Older Without Getting Old* (New York: Doubleday, 2020) 1-14 and 70-107. See also, Sue Armstrong, *Borrowed Time: The Science of How and Why We Age* (London: Bloomsbury Sigma, 2019); and David A. Sinclair with Matthew D. LaPlante, *Lifespan: Why*

We Age—and Why We Don't Have To (New York: Atria Books, 2019).

27 Carlos López-Otín, Maria A. Blasco, Linda Partridge, Manuel Serrano, and Guido Kroemer, "The Hallmarks of Aging," *Cell* 153, June 2013, 1194-1217.

28 Shinya Yamanaka, "Ekiden to iPS Cells," *Nature Medicine* 15 (2009), 1-4.

29 Andrew Steele, *Ageless*, 225-237.

Education

30 Erika Chen, "U.S. Spending on Public Schools in 2019 Highest Since 2008," *The United States Census Bureau*, May 18, 2021. Available at https://www.census.gov/library/stories/2021/05/united-states-spending-on-public-schools-in-2019-highest-since-2008.html

31 Digest of Education Statistics, hosted by the National Center for Education Statistics, available at: https://nces.ed.gov/programs/digest/d19/tables/dt19_236.55.asp?current=yes

32 John Dunlosky, Katherine A. Rawson, Elizabeth J. Marsh, Mitchell J. Nathan, and Daniel T. Willingham, "Improving Students' Learning With Effective Learning Techniques: Promising Directions from Cognitive and Educational Psychology," *Psychological Science in the Public Interest*, vol. 14, no. 1 (2013), 4-58.

33 Peter C. Brown, Mark A. McDaniel, and Henry L. Roediger, *Make It Stick: The Science of Successful Learning* (Cambridge, MA: Belknap Harvard, 2014), ix and 1-22.

34 Daniel T. Willingham, *Why Don't Students Like School?: A Cognitive Scientist Answers Questions About How the Mind Works and What It Means for the Classroom* (Hoboken, NJ: Jossey-Bass, 2021).

35 Benjamin Bloom, "The 2 Sigma Problem: The Search for Methods of Group Instruction as Effective as One-to-One Tutoring," *Educational Researcher*, vol. 13, no. 6, (June-July 1984), 4-16.

36 The philosopher Bertrand Russell sums up this view in his

treatise on education: John Locke and Rousseau "consider only the education of an aristocratic boy, to which one man's whole time is devoted. However excellent might be the results of such a system, no man with a modern outlook would give it serious consideration, because it is arithmetically impossible for every child to absorb the whole time of an adult tutor. The system is therefore one which can only be employed by a privileged caste; in a just world, its existence would be impossible." Bertrand Russell, *On Education* (New York: Routledge, 2010) 3. For a survey on the history of tutoring, see Edward E. Gordon and Elaine H. Gordon, *Centuries of Tutoring: A History of Alternative Education in America and Western Europe* (Lanham, MD: University Press of America, 1990).

37 King Phillip of Macedonia, Alexander's father, supposedly wrote a letter to Aristotle: "I give you notice that I have a son born to me, but I am not so much obliged to the gods for his birth, as for the happiness that he has come into the world while there is an Aristotle living." Edward E. Gordon and Elaine H. Gordon *Centuries of Tutoring*, 16.

Water, Soil, Air

38 For the negative consequences of California's drought, see Jay Lund, Josue Medellin-Azuara, John Durand, Katherine Stone, "Lessons From California's 2012-2016 Drought," *Journal of Water Resources Planning and Management*, vol. 144, no. 10, October 2018.

39 Emma Newburger, "Ghost Towns and Toxic Fumes: How an Idyllic California Lake Became a Disaster," *CNBC* November 6, 2021, accessed at https://www.cnbc.com/2021/11/06/californias-salton-sea-spewing-toxic-fumes-creating-ghost-towns-.html.

40 Seth M. Siegel, *Let There Be Water: Israel's Solution For a Water-Starved World* (New York: Thomas Dunne Books, 2017), 224-225.

41 David Dunlap, "Far, Far Below Ground, Directing Water to New York City Taps," *The New York Times*, November 19, 2014.

42 Marc Reisner, *Cadillac Desert: The American West and its Disappearing Water* (New York: Penguin, 2017), 9-10.

43 Wolfgang Saxon, "Bernard Vonnegut, 82, Physicist Who Coaxed Rain from the Sky," *The New York Times*, April 27, 1999.

44 Amanda Little, "Weather on Demand: Making it Rain is Now a Global Business," *Bloomberg Businessweek*, October 28, 2015.

45 Courtney Johnson and Brain Kennedy, "U.S. Adults Have Mixed Views on Whether Geoengineering Would Help Reduce Effects of Climate Change," *Pew Research Center*, June 11, 2021.

46 Marc Reisner, *Cadillac Desert*, 550-551.

47 Seth M. Siegel, *Let There Be Water*, 74-75.

48 Bill Gates, *How to Avoid a Climate Disaster: The Solutions We Have and The Breakthroughs We Need* (New York: Knopf, 2021) 179-181. See also, Binyamin Appelbaum, "Enough About Climate Change. Air Pollution is Killing Us Now," *The New York Times*, April 19, 2022.

49 Howard J. Herzog, *Carbon Capture* (Cambridge, MA: MIT Press, 2018) xiv-xv.

50 Bill Gates, *How to Avoid a Climate Disaster*, 94-95.

51 Howard Herzog, *Carbon Capture*, 42-58.

52 Christa Marshall, "In Switzerland, A Giant New Machine Is Sucking Carbon Directly from the Air," *Science*, June 1, 2017.

Human Flourishing

53 All of Stockdale's quotes in what follows and the details of his life and prison experiences are drawn from two of his moving books: James B. Stockdale, *Thoughts of a Philosophical Fighter Pilot* (Stanford, CA: Hoover Institution Press, 1995) and James B. Stockdale, *A Vietnam Experience: Ten Years of Reflection* (Stanford, CA: Hoover Institution Press, 1984). On Stoicism, see William B. Irvine, *A Guide to the Good Life: The Ancient Art of Stoic Joy* (Oxford: Oxford University Press, 2009); A. A. Long, *Stoic Studies* (Berkeley: University of California Press, 1996); F. H. Sandbach, *The Stoics* (Indianapolis: Hackett, 1989). For criticisms of stoicism: Martha C. Nussbaum, *The Fragility of Goodness: Luck and Ethics in Greek Tragedy and Philosophy* (Cambridge, UK: Cambridge University Press, 2001) and

Robert Nozick, *The Examined Life: Philosophical Meditations* (New York: Simon & Schuster, 1989).

54 Epictetus, *The Discourses: The Handbook, Fragments* trans. Robin Hard, ed. Christopher Gill (London: Everyman, 1995).

55 James B. Stockdale, *A Vietnam Experience: Ten Years of Reflection* (Stanford: Hoover Institution Press, 1984), 123.

56 Philip Delves Boughton, "Silicon Valley is Philosophical Over Trump's Victory," *The Financial Times*, December 16, 2016.

57 Elif Batuman, "How to Be a Stoic," *The New Yorker*, December 11, 2016.

58 Ryan Holiday, *The Obstacle is the Way: The Timeless Art of Turning Trials into Triumph* (New York: Portfolio / Penguin, 2014), 5.

59 Ryan Holiday, *The Obstacle is the Way*, 22.

60 Ryan Holiday, *The Daily Stoic: 366 Meditations on Wisdom, Perseverance, and the Art of Living* (New York: Portfolio / Penguin, 2016), 5.

61 D. T. Max, "The Unfinished: David Foster Wallace's Struggle to Surpass Infinite Jest." *The New Yorker*, March 9th, 2009. See also, Jonathan Franzen, "Farther Away" and "David Foster Wallace" in *Farther Away: Essays* (New York: Farrar, Straus, and Giroux, 2012), 15-52 and 161-168.

62 David Foster Wallace, *This Is Water: Some Thoughts, Delivered on a Significant Occasion, about Living a Compassionate Life* (New York: Little, Brown and Company, 2009).

63 Craig J. Bryan, *Rethinking Suicide: Why Prevention Fails, and How We Can Do Better* (Oxford: Oxford University Press, 2021), 1-76.

64 Allan V. Horwitz, *DSM: A History of Psychiatry's Bible* (Baltimore, Johns Hopkins University Press, 2021), 1-13.

65 Anne Case and Angus Deaton, *Deaths of Despair and the Future of Capitalism* (Princeton: Princeton University Press, 2020), 32.

66 Emile Durkheim, *Suicide: A Study in Sociology* trans. John Spaulding and George Simpson (New York: Free Press, 1997).

INDEX